The River's Daughter

The
River's
Daughter

A Memoir

Bridget Crocker

**Spiegel
and Grau**

Spiegel & Grau, New York
www.spiegelandgrau.com
Copyright © 2025 by Bridget Crocker

This is a work of nonfiction that includes the author's present recollections of her experiences over many years. Names and identifying characteristics of some people have been changed.

Quotation from *The Way It Is: One Water, One Air, One Mother Earth* by Corbin Harney (1995) is reprinted by permission of the publisher, Blue Dolphin Publishing.

Photograph of Bridget Crocker by Tony Demin, used by permission of tonydemin.com.
Interior design by Meighan Cavanaugh.

Library of Congress Cataloging-in-Publication Data Available Upon Request

ISBN 978-1-954118-54-6 (hardcover)
ISBN 978-1-954118-86-7 (ebook)

Printed in the United States

First Edition
10 9 8 7 6 5 4 3 2 1

For my parents

and the rivers who raised me.

You see, this water has a Spirit. It's got a life like we do, the same thing. . . . I can hear what it's saying. I've talked about what the Creator tells me, but here I can actually hear the voice coming from the water itself, saying those things. But I tell you, the water's not going to continue saying these things. Once we kill the life that's in it, it won't have a voice like we have any longer. It won't have the strength.

—Corbin Harney, Western Shoshone spiritual leader, *The Way It Is*

Contents

Author's Note

Before every guided river trip, passengers are provided with a safety talk. During this talk, the trip leader touches upon three important concepts: how to stay in the boat, what to do if you fall out of the boat, and how to get back in the boat. Passengers are instructed in the dangers they're about to encounter downstream and how to avoid trauma or death.

This is the story of how I fell out of the boat when I was a girl, how I survived a harrowing, treacherous swim, and how I was restored through my relationship with rivers.

This book represents my story as I experienced it and is recreated from my memory, journals, photographs, interviews, and research. I've changed the names and the identifying characteristics of certain people, groups, and companies to protect their anonymity and privacy. I have recreated dialogue in some places, approximating, combining, or moving it in time. In a couple of instances, I compressed or altered time sequences and created composite characters for clarity. Specific people and events have been omitted when they had no impact on the substance of the story. I have taken care to represent others' stories, cultures, and languages only where they intersected with my own, recognizing that these renderings are entirely subjective and filtered through my own experiences and enculturated point of view.

Like any extreme Class V whitewater run, this story is filled with obstacles, and trigger warnings for domestic violence, child abuse and neglect, sexual assault, sexual harassment, and racism apply. It's possible to portage (walk around) the sections that feel too difficult for you, then rejoin the boat downstream.

Paddles ready now, it's time to go forward.

The River's Daughter

Baptism

I was forbidden to play in the Snake River. Mama said if I fell into the river, I would die. She was a nurse at St. John's, and she'd told me plenty of stories about people fishing or fooling around onshore only to be swept downstream, their decomposed bodies recovered weeks or months later, completely unrecognizable to their own families.

"I don't want to get a call to come identify your stinking little nine-year-old corpse," she'd say, shaking her head. Mama was from the barrio in East Los Angeles, where most of the riverbed was covered with concrete and bodies were dumped into the channel. "Spare your poor mother, okay? Stay out of the river."

Behind our trailer court, a grove of cottonwood trees spread out like gracious giants, nestled between our winter sledding hill and the lumbering Snake River. It was impossible to wander far among the cottonwoods without stumbling upon the water's edge. The river spoke to me in gurgles and shifting riverbed rocks. From anywhere in the grove, I could hear her voice, which served as a constant reminder that she was alive and powerful.

Once, I'd watched a full-grown moose try to swim across the Snake to the other shore. She was carried around the bend, clear out of view, before she even reached the middle of the river. As a skinny switch of a girl, I didn't stand a chance against such strength. That's why, when it was warm enough, I went in up to my calves only, and never in the fast downstream current. I knew I wasn't supposed to get in the river at all, because *if you fall in the river, you will die*, but nine-year-olds in search of gold and tad-poles sometimes break the rules.

After school, I'd spend afternoons by myself or with Justin, a friend my age from the trailer park. We liked building forts in thick, hollowed-out trunks or scouring leaf-littered ponds, hoping to spy water skippers, known as Jesus bugs because they walk on water. I preferred the company of the river to that of most other kids, but I liked playing with Justin because he wasn't much of a talker. All he wanted to do was explore the river like me. And he didn't treat me like I was nothing because I lived in a single-wide, the way the kids at school did, since he lived in one too. We never went into each other's homes. Instead, we met up at the river.

One spring afternoon, Justin and I were lured outside by a crystalline sky and a warm chinook wind. We discovered a fallen cottonwood perched on the edge of the steep riverbank, its scoured-smooth bark freshly uncov-ered from the heavy Wyoming snowmelt. It was difficult to walk the length of the slimy log without sliding off, but Justin and I imagined ourselves to be great gymnasts working the beam and managed to twist our bodies safely toward shore, rather than the river, whenever we lost our balance. We perfected our routines over the course of the afternoon, working out the kinks in our combinations of tricks. So when my feet slipped from beneath me during a simple hop landing, I was stunned. Instead of landing onshore, I was launched headlong into the Snake, which was filled to the brim with a winter-load of snow from the nearly fourteen-thousand-foot Tetons.

Immediately I surfaced, my lungs already so shrunken from the stab-bing forty-degree water they wouldn't take air. Wide-eyed and wheezing, I bobbed next to the steep cutbank just long enough for Justin to lean out from the log and grab my outstretched hand. But the river was far stron-ger, and Justin was yanked into the current with me.

We became part of the flushing surge. The Snake swiftly carried us downstream from the cottonwood grove, past the trailers, and toward

Swinging Bridge, with miles to go before the confluence with the Hoback River.

From somewhere, a voice called out, *SWIM!*

I didn't want to end up like Mama had warned, bloated and purple on a gurney, so I put my face in the water and flailed out a crawl stroke like some possessed water skipper. Justin did the same, and we both made it into an eddy, where we grabbed some stout willow branches and flopped onto shore.

"I can't believe we made it," I said.

"We could have died," Justin panted. "We can't ever tell our parents."

Telling would put an end to fort building and interfere with morel mushroom–gathering season, which was fast approaching.

"I'm glad you yelled to swim," I said. "It was so cold, I forgot."

"I didn't yell."

"Who was it?" I looked around. There was no one, not even a deer or a moose. It was just us and the river.

"I don't know. I didn't hear anything." Justin looked at me like I'd lost it.

This wasn't the first time I'd heard the river talk. Since we'd moved to Wyoming from California two years earlier, I'd heard the Snake's voice several times. It happened mostly when I was so focused on watching the river that I felt as if I'd blended into the surrounding shore. I knew it was strange to hear voices in the water, so I'd never mentioned anything to Justin, or to anyone.

If you fall in the river, you will die. I'd fallen in, and the river had told me what to do: *SWIM.* Even though I carried the grief of a violently broken home and endured shaming at school, I decided that I must be a very lucky and special person. The river must have developed a fondness for me and protected me, like a cow moose protects her baby.

Afterward, I quit listening to Mama whenever she talked about the river. She didn't know the water the way I did. The Snake had touched me, and in some way, I now belonged to the river.

Easter Sunday

A s Sully drove our green van past the sprawling pastures of South Park, I looked out of the open windows at newborn calves nudging their mothers' bulging teats. Sully wasn't my real father, although I called him Daddy. He took care of me more than anyone else and had raised me for ten years, since I was four.

It was a bit cold to be traveling with the windows down, but since Mama wasn't with us, Sully had stopped at the drive-through window at the Virginian Saloon and, along with his usual twelve-pack of Milwaukee's Best, had bought cigarettes. As he drove, Sully inhaled from his shaking hand and blew smoke out the window so it wouldn't poison the rest of us. It was the first time I'd seen him smoke. Mama said he used to smoke before he moved in with us when we lived in California, but she told him he had to give it up and he did.

None of us in the van—my aunt Theresa, cousin Lana, half-brother David, or I—said anything about the cigarettes. Mama's baby sister, Theresa, was nineteen, only five and a half years older than me. Since she was three, Theresa had been raised mostly by Mama after their mother died, and she'd lived with us on and off over the years. She was more my sister than my aunt. She and her daughter, Lana, had recently moved into their own apartment in town, although on occasion they still spent the night with us.

Because she was older, Theresa got to ride in the passenger seat where Mama usually sat, clearing her throat in the same strained way Mama did when she was tongue-tied. The throat clearing had my attention, since usually Theresa talked so much it gave me a headache. I was stuck in the back of the van on the foam bed entertaining two-year-old Lana and six-year-old David. I felt like throwing up, even though Sully was driving steadily and there was a cool breeze coming in the windows. Aside from the smoking, the silence, and the nausea, we all pretended nothing had happened. It was as if earlier that morning our world hadn't been demolished in the time it took to tie your shoes.

It had only been a couple of hours since we'd waited in the living room for Mama to get ready for Easter Sunday Mass. Sully watered the plants while the Eagles played on the eight-track stereo. He had smoothed back the little hair he had left and was wearing the orange flowered western shirt that Mama had bought him, even though he was a motorhead mechanic whose dream was to buy a Harley and ride to Sturgis. Moving to Jackson Hole had been Mama's dream, but Sully never complained about wearing the western shirts and boots, cutting the wood, or shoveling the driveway. He kept our lives running predictably, like a well-maintained engine.

As we waited for Mama, David drove his favorite Matchbox cars along the yellow shag carpet, drooling as he mouthed motor noises. Aunt Theresa smeared gel into Lana's wispy toddler hair, while I complained about my braces and tugged at last year's Easter dress in a futile attempt to pull it down over my knees. It was the first year there weren't new Easter outfits in our baskets.

Mama's bedroom door flung open, and she walked into the living room. She was still in her flannel nightgown, her permed blond hair ferociously undone.

"I'm not going to church today," she said. "In fact, I'm not going to church anymore. I don't believe in God. I never have."

This was news to me. A Catholic school graduate and committed parishioner of Our Lady of the Mountains, Mama made special trips to town every Saturday to take me to catechism. She washed my mouth out with soap whenever I took the Lord's name in vain, and I got hauled into confession after asking if Aunt Theresa might get an abortion when, at seventeen, she accidentally got pregnant. In the seven years we'd lived in Jackson, I could remember us missing church only once, because we were snowed in and couldn't get to town. Mama not believing in God was like the Tetons not having snow. It seemed to me she'd come down with a disorienting case of the flu.

Fueled by our silence, Mama continued. "I believe in the earth. I believe in wildness. I don't want to put off living anymore. I don't want to waste my life waiting for the day when we retire and buy an RV. I want to go somewhere now. I want to live now." Mama paused and puckered her thin lips together, making her mouth wrinkled and small. She turned her gaze outside the window, beyond the trailer park, and said in a distant voice, "I want a divorce, Sully."

None of this made any sense. Divorce Sully? He was the anchor that steadied us. Mama and Sully were a team; they'd moved us from California and created our life next to the Snake out of nothing but hard work and devotion. Had Mama lost her mind or become someone else in her sleep?

"What are you going to do today, Eliza, if you're not going to church?" Theresa said to Mama, her voice several octaves higher than usual.

"I'm going backcountry skiing with friends. We're going to celebrate the spring equinox, howl at the moon, and dance naked if we damn well please. I'm going to do what I want to do, instead of rearranging myself to accommodate everyone else."

As she spoke, Mama's deep blue eyes pulsed and flickered yellow. She didn't look like herself at all. I stole a glance at Sully, hoping to get an understanding of what was happening. I waited for him to say something so she'd snap out of it, but he just stared at her. Panic took root in my chest.

"But, Mama, you don't ski," I pointed out. "You don't even sled." Mama was a fifth-generation Angeleno who jogged when the weather was pleasant. She usually didn't get out of the car while picking me up from my ski lessons and did backcountry snow trips only when we skied into the forest to cut down our Christmas tree each year, with Sully breaking trail.

Who were these friends, anyway? Mama's friends would all be at church with their families, not tromping through backwoods snowdrifts, howling or naked. Surely, she would change her mind, change back into Mama again.

Sully set down the watering can. He stroked his long ZZ Top beard as he moved over to the closet, where he began pulling out coats. The wire hangers pinged off one another, jangling in the emptiness.

"Come on, kids, let's load into the car now," he finally said. "It's time to go to church." Sully's sturdy, grease-stained hand steadied my back as I opened the front door, letting the chill blow inside.

"Theresa, put your coat on." Sully talked to her like she was his girl too; he'd helped raise her since she was nine. Sully never said no when Mama wanted one of her brothers or sisters to stay with us. Five of her eight siblings had lived with us at one time or another. Their mother had died when Mama was eighteen, and they were left with their father, whom I had met briefly in LA once and who by all accounts was Lucifer himself. Mama was their lifeboat.

Theresa moved her thin body around the living room like a bewildered hummingbird, frantically trying to make Mama see the ridiculousness of it all. "Who's going to make Easter dinner?" Theresa bordered on hysterical. "You always make it. Nobody else knows how to do it."

Mama sighed. "I really don't care, Theresa," she said. "Since I was a toddler, my life has been about taking care of other people. That's not my job anymore." Mama returned to her bedroom, gently shutting the door behind her.

We went to church without Mama; then Sully stopped at the Virginian to buy himself cigarettes. Now we were almost home, passing our sledding hill and my secret fort-building spot next to the Snake. Often after church, if the snow was good, we did laps on the sledding hill, careening down into the cottonwoods while Mama stood off to the side, taking pictures. I thought of Mama giggling, her freckles scrunched up on her nose as our toboggan bounced down into the trees. Whenever we'd get close to crashing into one, Sully would yell, "Roll!" We'd bail off the side then, screaming and laughing, wiping snow off our faces as the empty sled thumped against the tree trunk. Sully's whole face would lift into a smile when he watched me sprawled across the snow, laughing next to the cottonwoods.

Nobody was laughing now as Sully pulled up onto the gravel in front of our trailer.

Mama's car wasn't there, but I still fantasized that she'd be inside waiting with hot chocolate ready for us. Maybe when we walked in, the trailer would be filled with the sweet smell of sizzling honey-glazed ham in the oven. I would scratch out a spirited version of "Buffalo Gals" on my fiddle—Mama's favorite—and David would spin around wildly, singing the only words he could remember, "and dance by the light of the moon," over and over.

We walked across the driveway, carefully avoiding the ice patches that refused to accept the inevitable change of season, and opened the door. The house was cold and silent; not even an ember smoldered in the woodstove. Mama was gone.

Three

Sinking Ship

Theresa and Sully threw together Easter dinner from the meager supplies we had on hand, and we ate it without Mama. Afterward, Theresa and Lana drove home to their apartment in town. Long after I went to bed, I lay awake worrying that Mama had permanently run off or been killed in an avalanche. Finally, around midnight, I heard Mama's Oldsmobile Cutlass creep into the driveway, and I relaxed under my comforter.

The next morning, I got up early to hitch a ride to school with Sully. He came from a family of mechanics and owned a small engine-repair shop across from our church in the center of Jackson. Sully went into town at four every morning to get a jump on fixing motors before the shop opened. He worked alone thirteen hours a day, except Sundays, fixing and selling chainsaws, snowblowers, and lawn mowers.

I often caught a ride with him to avoid taking the bus with all the other south-of-town kids—from elementary to high school—between Hoback Junction and Jackson. On the bus, I usually got a ration of shit from the trailer park kids for being a stuck-up honors student, which could escalate into physical brawls in the back of the bus or even at the bus stop. The second half of the ride, I got shit from the rich kids in my honors classes who caught the bus closer to town, where there were grand wooden houses and barns with acreage and pastured horses. They called me trailer park trash and made fun of me for having a different last name—my real father's name—while Mama and David shared Sully's name. I could get scrappy when I needed to and talk trash just fine, but the thing I did better than any of them was run. Even the high school kids couldn't catch me.

While I was the only Crocker in Jackson, these kids had families that went back generations. Mountains, roads, and parks carried their last names. Their parents owned construction companies or shops along the town square with their names hung up in lights. These businesses catered to the millions of tourists who came through our small town each year to visit Jackson Hole Mountain Resort and Grand Teton and Yellowstone National Parks. Their families profited handsomely from tourism and development. Like the other trailer park families, mine eked out a living in the service industry, barely able to make ends meet in the inflated resort economy.

In Jackson, it was so unusual to have a different name from your family that even the trailer park kids used it against me. On the bus the week before, a high school girl sitting in the seat in front of me had said, "Where *is* your real dad, anyway? Nobody's ever seen him. You probably just made him up." She turned back smugly and carried on talking to her friend. In my backpack was a curling iron that I took to and from school to use after PE. I wrapped my palm tightly around the handle, waiting for the right moment. When the bus door opened for my stop, I stood up behind her and cracked her on the top of the head with the metal shaft as hard as I could.

"Shut your damn mouth," I said, then ran off the bus.

It wasn't her stop yet, but she chased me off the bus, yelling, "You better run, you little bitch. I'm going to kill you." Even though she was four years older and much stronger, I made it to my house without her catching me.

But I didn't want to ride to town with Sully just because I was trying to hide from all the unpleasantness on the bus. Going early with Sully was special. We would talk about things without any distractions, and I sure needed that the morning after Easter Sunday. As was our habit, we pulled into the twenty-four-hour Elkhorn Café near Sully's shop. Our boots chomped against the granular snow as we trudged from the van to the restaurant in the blackness, breathing air so cold it made me sneeze. Sully held the door open for me, and I stepped into cinnamon-and-bacon-scented warmth that made the skin on my face feel instantly dewy. We took our usual red booth and looked over our menus silently.

"What was Mama talking about before church?" I said, trying to sound real casual.

Sully stopped stroking his long brown beard. He turned his head toward the darkness outside the window, giving me a good view of his hooked nose. Sully wasn't classically handsome like my real father, who was a Robert Redford look-alike, but he had a knack for making you feel comfortable and safe. Being near him was like curling up next to the woodstove.

Sully looked back at me and shrugged.

"It was confusing," I said. "It didn't seem like her at all."

Sully rolled his eyes dismissively. "Women."

Bill, the owner, hobbled over on his wooden leg to pour Sully's coffee. At this hour, there was a specific clientele: drunks trying to stay warm after the bars closed and men who wore knife tools on their belts and carried towing chains in the back of their rigs. I was the only child in the place, and the only female, which was fine with me. I'd always felt at home among men with callused hands.

"Made it in okay, Sully?" Bill asked. Meaning: You didn't slide off the road or hit a moose on the way into town?

Sully nodded. "You bet."

Sully watched Bill limp off before saying, "See, now, there's a guy who keeps it straight. He's open round the clock. You always know you can come in here and get breakfast anytime you want it. You can count on him."

"What would we do if the Elkhorn shut down?" I asked. *Like Mama.*

"Bill ain't going nowhere." Sully took a swig of black coffee.

"But what if Bill died or something, or decided he was tired of serving people twenty-four seven?"

Sully shrugged. It seemed clear to me that he'd never considered that things might change. He'd been blindsided too. If Sully didn't know how to fix this, we were screwed. A buzzing terror rushed up my spine. I felt like screaming right there in the restaurant.

Sully could see I was struggling to act normal and changed the subject. "Ever see Mike around school?"

I nodded. Sully's buddy Mike often hung around the shop in the evenings near quitting time, after finishing up at my school, where he worked as the janitor.

"He said something about kids at your school giving him shit."

I felt sorry for Mike because he got it hard from the rich kids at school. Just a few days earlier, some boys had taped a sign on his custodian's cart that read "Trash man." Mike didn't see it right away, and people laughed as he pushed his cart down the hall. I didn't know what to do, so I just nodded to Mike on my way to class, lingering long enough to tug off the sign and crumple it in my palm.

"I know you're not in on any of that," Sully said matter-of-factly. Sully always believed in the best version of me, believed me to be like him and Mama, unfailingly kind, no matter what. Like the time his only sister got married in California and his whole family refused to go because she married a Mexican. The party was a giant *asada* in the park, packed with the groom's family all laughing and dancing. Sully, Mama, and I were the only family members who showed up for the bride.

"Imagine if we hadn't gone," Mama had said.

Of course, I couldn't imagine it, because family was everything to Sully, and especially to Mama. Mama was always thinking of her younger brothers and sisters. The year we'd moved to Jackson, she'd started sending for them immediately. She'd prepared the big master bedroom for her sister Peggy to live in, and another room for Theresa. Mama and Sully slept in a makeshift bedroom next to the washer and dryer. My parents gave every last drop of energy they had to their family. You could bet your breakfast on it—until yesterday, anyway.

After the Elkhorn, we headed to the shop so Sully could get to work, even though it was still dark. The place had no heating system, and its cinder-block walls and cement floors made it miserably cold. Sully set me up with a space heater in the parts room, where he'd put a little desk for me so I could study. He was proud of my good grades and said I was smart enough to go to college in Laramie and be a teacher if I wanted.

Sully had the skills to fix anything—cars, boats, snowmobiles, water heaters, you name it. Mama sometimes made comments about how he was too nice, doing things like sharpening scissors for ladies from church when he could be making real money fixing cars. Sully had never meant to have a small engine-repair business. His former boss, Cecil, who used to own the shop and was like a father to Sully, had been a volunteer firefighter and died tragically in a fire at the Wort Hotel, a few blocks east of the shop. His widow couldn't sell the business, and so Sully stepped up and took it off her hands. Mama thought Sully should change the name of it, but he kept the sign and everything in the shop the way Cecil had it. Sometimes when Mama was mad, she threw this at Sully—"You can't even put your name on the sign outside." She wanted him to take ownership, build the business into something that was his instead of working day and night to make payments to Cecil's widow. Mama wanted him to someday turn a profit, so she wouldn't have to work so hard at the hospital, carrying the load for all of us.

After getting me sorted out in the parts room, Sully flipped on the radio for company. Listening to Paul Harvey's show, *The Rest of the Story*, made the leaden, predawn air around us less lonely. I worked ahead on my homework, then read from my library book until it was time to walk the mile across town to Jackson Hole Junior High School, built along the edge of the town elk refuge. By the time I got to school, my toes and fingers were numb. Before I walked into the building, I paused to look at the elk surrounding my school. The herd wintering at the refuge was still in the hundreds, even though things were thawing and the backcountry was opening up. I could see that the animals were tired from the strain of a heavy winter by the way they took extra time to eat tender valley grass and build energy for their move. Then I opened the school door and prepared myself for another day of eighth grade.

Before class, Justin cruised by my locker. He had on stained red parachute pants and a Van Halen T-shirt with the sleeves ripped off. We had outgrown fort building by now and moved on to fishing. Justin and I didn't really hang out together at school. We didn't want anyone to get the wrong impression that we *liked* each other or something. There was a kinship between us, though, as people who've nearly died together often have.

"You okay?" Justin said, raking up his hair into spiky clumps that made him resemble Kevin Bacon.

I didn't nod, only looked at him. *No.*

He cocked his head, asking for more.

"It's my mom," I said. "Something's happened to her."

"Hey, where's the flood?" Julie Shannon cackled as she passed me with her posse, all of them clad in rabbit fur coats. I rolled my eyes. My pants were always too short; it had been pointed out to me every day since third grade. We couldn't afford the clothes sold in the fancy Jackson stores, so every September, Mama drove me two hours each way to Idaho Falls to go school shopping. The way I grew, it didn't take long for my pants to be up past my ankles. I had to wear them like that until Christmas or Easter, when my parents would scrape together the money to get me a few new things. That is, until this Easter.

A couple of years earlier, I'd asked for a rabbit fur coat for Christmas, like Julie and the other girls had, but when I unwrapped the long box under the tree, it was a .22 rifle. Sully said, "This way you can hunt the rabbits yourself and make your own coat." Sully and I went out for target practice a few times, but I only killed one rabbit before I gave up on the coat. Even though I'd killed plenty of fish, I didn't have the heart for killing bunnies. When I told Sully as much, he said, "That's okay. At least now you understand the responsibility of wearing a coat like that."

Justin ignored Julie and her crew as they passed us. Their taunts were the air we breathed. "What happened to your mom?"

"It's like an alien came and took over her body. Looks like her. Sounds like her. But it ain't her."

He started to smile, thinking I was making a joke, but then stopped when he saw I wasn't kidding.

I banged my locker shut. Neither of us knew what to do about an alien mom.

In first-period PE, Mrs. Widman made us go out in the bitter wind to run a timed mile. I made it halfway around the track before my limbs stopped. It didn't matter that my brain was telling my legs to go. I was as surprised as anyone when I collapsed onto the asphalt like a horse with a busted tendon.

"Let's go, Miss Crocker," Mrs. Widman yelled. The wind jangled the whistle and keys hanging around her neck and blew her thin blond hair across her glasses.

"I can't."

"That's not like you," she said, jogging across the track to me. "You're usually one of the fast girls. What's going on?" She reached out her hand to pull me up.

I tried to think up some lie to explain my collapse, but I couldn't. Mrs. Widman wasn't just my PE teacher, she had also recruited me the previous year for the volleyball team. She was tough on me, but that was because she was cultivating an athletic ability in me I didn't know I had.

"My parents are getting divorced," I blurted. The grief of saying it sliced through my center.

"Oh, honey," she said. "Are you sure?"

I managed a nod before starting to cry. She put her arm around me and guided me back inside. When it came to living with divorce, I was more experienced than most people in our conservative small town, where only a few kids at school had divorced parents. Mama and my father had split when I was four. But this divorce felt different, and worse. Already, I was a broken girl from a broken home, who'd been ripped in half once. How was I going to survive being ripped apart again?

"Where will you live?" Mrs. Widman asked.

I looked at her blankly. I hadn't thought of that.

Mrs. Widman said things to encourage me, but she never said it was going to be okay.

"Do you know why they're splitting up? Have they been fighting?"

I never really saw Mama and Sully fight, not like Mama and my father. My earliest memory is of squatting underneath the kitchen table on the faded yellow linoleum, gripping wooden legs with my tiny hands as my father dragged Mama across the floor by her long blond hair. Mama's eyes stayed on me as she wriggled, trying to get free, begging, "Not in front of Bridget!" while I screamed, "Stop!" and "Mama!" over and over. My father didn't listen, just dragged Mama to the living room and then overturned a fully loaded bookcase onto her, pinning her to the floor. My father was shaking and spitting while he yelled, but I don't remember what he said. Finally, he caught his breath, looked down on Mama, and gave her a twisted smile before striding out of the apartment.

After the door slammed shut, Mama sniffed a few times and tried to act like she wasn't crying. She was still trying to be my strong mama, even though she was broken under the bookcase. I ran out from under the table to help her and struggled to lift the heavy bookcase. I felt so desperate and small. I started screaming all over again, until Mama told me to go and get the woman who lived next door to help us. It wasn't long afterward that Mama enrolled in nursing school and started planning our escape.

As far as I could tell, there was nothing like that going on with Mama and Sully. Mama had simply woken up as someone else. Mrs. Widman's questions—*Do you know why they're splitting up? Have they been fighting?*—rattled around inside me all day, and then in English class, I remembered something.

The week before, instead of making dinner for us at home like he always did, Sully had taken David and me to the hospital on a school night to have dinner with Mama while she was working the night shift. I'd never been to the hospital when Mama was working. I didn't even know you could do that. Sully had her paged over the intercom, and she met us in the cafeteria, walking so fast she nearly glided in, white-blond hair billowing behind her. Even in scrubs, Mama was a knockout, with her delicious smile, long legs, and deep blue eyes. She kissed me and David but turned her head when Sully tried to kiss her.

"What's with you, Eliza?" Sully asked as we sat down with our food.

"I can't believe you just went and did that," Mama said to him from across the table. "You can't make big decisions like that without consulting me. Especially when it's my car and my insurance."

"I didn't think you needed to know," Sully said. He was slumped over his tray a little, unable to look at her. The glare from the fluorescent lights bounced off his mostly bald head.

"So it's okay to cancel my insurance without telling me?" Mama was mad. "Imagine how humiliated I felt after telling those people, 'Don't worry about the dent, we have insurance.'" Mama lowered her voice to a whisper, but it still sounded like yelling. "Then you try to give them a fucking chainsaw to buy them off, because it turns out that no, you've actually been letting your wife and children drive around uninsured *for months*."

"You know the shop hasn't been doing well. I was going to fix the insurance as soon as we got the money. Summer's almost here, and people will be buying new lawn mowers."

"Well, canceling an insurance policy is a decision we make together."

"Nah." Sully looked at her without blinking.

"Excuse me?"

"I'm the head of the household, and I'll make the decisions."

Mama got a look I'd never seen on her before. When Mama was with my real father, her face was permanently gripped by terror and shame, and it had taken years of Sully making her laugh for it to settle into an open happiness. I knew because I was in the habit of gauging Mama's every expression. Were we safe? Would we be able to pay the rent? Would we be buying hamburger or ramen to eat this week? Mama's face laid out our situation when her words couldn't. This new expression was more like outrage and not like Mama at all.

"You wanna say that again in front of our daughter?" She pointed her chin toward me.

I did not want to be dragged into this argument. I wanted to be quietly tucked in the corner like David, who was obliviously eating a giant bowl of tapioca pudding, even though it wasn't nearly as good as Mama's homemade version.

"I'm the head of the household," Sully said slowly, his eye twitching. "And I'll make the decisions for this family."

Mama snorted, then looked at me and gave a sad smile.

"I've got to go," she said, looking at her watch. Then she stood up and walked away.

Nothing more happened after that dinner. Mama and Sully were rarely together, each of them working more than full-time and tag-teaming as parents to keep things afloat. Throughout the week, we'd carried on with school, work, grocery shopping, and fiddle lessons. It seemed like the whole insurance thing had blown over, but maybe it had just been gathering into a storm, to be released on Easter Sunday morning in an unexpected torrent.

After school, Aunt Theresa had a hot date and wanted me to babysit, so I walked over to her place near Cache Creek. Luckily for her, nineteen was the legal drinking age in Wyoming, since she spent plenty of time at the bar. I babysat Lana when Theresa went out, usually staying the night at her motel-like Section 8 apartment littered with *People* magazines, dirty laundry, and half-empty bottles of nail polish. Usually, she'd bring home some random drunk guy from the bar to spend the night, and I'd lock myself in Lana's bedroom if I was staying over. Today, though, she'd made plans for an afternoon date, since it was a school night for me and Sully would come pick me up on his way home around six-thirty.

I arrived to find Lana napping and Theresa, hot rollers in her hair, filing down plastic yogurt lids to the shape and size of quarters to use in the shared coin-op laundry machine. She was going on about her date, Steve, a guy she'd recently met at a party, who according to her was like an outdoorsy Rob Lowe with glasses.

"You mean he's a gorper?" That's what we called ski bum hippies because all they ate was gorp—good old raisins and peanuts. Gorpers could be college dropouts who were working as ski lift operators or old hippies who lived in yurts and went backcountry skiing, like the new friends Mama had described on Easter Sunday.

Theresa moved to the bathroom to take the rollers out. "What's wrong with gorpers?"

"They don't shower. Also, they smoke pot." A girl at school who babysat for our science teacher—a gorper—said there was a big bag of marijuana in his cabinet.

Theresa laughed.

"Do you think Mama is turning into a gorper? Maybe that's why she wants to divorce Sully." Sully was definitely not a gorper. As far as I could tell, gorpers weren't big on working—it interfered with skiing—and I'd yet to meet one whose hands were greasy from being in engines all day.

"She wants a divorce because she's having an affair."

"What are you even talking about? She is not."

"She is too." Theresa's eyes glittered with excitement. She relished any opportunity to be right, especially if she knew something I didn't. "With a doctor. Or maybe that's done. I think she's moved on to the doctor's friend now."

"How do you know?"

"Everyone in town knows."

I leaned against the bathroom door to steady myself. "Sully doesn't."

"He has to suspect something. Who does he think she went backcountry skiing with? The thing with the doctor's been going on for a couple of months." Theresa shook her fresh curls to give them more body. "But now she's more interested in his friend. He's *definitely* a gorper." She laughed.

None of this was funny. "Why didn't you say anything?"

"She told me not to, but since the shit's hit the fan, fuck it. She can deal with her own mess."

My aunt put on lip gloss and an embroidered, gauzy peasant blouse. "What do you think?"

Theresa trying to pass herself off as a gorper was nearly as ridiculous as Mama having an affair. Theresa didn't ski or do anything outside. She didn't listen to the Grateful Dead or Bob Marley. Instead, she'd nearly broken her Madonna cassette tape playing "Material Girl" over and over, and she was always going on about landing a rich guy to get off food stamps.

"You need underarm hair to pull off that shirt," I said absently, still stunned from the news.

"What about your beanie?"

I threw it over to her as she blotted her lip gloss to be more natural.

"I've left you guys a box of mac and cheese, and you can watch MTV." We had only two channels in the trailer park, and Theresa knew that MTV was a big reason I liked to babysit. "If you want, you can keep working on filing these coins down to fit in the washer. Damn landlord thinks he can charge us single mothers fifty cents a load? Asshole can think again."

Mama would disapprove of Theresa's laundry scam, say it was stealing or cheating. Theresa never really listened to Mama or took her advice. Apparently, Mama didn't take her own advice either, if she was going around cheating on Sully. After Theresa left, I turned up the volume to Prince's "Let's Go Crazy" video and got to filing.

⌒

I didn't see Mama until the next day after school. When I ran home from the bus stop, she and David were there making chocolate chip cookies. It was the first time I'd seen her since the Easter Sunday episode, and I had questions.

"How was skiing?" I asked.

"Oh, it was a challenge, but I made it off the mountain alive," she said. "How was church?"

"Horrible," I said. *Because you weren't there.* I bit into a cookie to avoid crying.

"Well, that's what I've thought for years," she said. "That's why I'm not going anymore."

Mama was incredibly smart, but she missed that our horribles were for different reasons. Plus, going for years and pretending to like it was sort of like lying. Had she been lying all these years? And, if she was lying about believing in God, was she lying about believing in family too? The list of things she might be lying about was getting pretty long.

"Why do you want to divorce Sully?"

"Honey, don't you see? I can't keep letting him control all the family decisions." Mama shook her head.

I'd understood why Mama had had to leave my real father. But saying that Sully's control over her was worthy of divorcing him was something I didn't understand. Her deciding to break up the family without consulting anyone seemed far more controlling than his canceling the insurance. I wanted to ask Mama about having an affair but didn't actually want to hear any details. I hoped Sully never found out because it would break him. Anyone could see from the way he looked at her that he adored Mama.

"Where are we all going to live?" I managed.

"Here," she said. "Nothing will change."

Everything was changing. Didn't she get that?

"We'll just split the trailer in half," she said. "I'll use the back door and Sully can use the front door. You kids can just go between us."

"Then Sully is going to move into my room?" I grasped at logistics. *Also, was he still my daddy? Was I still going to be his daughter?*

"That would make the most sense."

None of this made any sense. I couldn't sit listening to her insanity another minute.

I flew out the front door then, headed for the cottonwoods. I had to get to the river.

I reached the water's edge and fell to my knees, hitting the river rock like a pew. I couldn't get the words out through my hiccupping sobs, so

I put my fingers into the river's swollen waters and imagined the story in my head, releasing it to her through my fingers. Then, I steadied my gaze on the glare burning off the Snake's surface. Over the years, I'd discovered that if I focused like this, I could make out the river's voice. More than ever, I needed an answer from her. A sign.

It's time for you to go.

Go? Where?

The gleam off the river's surface shone whiter, until it was all I could see. A tidy yellow house not far from the ocean emerged in my mind's eye. It was my real father's house, where I visited him during school breaks, flying as an unaccompanied minor between Jackson Hole and LAX. I saw the solid branches of the avocado trees I loved to climb in the back-yard. Inside lived a picture-perfect family; they appeared like a lifeboat out of the river's glare. My father was a real estate agent, and his new wife, a schoolteacher. They and their toddler son wore designer clothes. They drove luxury cars to the mall and ate ice cream on weekends.

After my mother divorced him, my father had worked to get himself to-gether. He moved into a beach shack in Ventura and started going to coun-seling. For a time, he took up the banjo and listened to Neil Diamond. In a grueling *Kramer vs. Kramer*–type custody battle, he fought for and was awarded joint custody of me, which was a rare feat in California in the mid-1970s. Before Mama moved us to Wyoming, I spent every other weekend with my father. During my visits, he was never violent with me. He didn't hit me like he had Mama. We spent our time catching crabs in the jetties and walking barefoot to the fish market to get dinner.

After Mama left him, my father threw his energy into improving his career options to make more money for his family, which at that time con-sisted of me, and he'd been court-ordered to pay child support. It wasn't easy, since he hadn't graduated from high school. He went from pumping gas to selling jewelry at a department store to selling commercial real estate. He met his wife, Shiray, while playing tennis, and together they bought the yellow house and forged a new family. They seemed to get along great, always joking and laughing. He bought her diamonds and kissed her every morning before leaving for work in his silver Porsche.

Mama was always telling me that my father was a monster and that's why we had to leave California. I had only a couple of clear memories of the violence, and often wondered if Mama was exaggerating how bad it had been to poison me against him. I'd witnessed with my own eyes that he'd changed, and he'd never hit me before, or Shiray as far as I could tell. In any case, divorce and disaster were wired together in my mind, and now that divorce had been spoken, I didn't have the stomach for what would happen next. I had to get off the sinking ship, fast. While I didn't think Sully was capable of overturning a bookcase, I didn't want to stick around to find out.

Go, the Snake said.

How could I leave Mama, Sully, the river? Abandon my baby brother, David? Leaving felt like trading them in for a new family, but I didn't know what else to do.

Go, she said. It was as clear as the day I heard *Swim*.

Four

Hotel California

I didn't notice the forest-green van with the macramé curtains driving alongside us on the Ventura Freeway until my stepmom, Shiray, said, "Is that Sully?"

It had been two years since I'd moved to California to live with my father, but it felt like a lifetime since I'd heard Sully's name. I'd almost forgotten who she meant—*Daddy*. It was strange to hear Shiray mention him, since they'd never met, even though they'd both been involved in raising me since I was a kindergartner. Shiray knew about his van, though. There was a lot of car talk in our house. My father was obsessed with them, and he dragged us to car shows every weekend, where his cars would win prizes. Naturally, my father didn't much care for vans, maintaining they were for homeless drifters and scam artists.

There was no mistaking Sully's rig, with its Wyoming plates and sparkling metallic green paint job, which stood out on the colorless freeway. As I laid eyes on it, my stomach dropped into my pelvis; I felt like I was still lurching around on Mr. Toad's Wild Ride at Disneyland, where we'd just spent the day celebrating my sixteenth birthday.

For the occasion, my father had rented a white luxury passenger van for the day. He'd missed nearly all of my birthdays growing up, so he'd decided to go all out for this one: taking the rare day off work, paying for me and six of my friends from school to go to "The Happiest Place on Earth," and renting a passenger van to haul us all in, despite his aversion to them.

As I climbed over the rows of bench seats toward the front for a better look, my father gunned the engine. He sped up to put his van next to Sully's, as if drag racing.

"Do you think it's really him?" Shiray asked, incredulous. She moved my five-year-old half brother, Garrett, into the seat behind her and motioned me onto her lap, even though we were both the same size.

It had to be Sully. The macramé curtains were the clincher. How many hours of my life had I studied those curtains while lying on the foam bed in the back, trying to make sense of their pattern? Eventually, I'd discovered that the two ivory curtains didn't match at all.

It was such a weird coincidence, seeing Sully on the freeway like this, a thousand miles away from Jackson. I hadn't seen him since I'd left. Maybe he was visiting his family, who lived in the area, or maybe he'd moved back to California. It was February, after all, and he never did like the snow.

I rolled down the window and hung out up to my waist, waving both hands outside Sully's window.

"Honk the horn," I called to my father. I'd imagined a friendly *beep-beep* honk, but my father laid on the horn as if Sully had sideswiped his lane.

Sully turned and looked at the noise. His long beard had changed from brown to mostly white now. He didn't recognize me at first. I kept waving and stretching toward him until he rolled down his window and smiled, with all his teeth showing, which he only did when he was really happy. Over the roar of road, wind, and tires, he yelled across the lanes, "Happy birthday!" We flew down the freeway together, my sixteen-year-old body almost bridging the two vans.

"Thank you!" The wind ripped my tears, launching them into flight before they could touch my cheeks.

"Have a good one!" He waved his thick, sturdy hand before rolling up his window.

Shiray pulled me back in by my shirt. I tried to wipe my snot and tears before any of my friends noticed.

"Who's that?" Garrett asked.

I didn't know what to call him. My ex-stepdad? The man who raised me but was no relation to me now?

"Her mother's second husband," Shiray said.

I returned to the back of the van and burrowed between my friends Ryan and Michelle. Although Michelle was my best friend, she didn't know about Sully or the life I'd lived next to the Snake. I'd told her that I'd moved to California to live with my father because I couldn't live with my mom anymore. I'd never said why. My life before had simply ended, along with the girl I'd been.

I leaned forward and hid my face behind the faux-leather seat of the rental van, willing myself to turn back into the California girl who was coming home from Disneyland on her sweet sixteenth, the girl whose father had gone all out to make it special. I conjured up images of fresh-squeezed lemonade and funnel cake. Cute boys and Guess jeans. But then over the radio George Michael crooned, "Guilty feet have got no rhythm," and the guilt I had over abandoning that life and my family before—Mama, Daddy, David, the Snake, and the girl I was—pressed against my forehead thick as cement, until I felt as if I might collapse.

Michelle saw that I was struggling not to lose it. She stroked the back of my hand as if it were a tiny wounded kitten. I looked straight ahead, catching my real father's glare in the rearview mirror. His usual charming, joking persona was gone. His ice-blue eyes were brimming with tears, but also narrowed, and firing rage. He glowered at me as if I'd betrayed him, then looked back at the road, eerily silent.

I'd never seen my father cry before and had heard about him crying only once, from Shiray, who said he cried when I moved to Wyoming. I'd always wondered why he hadn't fought harder for me to stay in California if he was that devastated to give me up. Right now, though, I wondered what would happen later when we got home and there were no witnesses. Would he take out his hurt on me with his fists, as he'd often done since

I'd come to live with him? Or leave it to Shiray, who dished it out just as brutally as my father, preferring choking to punches?

I was reminded of the time Mama drove me home from dance class when I was five, before we'd moved to Wyoming. As we pulled up to the house my mother shared with Sully, we came upon my father and Sully locked together on the front lawn. In the dusky twilight it took a moment for me to work out that they were fist-fighting. Sully held my father at arm's length, and only half of my father's punches were landing. Mama screamed through the car window for them to stop. They both dropped to the ground and rolled around on the freshly cut lawn in front of the house, my father still trying to punch Sully in the head, shouting, "You piece-of-shit chrome dome." Sully wasn't instigating punches, just holding my father's arms, as if he were a human straitjacket. I knew they were fighting because Sully had taken my father's place in Mama's bed and I had started calling him Daddy. While they rolled around, Mama threatened to call the police, so my father got into his car and drove away without even looking at us or saying goodbye, even though the whole thing had been over Mama and me.

Ten years had passed since their fistfight on the lawn, but my father still resented Sully for stealing his family. I sat in the rental van, torn by conflicting loyalties, unable to reconcile my fractured identities. I'd gotten used to suppressing my emotions and being the daughter my father expected, especially since he beat me whenever I reminded him of my mother or Sully. But now, after seeing those macramé curtains and the man who for most of my life was my loving and tender daddy, the girl from the Snake River who lived inside me was fighting to get free.

"Lie down," Michelle said. She stroked my hair and gently pushed my head toward Ryan's lap. She lifted my legs up onto hers and patted my tanned calves. Ryan rested his wide hand comfortingly on my shoulder. The steady rhythm of tires humming over the road lulled me into a thick sleep. I drifted in and out during the hours-long drive as if I were drugged.

It seemed like the middle of the night when we finally returned to our tidy yellow house in Ventura after dropping off my friends. I lagged several minutes behind my father and Shiray, who had already disappeared into the house, carrying my sleeping brother to his room. Groggily, I gathered my mouse ears and bags of gifts and shuffled to the front porch.

As I entered the house, I didn't notice my father standing in the foyer until I felt his fist land solidly next to my left breast. The blow forced me back on my heels. I braced for another hit, but instead of winding up his fist, my father stepped closer to me. He was only an inch taller than me, and his face came right up to mine.

"You think I don't know what you were doing back there?" he sneered. His eyes rolled back into his head like a mad horse. He wrapped his pale, smooth hand around my upper arm and jerked me over the threshold, then threw me against the foyer's flowered wallpaper. My bags dropped from my hands, landing on the threshold. He slammed the front door, but it didn't shut because my mouse ears were in the way. He kicked them, now crumpled, across the shiny oak floor and latched the front door shut, clicking the dead bolt.

"What? I wasn't doing anything!" I yelled, holding my hand against my throbbing breast.

Shiray appeared in the foyer. "That was some ballsy move, young lady, doing that in the back seat with Ryan." Her flaming red cheekbones overpowered her flat blue eyes, which were dull and small. Her earlier compassion had switched to fury, which wasn't unusual. Shiray felt things quickly and deeply and was seemingly unable to control the changing tide within her. In the two years I'd been living with her and my father, I'd come to understand that determination and loyalty were the glue of their marriage. Their passion was so fierce, it often spilled into rage.

"Do you think I couldn't see you giving that boy a blow job back there?" my father asked. "I could see you in the rearview mirror!" He punched me again between my breast and my shoulder, then stepped toward me, leaving little space between our bodies. I was boxed between him and the wall, my shoulder and breast throbbing.

I instinctively brought my arms up and crossed them in front of me as a barrier, hunching forward to protect my chest. "I wasn't, I swear!" I didn't exactly know what a blow job entailed. I'd never had a boyfriend. The guys I hung around with were from my church youth group. They never even swore and they went on house-building missions to Mexico. All of us were virgins.

"Don't lie to me! You're fucking lying!" Bouncing up and down on the balls of his feet, he slapped my head with both hands. Shiray stood behind him, disdain flickering across her puckered mouth. Sometimes, she took turns with my father, either hitting me or holding me down, but she seemed content simply to cheer him on this time.

"I'm not lying! I was sleeping." I hiccuped the words now, wheezing them out in wispy spit strands.

"You're a fucking liar and a slut, just like your mother!"

Something clicked in my father's eyes, and they were no longer rolling back but fixed and black. I suddenly remembered that this was exactly what he yelled at Mama—that she was a liar and a slut—before he over-turned the bookcase onto her.

Once my father's eyes were fixed like this, I knew there was no hope of calling back his rage. My spine to the wall, I slid down until I was folded in as small as I could be and covered my head with my forearms while he slapped and kicked me, screaming that I was a liar and a slut over and over. The only thing to do was harden myself and weather the beating. It was something Wyoming had trained me for—all those years of hauling wood in subzero temperatures, postholing through snowdrifts along the river, enduring the suffering that came with living in an inhospitable place. I knew well how to separate myself from physical pain. This form of numb-ing myself worked just as well to shield me from emotional pain too.

While my father beat me, I went deep inside myself, into a small cave in the back of my being. It was quiet and calm there, and I was safe, en-veloped by still, silvery air. What was happening inside me and what was happening outside were two different realities. I'd been to this internal cave so often, I'd come to think of it as a sacred place where I sat with God.

I could still hear Shiray shrieking. "Stop it, you're hurting her. I think you're really hurting her!" A sturdy woman, Shiray yanked my father off me in one motion. I rolled over onto my hands and knees and crawled down the hallway to my room. I could hear my father panting behind me, spent. I shut my bedroom door, then scooched into my closet and slid the mirrored door closed. Inside my closet, I'd created my own world. There was a flashlight, throw pillows, George, my sympathetic monkey, and hundreds of pictures cut out from *National Geographic*. I'd collected photos of the African savanna and taped them to the closet walls in an uninterrupted collage.

"Someday, I will escape," I told the glossy lions, wildebeests, and giraffes. "I will come to you, and they will never find me."

I only had to survive long enough to make it through high school. I couldn't yet imagine how difficult that would be.

Five

A Perfect Beach Day

Garrett burst into my bedroom, his little feet thumping against the polished oak floor. "Bwidget! Michelle wants to talk to you." Through the crack of my closet door, I saw him jump onto the frilly lavender bed that I hardly slept in, expecting to land on my curled-up body. Not finding me, he froggy-hopped over to the closet and pressed his silky blond head up against the crack of the sliding door, squinting a blue eye into the darkness.

My whole body was sore from the previous night's beating. Even though I was exhausted, I hadn't slept.

"What are you doing in there?" I could smell the strawberry juice circling Garrett's lips.

"I'm hiding."

"Fwom who?"

"The strawberry-lipped froggy monster, who do you think?" I thrust my hand out and grabbed his mini polo shirt as he shrieked and twisted away.

Garrett tauntingly wiggled his hips back and forth. "I'm going to hang up on Michelle!" He giggled before running down the hallway.

"Garrett!" Shiray called from the kitchen. "Did you tell your sister?"

"Yes. She's in her cwoset again."

I moved slowly from my room through the foyer into the glaringly sunny kitchen. Shiray was singing along to Motown hits while preparing a batch of fresh waffles with strawberries, my favorite. She'd even bought a spray can of whipped cream.

"Michelle's on the phone, sweet pea," she chirped.

I felt nauseated, trapped in a shifting fun house with piped-in happy music. I avoided looking at Shiray as I picked up the phone by the long, twisted cord.

"Okay, so I'm looking out my window, and it's gorgeous blue, no wind. A perfect beach day. Come pick me up."

Long pause.

"Or are you grounded?" Ninety percent of the time, I was on restriction: no phone, no outside contact.

"Can I go to the beach with Michelle?" I asked.

"Sure. Take the Jaguar if you want. Your dad washed it before he left."

On weekend mornings, my father pounded out eighty miles on his road bike before noon; this in addition to the twenty miles he did every weekday morning. On weekends, it was my responsibility, as part of my chore list, to wash and wax the Jaguar and the Mercedes. My father didn't trust me alone with his silver 911 Porsche or his restored '51 Chevy, so after his bike ride, we detailed those cars together. He'd gone easy on me this morning, his way of making up for going hard on me last night.

Michelle heard Shiray over the line and squealed, "The Jag?! Get over here already!"

I hung up and turned to leave, but Shiray handed me a waffle plate. "Uh-uh, not so fast. Breakfast for the growing girl. It was such a long day at Disneyland," she said, bringing me a glass of milk, "I don't think we even had dinner." She laughed. "No wonder everyone got so cranky."

Shiray's denial coupled with the relentlessly cheerful Motown had my head throbbing. Still, I choked down sticky spoonfuls from my plate, intent on getting out of the house, away from her. I only had to say my lines.

"It really was a tiring day," I said, "but I had so much fun. Thank you."

"You're welcome, honey. We really wanted to make your sixteenth birthday special."

It was one I'd never forget.

In the two years I'd spent living under Shiray and my father's rule, lying for the sake of survival had become my shield. At night, in my closet, I wrote stories about a lost moose trapped in suburbia. The bewildered moose tried to find her way home and mistakenly broke into a fluorescent-lit real estate office. Everything was foreign, and she became terrified and angry, trampling the furniture with long, powerful legs meant for crossing rivers. When the real estate agents tried to subdue the moose, she twitched her ears, conjuring a plague of stinging hornets until all the real estate agents were swollen and dead. In the end, the moose couldn't escape the air-conditioned office. Even though she navigated the wreckage of busted furniture and bodies, she couldn't turn the doorknob with her hooves. My English teacher frequently asked how I came up with such crazy stories.

I finished eating Shiray's sickening waffles and wandered back to my room to begin the long process of "getting ready," which meant checking for bruises and, if I had any, figuring out how to hide them. I flipped on Rick Dees dishing out the top forty hits and faced the mirror. There was a purple welt close to my left eye that looked like a mascara smudge. Concealer and sunglasses would cover that. Red and purple streaks up and down my rib cage could be hidden by a one-piece swimsuit. Welts on my shins, easily explained away by Disneyland rides. While the eighties teen singing sensation Debbie Gibson crooned about secrets over the airwaves, I pushed down my simmering shame by dancing around as I hair-sprayed my bangs into a defiant claw. I blended concealer and a little blue eye shadow over the bruise near my eye.

I threw together a couple of sandwiches for Michelle and me. Michelle never had any food at her house because her parents were too self-absorbed with their divorce to notice her. Her father worked twenty-four-hour shifts as head of maintenance at a fancy hotel, where he often stayed, while her mother rarely left her bed, sobbing and sleeping in turns.

"Bye," I yelled to Shiray, who was watering her fuchsias in the backyard.

"Bye, hon. Have fun. Keys are on the table."

When I rolled up to Michelle's ocean-view house, the purring Jag motor was almost silent. I didn't honk (Mama always said that was rude), but I didn't get out either. Instead, I busied myself cueing my cassette tape of Paul Simon's *Graceland* to my favorite part as Michelle ran down the steps with her neatly rolled towel.

"Ooh, turn it up," she said as she slid into the black leather passenger seat.

Giddy with freedom, I peeled out and laid tracks down the sleepy street, then turned onto the steepest part of the hill. Michelle nodded as I pushed the gas pedal all the way down, gunning for the dips below. We launched off the first dip and flew through the air *Dukes of Hazzard* style, landing solidly onto the lip of the second dip before careening to a halt at the stop sign.

"Good one." Michelle gripped the seat and smiled. It might have been the best air we'd ever gotten.

Our youth pastor, Byron, once told me that I was a reckless driver. I had driven into the church parking lot with such force that smoke rose from the pavement when I squealed to a stop.

"This is an exquisite vehicle," Byron had lectured through the driver's window. "You need to take better care when you drive it, not only so you don't wreck it, but for safety reasons."

Reckless driving was an outlet for my curbed adrenaline, sure, but it was also my revenge. Every time I laid down tire tracks, cornered at high speeds, or jumped through the air, it was a fuck you to my father. *Fuck you for caring more about steel than your own flesh and blood.*

After his reprimand, I added Byron to my Reckless Driving Fuck You list. I'd told Byron several times about my situation at home, and all he did was point out Bible verses for me to read. He didn't visit me outside of youth group or read over verses and give counsel during long, unsupervised walks at the beach like he did with Michelle. I'd started going to church with Michelle because I thought I might find some help there, and it was one of the only places my father and Shiray, who weren't at all religious, would let me go without them. But instead of helping me, all Byron did was brush off my pleas while creeping around with my best friend, despite being married with three kids. I felt uncomfortable when Michelle told me stories about Byron taking her on long motorcycle rides, her clinging to his waist from behind. Eventually, I gave up on listening to anything Byron said. As far as I could tell, there wasn't a passage where Jesus behaved inappropriately with some of his underaged disciples while abandoning the others.

But Michelle and I weren't thinking about Byron or Bible verses as we cruised along the palm-lined streets of Ventura listening to *Graceland*. Our objective was to get down to the pier. We routinely avoided the cool kids at Schoolhouse Beach a few jetties down, even though we qualified as popular thanks to student council and track. Our main goal at the beach wasn't to be part of the scene, putting on some big act. We were intent on being supreme dorks, and we didn't want any witnesses. We liked the pier because the only people we ever saw there were passed-out homeless junkies and drunks.

We laid our towels down and ran straight for the water. We screamed and laughed, diving under waves and swimming out until we couldn't touch ground anymore, beyond the break zone. The water was cold and silky, and the salt stung my cuts.

"Dolphins or mermaids?" I asked Michelle.

"Dolphins," she said decisively.

"EEEEE, EEEEE, EEEEEE," I screeched, legs pressed together in a dolphin tail. Michelle and I swam next to each other, trying to synchronize our dolphin kicks. We came up for air, rounded our backs, and went under again.

My body went numb from the cold water. No more stinging or throbbing. We rested on the water's surface, just floating, relaxing in the expansiveness of the water.

I thought about how the Snake made its way from Jackson through Idaho and Oregon, then joined the Columbia River in Washington before spilling into the Pacific Ocean. The water I was swimming in now was part Snake water. More than Michelle or anybody else, I felt that the water understood me. When I went under, I felt washed clean of my burden, more so than the time Byron dunked me in the church baptism tank. Unlike humans or their constructions of God, I knew that the pure power of the ocean wouldn't fail me. I was reminded that I was a special child, that I was loved. I knew this like I knew my own name.

"I'm hungry," Michelle said, as we floated among amber kelp fronds.

"I brought sandwiches."

We bodysurfed back to shore and dripped over to the towels. As we ate, a man with pee-stained jeans and matted brown hair approached.

"Good afternoon," he said. "I'm the Son of God."

We squinted up at him.

"How nice for you," said Michelle.

With the sun in our eyes, we couldn't see him as well as we could smell him. His stench reminded me of the kids back at the trailer park, who smelled of urine and neglect.

"I bless you. On this glorious day, I bless you." The Son of God went into some sort of trance, as he prayed unintelligibly over us.

Michelle gave me a look. This guy blessing us was sort of ironic, since she'd spent her entire summer vacation the year before with Byron proselytizing to vagrants around Ventura as part of the summer missionaries program. I hadn't wanted to spend that much time with Byron, so I'd opted to go to summer school in order to open up my schedule for student council in the fall. I had a hard time not laughing at this poor homeless guy who thought he was Jesus, so I lay down on my stomach and hid my face deep in my towel until I could smell the dryer sheet perfume mixed with salt. Disappearing had become my way of saying no.

"Thank you," Michelle said, midway through his chanting. "We're going to finish our lunch now. Good luck."

After an awkward minute of silence, I whispered, "Is he still there?"

"Nah, he stumbled off."

We laughed so hard we had to go back in the water to pee.

"Hey, are you wearing mascara?" Michelle swam closer until her face was right next to mine. She rubbed her thumb near my eye, on top of the bruise. I backed away from her, wincing. "What happened?"

"It's so stupid." I started to tear up. "It's so stupid I can't even say it. It's embarrassing."

"Don't be embarrassed. Don't ever be embarrassed around me." Michelle was the mom right now, a part we took turns playing.

"My father accused me of giving Ryan a blow job in the back seat yesterday." I sank down in the water until only my eyes poked out.

"What? Are you serious?"

I nodded, still partly underwater.

She shouted upward, toward the sky, "That is the lamest thing ever," then smacked the surface of the water with both hands. "We have to tell someone." Michelle meant an adult. That was what she said every time, but it was pointless. Telling other adults over the years had gotten me nowhere.

"Who is there left to tell?" I asked. "I've told three teachers, the school counselor, the nurse, two youth pastors, not to mention how-many-people's parents. Nobody believes me." I was yelling from the frustration of being ignored and dismissed by adults who were too busy or afraid to get involved. Some of them knew Shiray, a teacher from a neighboring school district, or they knew my father, a prominent businessman. They brushed me off, saying they couldn't imagine it was as bad as all that. I was an honors student from a wealthy family, on the track team, student council, and newspaper. I drove a red Jaguar with whitewall tires to school, and Shiray had me into modeling. To them, I didn't look like someone whose homelife was a hellscape. I had started to believe that they weren't helping me not because they lacked courage but because I wasn't worth protecting.

"I believe you," Michelle said, her blue eyes looking squarely at me.

"Well, you're the only one." My throat felt raw.

"What about your mom?"

"She'll make me go back to Wyoming. Like that's any better."

We held hands in the water for a while, not knowing what else to do.

"Let's play mermaids," Michelle suggested brightly.

I wiped my face clean and we went under again, swimming with our legs stuck together in the same way we did when we played dolphins. The main difference between playing mermaids and playing dolphins was that mermaids could use their arms and could speak English. Dolphins didn't have arms. They spoke a language we only pretended to know.

That night, I sat in my closet, rereading my favorite part in *Roots*, where Kunta Kinte's father holds up Kunta to the world after he is born and says, "Behold, the only thing greater than yourself."

"Bwidget," Garrett called through the crack in my door. "Your mother is on the phone."

I steeled myself before going into Shiray and my father's room to take the call.

"Happy birthday a day late! It's your mama callin'."

I hated it when she said she was my mama. She'd stopped being Mama the day she gave up on our family to become someone else.

"I called earlier, but you were gone."

"Michelle and I went to the beach. It was rad."

"Rad?"

"You know . . . radical?"

"Did you get the newspaper clipping I sent of your brother and me?"

"Yeah." In the cutout photo, she pretended to ski over David, who was dressed in a baby bear costume, to protest a proposed ski area in Yellowstone.

"Talk about radical," she said. "The news crew from Idaho Falls showed up, and people were chaining themselves to the federal building. A few people got arrested. It was so much fun. Mark wasn't there, of course. He's still in the slammer."

Mark was the guy she'd gone backcountry skiing with on Easter Sunday, the one she'd left Sully for—not the doctor but his friend. He had recently been thrown in jail for pulling up road survey stakes to protect a roadless area from oil and gas drilling.

"Wow," I managed to say.

"Anyway, that's what's going on around here. What did you do for your birthday? I guess you went out, since I got the answering machine." She hadn't left a message.

"My father took me and my friends to Disneyland. We had so much fun, we rode everything and got sick on funnel cake." I considered mentioning that I'd seen Sully driving on the 101 but decided against it. We never talked about him.

"You know there are so many preservatives in funnel cake. I really don't want you eating it."

"Okay." I rolled my eyes while flipping off the phone.

"I'm serious, Bridget. I am still your mother, and I don't want you eating stuff with nitrates and corn syrup in it. Do you understand me?"

"Yes," I said, even though I didn't understand her at all.

"Anyway, I'm just calling to make sure that *everything's going okay* and that you had a good birthday." She spoke in a deeper, weighted tone of voice, code for what she really wanted to ask: *Is he beating you?*

I picked at a scab on my shin and thought about coming clean. All I had to say was *You were right, he's a monster*, and I could be on a plane back to Wyoming that night.

"Everything's terrific," I lied. "I'm having the time of my life: going to Disneyland, driving around with Michelle in the Jaguar, swimming in the ocean . . . it's a dream."

I was too proud to admit I'd made a mistake in moving, and I would endure a thousand beatings to prove I knew how to manage my life better than she did. Besides, there wasn't much for me to go back to: the trailer was long gone. My mother now lived in a rented one-room shack that was smaller than my bedroom in the trailer had been, and there was no shower or hot water.

Beyond my pride and need to prove her wrong was the rock-bottom truth that I would rather live with the physical beatings—at least I knew

what I was in for—than deal with the feelings of abandonment and instability I fell victim to with my mother. My skin was far tougher than my
heart.

"I love you, Bridget. As long as there are stars in the sky, I will love you.
You will always be my daughter. Don't forget that."

But loving me wasn't enough. I needed my mother to take care of me,
too, and even though I was only a kid, I knew that she was no longer capable of that.

Six

The Adventure Is Just Beginning

I flopped down in the seat next to Michelle's in our AP English class. "Shiray wants me to bring Jai over to the house," I told her. "She overheard us on the phone."

"Oh, God." Michelle squirmed in her chair. "Do you think that's a good idea? I mean, he's so . . . innocent."

Michelle and I were juniors, but Jai, whom I'd been seeing the last few weeks, was only a freshman. It wasn't just his age that Michelle was talking about, though, it was the way his idealism glistened like ocean sparkles. Not only was he BEAUTIFUL, with dark skin, green eyes, and a smile that melted me, but he was the smartest person I'd ever met, with ambitions for the Ivy League. He was on student council with Michelle and me, and he'd been voted freshman prince at homecoming. Jai had a softness and quiet confidence to him, a knowing that he could do anything. Being near him was like being with the Snake River: Jai reflected to me the best part of who I was, and I caught glimpses of myself in the way he looked at me and talked to me with such respect. When I was with him, I felt I could do and be anything I wanted. He was the guy I wanted for my first boyfriend.

"They won't let me go out with him if I don't bring him over."

"Could it be a quick thing, like studying for a school project or something, and then you drive him home? Not like a coming-for-dinner thing?"

"You mean not like a *Guess Who's Coming to Dinner* thing?"

"Well, yeah."

"I can't take him over there." I sighed, coming to my senses. "They'll crucify him." I'd heard my father use racial slurs many times, although never to someone's face.

"That's why it has to be quick. It can't get ugly that way."

I saw how much she wanted to believe this was true. We both wanted to believe it so badly that we convinced ourselves.

By now, I'd figured out that staying very busy with school and church kept me out of the house, minimizing opportunities for beatings. I maintained high grades in honors classes, dressed modestly in long skirts and cowl-neck sweaters, and worked hard at my chores. I'd become skilled at saying my assigned lines and keeping my feelings confined to my journal and closet.

I hadn't yet told Jai anything about my homelife or past. I hadn't wanted to tarnish the way he saw me, or worse, make him feel sorry for me. I was also worried that bringing him home might throw my life into complete chaos. But things had been going a little better, and maybe what Michelle said was true: if I kept it short and sweet, everything would be fine. I really wanted to date Jai, so I decided to risk it.

When we pulled into my driveway one day after school, I looked over at Jai in the passenger seat, holding several poster boards for my campaign for senior class president, and knew there was still time to turn around.

"I'm excited to meet your family," he said, opening the car door. I followed him, despite the buzzing adrenaline in my limbs that told me to run.

No one was home yet. After spreading the posters across the kitchen table, we got to work coloring in a green-foliage background to go with my Indiana Jones–themed slogan: "Bridget Crocker for Senior Class President: The Adventure Is Just Beginning."

"I wonder if I can get a big rope and swing onto the stage to deliver my speech?"

"That would be rad." Jai smiled at me.

Soon, Shiray and Garrett arrived home from work and day care.

"Oh . . . hi." Shiray's voice echoed through the kitchen.

"Hi, Mrs. Crocker." Jai was on his feet and had somehow managed to take a grocery bag from her arm before she could respond. He set it down on the counter.

"Jai, meet my stepmom, Shiray," I said.

"Hi, Ty."

"Oh, it's Jai." That smile again. "What do you think of these posters? Pretty good slogan, right?"

"Bridget certainly is creative." She set down her purse, then said to me, "Can you help me with Garrett for a minute?"

I followed her into the next room, where she put a Gumby tape into the VCR for Garrett. She motioned me to follow her to the back of the house, away from Jai.

"Your father's not going to like this," she whispered. "I didn't realize your friend was Black."

"So?"

"I agree with you. He seems like a really nice boy. But your father is pretty old-fashioned about a lot of things." She let out a nervous laugh.

My father's silver Porsche pulled up outside, and we both hustled back into the kitchen, not sure what to do.

The front door opened, and my father strode in, burgundy tie, hair perfectly in place.

"Hello, Mr. Crocker." Jai looked my father in the eye and extended his hand while flashing his gleaming, hopeful smile.

My father dropped his leather briefcase onto a chair. Instead of taking Jai's hand, he sat down on the yellow love seat adjacent to the kitchen table, where we were gathered.

"Hon, this is Jai, Bridget's friend from school. They're working on a project," Shiray said.

My father picked up the newspaper and started flipping through it. I thought he might not say anything, but then from behind the paper came, "A school project, huh?"

Jai lowered his hand.

"Yeah. Actually, we were just finishing up. Jai has to go home," I said.

My father put down the paper and leaned back, crossing one leg over the other. The tassel on his leather loafer bounced as he methodically kicked his lower leg. "Let's see it."

Reluctantly, I held up the posters we'd been working on. My father studied them, making a point not to look at Jai or acknowledge him.

"Is that the jungle? You need some animals in there," my father suggested. "Like monkeys." He looked at Jai for the first time.

Oh shit. I locked eyes with Shiray and she motioned her head toward the door.

My father picked the newspaper back up, blocking us from his view.

I tried to catch Jai's eye, but he was looking at the ground, shoulders slumped.

"You know," my father continued from behind the paper, "I was reading that they've now traced the cause of AIDS to a queer flight attendant boinging a monkey in one of those African countries."

I was so stunned by his thinly veiled racist attack, it didn't register that my father likely hadn't read that, since he couldn't really read—he had severe learning deficits that had kept him from even graduating high school. If only I had pointed that out or ripped his newspaper from his hands or even slapped him—I still regret doing nothing to stand up for Jai in that moment. Worse, I had led Jai into my father's lair. I'd ignored my intuition, and in doing so had betrayed Jai, setting him up for abuse.

All I could manage was to grab Jai's hand and flee. Shiray had the door already open, so it was a clear shot out of the kitchen. She flashed me a hardened *I told you so* look and did her uncomfortable laugh again. "It was nice to meet you, Jai."

Jai and I got into the Jag and put on our seat belts slowly, as if un-derwater. I pulled out of the driveway, eager to escape the tidy yellow house, glancing at Jai only once we hit the stoplight. He was looking at his hands, carefully folded in his lap. I didn't know what to say about my father's behavior, so I studied how he sat in the seat, his clothes clean and well-fitting, shoes neatly tied. Anything to keep hot tears from spilling out. I wanted to drive screaming fast like I usually did to shake the horror of the trap I'd led him into. Instead, I drove like a mother might, feeling a delayed responsibility to keep him safe.

We pulled up in front of his house. "You have perfect ears," I said, finally.

"What?"

"I have a real thing about ears," I said, not sure where I was going with it but needing to say something. "It's important, you know?"

He looked up at me with a weighted sadness on his face. "Ears aren't important," he said. He spread his hand firmly over my heart. "This is what matters." His gaze was absent its usual bubbling admiration, re-placed by a sorrow that shifted until it hardened. "I think you know that." He opened the car door and shut it gently before walking toward his front door.

When I returned to my father's house, I could see through the window that he was still sitting on the love seat looking at the newspaper, which was baffling, given his inability to read. I'd excused his rage and beatings for three years because I felt sorry for him—I knew my father's past and how brutally he had suffered growing up. Just like my mother, as a child, my father had endured extreme poverty and abuse. It was the only thing (besides me) that my parents had in common, and surely what had at-tracted them to each other: they felt like home. Whereas Mama had never looked back after escaping her life in East Los Angeles (except to send for her siblings), my father had returned to rural Maine after he'd made something of himself as a real estate agent, in order to prove that he wasn't good-for-nothin' trash like they'd all said. He flashed wads of cash and built the showiest lakefront house smack in the middle of his hometown, leaving it vacant most of the year like a giant middle finger extended to them all.

Sure, my father was vengeful, but I had never believed that he was evil, even though Mama told me that my father had stabbed his sister. I asked him about it once; I'd waited until he was comfortable in the garage, working on a new car project, before approaching him.

"Did you really stab your sister?" I asked.

I wasn't sure he'd heard me. He just kept turning the socket wrench with the same rhythm. As I was about to leave, he lifted his head from the car engine.

"Yep. I did." He raised his eyebrows and then lowered his head back into the engine.

"How?"

"With a pair of scissors. I hid them in her favorite chair. She was so fat, you see. She was so fat because my father wouldn't leave her alone—he was molesting her. I guess she was trying to make herself ugly." He looked off, wistfully. "I couldn't do anything about it. Everyone teased her. I wanted her to be smaller, and that was the only thing I could think of. I was just a kid. I thought she would pop if she sat on the scissors."

Understanding the source of my father's suffering made me better able to excuse his rage and cruelty to the point where I was almost grateful for it. After all, he wasn't sexually inappropriate with me, as both of my grandfathers had been with their children. My father provided well for his family; we were not living in squalor without heat or warm clothes, racing to an outhouse to do our business in the dead of winter. I could almost dismiss my father's rage as the cost of breaking the chain.

Witnessing my father trample Jai had changed that.

I walked into the house and stood over my father. "Why are you so awful?" My fingers were folded into fists, ready.

He put down the paper. "You think *I'm* awful?" I thought he was going to grab me, but instead he was chuckling, like this was all great sporting fun. "Your grandpa Crocker would have called him a jigaboo straight out."

"Jai didn't deserve that."

"Look, I have no problem with Black people. But society won't accept a White girl and a Black boy dating. Granted, in business or school, everyone should have an opportunity to make something of themselves. But when it comes to dating, it just doesn't work. The cultures are too different."

"What cultural difference? He grew up in Ventura. Their house is on Pierpont, a couple of streets from where you used to live after you and my mom divorced."

He shrugged. "I have Black friends who would agree with me on this."

"What Black friends?" I had never seen my father talk to a Black person.

"Guys I was in the navy with in Vietnam. Guys I've done deals with, had lunch with."

"So, what you're saying is, we can eat together, go to war and kill people together, go to school and make money together, but not love each other?"

"Exactly." He sat back, pleased, like it was settled. As if, finally, we had an understanding.

The only thing I understood was how faulty my father's version of love was. Before Jai, I'd challenged my father about his abuse only once. I'd caught him spanking Garrett before bedtime and quickly wrenched my brother from his hands. "Are you spanking a toddler on the diaper?" I'd asked, my tone thick with disparagement. I held Garrett close to my chest to soothe his crying while giving my father a hard, unblinking stare until he looked at the ground, ashamed. Not once had I stood up to him on my own behalf. What my father did to Jai helped me fully understand that he was a sick man capable of great cruelty.

It was the week before spring break, and I'd arranged to spend it in Arizona and New Mexico with my mom, backpacking on an excursion led by her boyfriend, Mark. I was scheduled to be gone a week, but I knew then that I was never coming back. Living with crazy people in the woods, chaining myself to trees to protest environmental injustice, suddenly seemed a noble endeavor compared to this insanity. Signing up for anarchy would be my deliverance.

I went into my room and looked at my things—my paintings, clothes, journals, and books. I decided not to tell anybody, not my father, not Michelle, not my school, not even my mom. I planned to leave everything behind and shed this skin like a rattlesnake.

Seven

Riches to Rags

By the age of seventeen, I'd flown nearly seventy thousand miles as an unaccompanied minor, shuttling between my parents from the Rockies to the coast. My usual hubs were Jackson Hole, Idaho Falls, Salt Lake City, and Los Angeles. I'd never flown into Tucson, but that was where I was meeting my mom and Mark for our weeklong backpacking trip in the Gila Wilderness.

I almost didn't recognize my mom at the terminal. She had grown out her leg hair and was wearing tight camo shorts with a T-shirt that had a sketched image of a dam being blown up. After hugging me, she looked around mistrustfully. "Let's get the fuck out of here," she said.

I remembered when Mama used to wash my mouth out with soap for cussing back when we were Catholic and lived with Sully in the trailer park. I knew things were different in her new life as an eco-warrior, but that didn't change how scary it felt not to recognize your own mom. I briefly reconsidered my plan to shed my life in Ventura. Yes, my father was an asshole, but at least he was consistent. It wasn't too late to change my mind.

"Mark's at Travis and Rainbow's house, packing for the trip," Mom said as we headed to the parking lot.

Mom and Mark had been an item for three years now. He was thirty-six (two years younger than she was), and he owned a commercial backpacking business that specialized in taking paying clients through large wilderness areas throughout the West. He was also one of the cofounders of Save the Earth, a radical environmental group, with Travis, who lived in Tucson with his partner, Rainbow. I'd been introduced to Travis and Rainbow at a Save the Earth rendezvous two summers prior, although with all the revelry going on, they didn't take much notice of me. Mark ran his spring backpacking trips out of a shed in their backyard.

"I know we said we were going to stay at the hotel with the clients tonight, but it's just easier to crash at Travis and Rainbow's," Mom said. "There's a lot to do before heading out tomorrow."

I nodded, despite feeling weird about staying with relative strangers.

"This is a chance for you and Mark to get to know each other better," Mom said. "I hope you'll go easy on him."

Mark and I had met in front of the Cowboy Bar in Jackson when I was almost fifteen, before he went to jail. I was on Christmas break, visiting from Ventura. Mom drove past the town square, and I looked wistfully at the snowdrifts piled up around elk antler arches covered with twinkling holiday lights, feeling homesick for the life I used to have with Mama and Sully by the Snake River. Mom slowed at the corner and told me to head down the boardwalk to the Cowboy Bar.

"Go say hi to the bouncer out front," she said. "Tell him you're my daughter."

"Why?" I was puzzled. Mom had never encouraged me to go to a bar before.

"He's a good friend of mine. I want him to see what a babe you are," she said. "Go on." She smiled proudly at me.

My snow boots clomped along the wooden sidewalk toward the bearded, burly figure in front of the Cowboy.

"I think you know my mom," I said to the guy. "Eliza."

Mark smiled, looked me up and down, and said, "I could tell you were Eliza's kid just by the way you walk. Those legs. You're a dish, just like your mother."

Since our initial meeting, Mark and I hadn't spent much time together, since I'd been living in California and Mark had mostly been incarcerated during my visits to Mom's.

Mom pulled the truck in front of a stucco house surrounded by scrubby desert. We found Mark out back, stuffing tents into bags.

"It's The Daughter," Mark said, looking up from his work. Presumably, my brother David was "The Son," but David wasn't here, since he didn't meet the minimum age requirement for the trip and was staying with Sully for the week.

I waved nonchalantly at Mark before ducking inside the house to use the bathroom.

I didn't know what to think of Mark, who was a dead ringer for the woodsy lumberjack on the Brawny paper towel package that Mama used to buy. Only Mark wasn't a logger. He beat up loggers and wore a silver belt buckle that said, "You can have my gun when you pry it from my cold dead hands." There was a lot about Mark that didn't make sense. He came from a well-off East Coast family, but he had no trace of an accent and was flat-ass broke. His mannerisms were gruff, but he had tremendous charm. All his friends were nonviolent, tofu-eating hippies, but Mark had the mystique of a roughneck who savored bar fights and steak.

I came out of the bathroom and hid on the enclosed back porch, taking in the backyard scene through the window. In the far corner across from where Mark was laying out sleeping bags, I spotted a sun-weathered, shirt-less blond guy arranging pemmican to dry.

"That's Ivan," said Mom when she saw me spying on him. "He edits *Save the Earth Journal.* He graduated from Yale, but he refuses to participate in the economy. Travis and Rainbow let him crash in the backyard."

"How does he get food?" I asked as Mom and I walked over to help Mark with the gear.

"He pedals his bike around to grocery stores and takes the food they throw out," Mark answered. "He's a skinny fucker, but he's all muscle. Hell of an activist."

I watched Ivan across the yard as he carefully lined strips of meat onto racks he'd placed inside a rusted Chevy in the backyard. The Chevy was the same era as my father's, with cheatgrass growing through the frame. It sagged with neglect, as if sinking into the earth. My father would never allow a car in his care to succumb to that state—his custom-painted '51 Chevy was sitting on blocks in his garage, polished to gleaming.

I understood my father's world, and the mall-going, Guess jeans–wearing girl I'd been there, just like I understood the scrappy, river-loving trailer-park version of myself I used to be. This new world of Mark's—and now my mom's—was foreign and unfamiliar. I couldn't see who I'd be in it, even though Mom had done her best to paint a picture. She'd tried selling me on leaving my father's house plenty of times.

"You could be the darling of the environmental movement," she had told me. "With your looks and brains, you could get into places no one else could. You could infiltrate the machine and report back."

I'd been dragged along to a few Save the Earth events with the Northern Rockies chapter while visiting her during school breaks. They were colored by hard drinking and drugs and a feeling of intense rage reminiscent of my father's. I didn't see the appeal. There was always a group of people getting arrested.

"You should chain yourself to the federal building with everyone," Mom suggested once, trying to include me. "The arrest wouldn't go on your permanent record since you're underage."

I'd managed to avoid any real involvement during visits, but I wondered about joining Mom's new life permanently. How long would it be before I got roped into something with lasting consequences?

At the Tucson house, the reality of what living with Mom would be like made me dizzy. I suddenly felt faint, like I might pass out.

"I need to sit down," I said. "I don't feel well." I walked back into the house, but I couldn't find any furniture to sit on, so I hoisted myself atop an old washing machine in the laundry room. It surprised me that Mark's friends had a washer at all, with all their romanticizing of the Pleistocene. I'd expected a pioneer-era washboard at best.

Mom and Mark cornered me as I sat there trying to catch my breath.

"She's dehydrated from the flight," Mark said.

"It's more than that." Mom held my gaze with such intensity, I couldn't look anymore. "Tell the truth, has your father or Shiray ever hit you?"

I tried to sit up straight under the crooked shelves filled with Dr. Bronner's soap. I looked at the ground, a rumbling of emotion churning in my gut. Should I lie, go back to California, and try to survive another year and a half? Or come clean about the beatings and jump off a cliff into this new world, blindly hoping for a landing?

Mom let out a heavy sigh. She knew.

I looked at her and nodded.

"Well, you're not going back there," Mom said.

"Yeah," Mark said, "fuck that." I wished Mark wouldn't stand so close to me, smothering me with his musky stench. If Mama hadn't left Sully for him in the first place, none of this would've happened: Mama would still be herself, Sully would still be my daddy, and David and I would still be sledding next to the Snake River, our laughter light as sleigh bells.

"Omigod," I said to Mark, scrunching my nose, "do you, like, even wear deodorant?" I rolled my eyes for emphasis, playing the California girl. Given his penchant for tirades targeting yuppies and urban scum, I figured a thick Valley girl accent would annoy him, maybe even scare him off. But it was Mom who winced.

"You're coming home," she said, meaning back to Jackson. "You're getting out before they completely break your spirit."

Part of me was awash in relief and another part felt like this was all a dreadful mistake.

"Let's call the son of a bitch right now," Mark said. He led us to the phone in the office, where *Save the Earth Journal* was produced.

I dialed. I didn't trust Mark, or my mom, now that she was this eco-guerrilla person. But I also couldn't forgive my father, or forget what he'd done to Jai. I pictured Jai's hand stretched over my heart: *This is what matters.*

"Joe's Bar," my father answered. His name wasn't Joe, but he liked joking around on the phone.

"You don't have to pick me up at the airport next week," I said. "I'm staying with my mom." Mom and Mark stood inches from me, their eyes fixed on my face.

"You're doin' what, now?" My father's Maine accent blasted through the line.

"I'm moving back to Jackson."

He cleared his throat. It sounded like he might be crying.

I'd imagined this call would make me feel more commanding, even powerful. But with my pounding heart and squeezed-off throat, it was painful being inside my body. Instead, I detached and stood outside myself—as I'd learned to do during beatings—and coolly watched the scene go down. I did not yet know that there would be a price for delaying emotions this way.

"You're still my daughter," he said quietly. "Nothin's gonna change that. Let us know if you need anything."

His tenderness caught me off guard, and I wanted to cry out for my dad who was beneath the rage, the dad I remembered from our days walking barefoot to the fish market, the dad who often made me laugh with his quick-wittedness.

Mom pushed down the receiver button, cutting the line. "That's it." She smiled. "Slip out the back, Jack."

"Fuckin' A." Mark pounded his fist against the wall. He grabbed a bottle of Jack Daniel's from the kitchen and poured out shots.

At the sound of Mark's pounding, Travis, Rainbow, and Ivan all came into the office. When they saw us gathered around the telephone, their faces blanched with fear.

"Did you use the phone?" asked Travis, clad in camo shorts and T-shirt.

"Just to call her dad," said Mark. "Nothing that those FUCKERS AT THE FBI would be interested in."

When Mom called me in California, she always warned me about the phones being tapped by the government. I took this as further proof that she had lost her mind. Now, here they all were, talking about the FBI and phone taps. Was the whole group of them mad?

"Ow oooh," Mom howled like a wolf. "My baby's comin' home."

Mark handed out shots to everyone, including me. My insides felt like pointed obsidian blades striking against one another. A shot seemed like a good idea. I'd been sneaking hard liquor since I was eleven, mostly from my parents' liquor cabinets, and I appreciated not having to hide my drinking anymore. I threw it back quickly and waited for the jagged edges in my chest to smooth out.

"Another Luddite in our midst," Travis toasted.

"And a good-looking one at that," said Ivan.

Mom sidled up to me and whispered, "You should go talk to Ivan." She wiggled her eyebrows up and down. "He's got the hots for you."

I shook my head no. At seventeen, I had kissed a few boys, but nothing more. Ivan wasn't even a boy; he was a man ten years older than I was. I was uncomfortable with Ivan talking about how I looked, and even more unsettled by Mom pushing me to cozy up to him like some seductress. I held out my glass for another shot of whiskey. Like it or not, this was my new life now, and I was going to need something strong to help me settle into it.

Someone put on a Talking Heads cassette. Mom and Ivan danced wildly, like birds in formation. They swooped through the office, writhing around the center table littered with reports on virgin forest clear-cutting, mining, and natural gas drilling in roadless areas. Rainbow noticed me looking at the papers and, eyeing me suspiciously, scooped them up, moving them out of my view.

The whiskey bottle moved among us—shot glasses abandoned—until everybody was chanting "We're living on nuts and berries" along with David Byrne. Ivan, now deeply drunk, staggered while slowly pumping a defiant fist in the air. Mom raised her hands, howling skyward. Rounds of coyote yaps ensued until the bottle of Jack was dead.

I was officially inducted into the tribe.

We didn't know it then, but one year later, the office we'd danced in would be raided in the early morning hours by armed federal agents. Travis and other Save the Earth activists would be charged with conspiracy, a felony crime. The group had been infiltrated by the FBI and betrayed by an informant who lived among them, someone they'd mistakenly trusted.

The morning after I told my father I wasn't coming back, Mark, Mom, and I quietly packed up our sleeping bags at first light. We were careful not to rouse Ivan, who was passed out in his tarp lean-to behind the Chevy. While Mark finished loading our gear onto his truck's roof rack, Mom loaded a bowl in her pink ceramic pot pipe and handed it to me.

I wasn't a regular stoner, but I'd gotten high before with Mom and the Save the Earth crew. I took a long hit from the pipe as amethyst and peach tendrils tinged the early desert sky. She reached over and untangled my hair with her fingers.

"I've been waiting for you to come back to me," she said, low and soft.

Her breathy voice blew life into my fantasy that when we returned to Jackson—where she still worked at the hospital and kept the one-room cabin—Mark would fade out of the picture, leaving Mom, David, and me alone. Finally, things would resemble normal: I would come home from school and she'd ask me about the story I'd read in English class or inquire about my friends she knew from Girl Scouts. I might even pick up the fiddle again, take some lessons from my old teacher. When Christmas came around, we'd get a small tree and decorate it with the ornaments we'd made over the years. We would have our old life back; Daddy and the sound of the Snake River would be all that were missing.

I harbored my secret hope as we climbed into the truck and headed off to pick up the clients for the backpacking trip. The way my teenage mind saw it, since she'd gone missing the very day he came on the scene—Easter Sunday—all I needed to do for Mama to return was get rid of Mark.

At the Super 8 parking lot, we found the clients, a father-son duo and two women traveling alone, milling around, wearing zip-off pants and caked-on sunscreen. The father, Tom, sported a safari hat cinched under the chin, snapped up on one side. Next to Mark, who wore Wrangler cutoffs, muscles bulging underneath his T-shirt, the clients were pale and puny, hiding their lack of survival skills behind expensive gear.

After a four-hour drive to the trailhead, we unloaded the backpacks from the roof rack and Mom fitted my pack onto me.

"Heavy enough for ya?" Mark came toward me wearing a squinty smile, framed by unruly dark curls. His worn pack was fully loaded with the group's pots and pans, grill, and first aid.

I rolled my eyes at him. "Please," I quipped, "I've carried Macy's shopping bags through the mall heavier than this." Not only did I plan to annoy him, but I also intended to make it clear I had no interest in being like him or even near him. Whenever I looked at Mark, I thought only one thing: *Home-wrecker.*

We filed up the trail that would loop through the tributary creek canyons of the Gila River, taking us from the dry-sloped mesas of pinyon pine and juniper forests and through the world's largest remaining virgin ponderosa pine forest. Mark charged ahead in the lead, leaving the truck, roads, and civilization behind. Mom brought up the rear. I hung back with her while the clients darted like jackrabbits to the front, jockeying to be near Mark.

"The first day, everyone is focused on outdoing each other," Mom said to me once the group had gone ahead. She put on a mocking voice: "Check out how buff I am, I've been working the StairMaster."

"What if I can't keep up?" I asked, suddenly worried.

"Finishing first—so fucking what? Surviving the trip without blowing yourself up is where it's at. Just put one foot in front of the other at your own pace and pay attention to what's going on with your body," Mom advised.

The only reason I'd ever taken stock of my body was to assess for bruises.

"If you feel a hot spot on your feet, stop and deal with it right away so you don't get blisters. If you feel dizzy or short of breath, pause and drink some water. Don't wait until you're thirsty—by then it's too late," Mom said. "We're way the hell out here. If you get trashed, there's not much you can do about it. The only thing you have control over is managing the suffering so it doesn't take you out."

We didn't see the group again until we caught up to them having lunch next to a stream. Aside from Mark, who was laying out sardines, cheese, crackers, and salami, everyone was disheveled and sweaty, panting as they downed their water bottles and splashed creek water onto their faces. Mom raised one eyebrow. *See.* She shook her head. *Rookies.*

After lunch, one of the group members joined Mom and me at the rear of the pack. Kelly was a reporter for an outdoor magazine doing a story on Mark. It was her second time coming on a trip with him, and I got the impression there had been a previous attraction between them. She was petite and dark-haired, with a pert, upturned nose. I'd seen Mom sneaking glances at her on the drive and noticed how Mark stood a little straighter, his chest appearing a little broader, every time Kelly spoke to him.

"Most kids your age would hate a trip like this," Kelly said, addressing me.

"Bridget's spent lots of time in the wilderness. We don't believe in letting our kids sit around watching TV," Mom said.

A hot, buzzy feeling crept from my throat toward my temples—the feeling I got whenever Mom seemed to forget about who we were before Mark. Had she forgotten the seasons we'd spent glued to the tube watching *Dallas* with Sully, passing a bowl of peanut M&M's along the sectional couch? Also, the way she acted like Mark had been involved in raising me made me angry.

"That's a neat walking stick," Kelly said. "What's it say?"

"Ayla." I handed it to her so she could inspect the carved letters near the handle. Mom had brought the stick special for me to use on the trip.

"Like the character in Jean Auel's *Clan of the Cave Bear*? My mom and Mark think I'm like her."

"She is AYLA." Mom jokingly grunted the name like a cavewoman.

"How so?" Kelly asked.

"Because she's brave and strong and resourceful," said Mom in a normal voice, "and she rejects society's rules."

Kelly handed back the stick. "It's a beautiful piece." She smiled at me.

"One day Ayla will find her Jondalar." Mom teased me using the cavewoman voice again.

"God, Mom!"

"Maybe Ivan? Just like Jondalar," Mom grunted.

"Ew. He's, like, *old*. Plus he's homeless."

"Not homeless," Mom said in her normal voice. "He refuses to be a pawn of consumerism and the military-industrial complex. It's a conscious choice—there's a big difference."

"Whatever. He eats out of dumpsters and sleeps under a raggedy old tarp. That's pretty much homeless."

"He's got the N gene," Mom said.

"What's that?" Kelly asked.

"Neanderthal gene," I said. "Mom and Mark say it's essential in a partner. It's supposed to be like an alpha survivalist thing, but I think it's really an excuse to not shower."

"Come on, Bridget," Mom said. "When civilization collapses, only the N genes will be left. You don't want to mate with someone who is lacking essential survival skills."

"I'm not interested in *mating* with anyone," I said. "And by the way, can you please tell Mark to quit calling Ivan his future son-in-law? I heard him do it last night. He's not my dad, plus I don't think it's legal for Ivan and me to date, let alone get married."

"Tell him yourself." Mom pointed across a meadow, to where Mark and the rest of the group were setting up camp amid a scattering of juniper.

"I did. He laughed at me."

"Oh well." Mom dropped her pack and began building a fire ring for the grill out of rocks. Kelly and I joined Laura, our tentmate for the week, who was snapping poles together.

"Are your feet just *killing* you?" asked Laura.

"Yeah," said Kelly. "I remember that from last time. It took days for them to toughen up."

"You've been on one of these with him before?" Laura stared at Kelly across the tent fly. "What on earth made you come back?"

"Oh, I don't know," said Kelly, her eyes glancing across the meadow at Mark. She was looking at Mark the way Mom did. Maybe there was a way to get Mark to like Kelly back and we could be free of him. I didn't know how realistic that was, though. Kelly was cute and smart, but Mom was like a Norse goddess with flowing flaxen hair and an axe.

Tent set up, Laura, Kelly, and I headed over to the fire ring, where Mom was placing kindling to burn. She stacked twigs over dried juniper fronds, then set it aflame with one match.

"Wow, you're really good at that," said Laura. "A real wilderness woman."

Mom set the pot of water she'd just hauled from the creek onto the grill in one swift motion.

Laura turned to me. "I bet you want to be just like your mom when you grow up."

I smiled awkwardly.

"No offense," said Kelly, "but what teenager wants to be just like their mother?" She gave me a wink.

"I sure as hell didn't," said my mom.

"Me either," Laura agreed. "My mom was so uneducated and without a purpose aside from baking cookies. I think that's why I became a university professor who's allergic to sugar."

"My mom never did anything without getting my dad's permission," said Kelly. "He wouldn't have let her come on a trip like this without him."

"Thank God my husband's not like that," Laura said. "When I told him I wanted to come here, he kissed me on the forehead and said, 'Have fun, honey.' He takes care of the boys more than I do, so I didn't worry about leaving them."

"What about your parents, Eliza?" asked Kelly.

Mom looked up from stirring the pot. "They're dead," she said.

I looked sideways at her. It was true that my grandmother had died shortly after giving birth for the eleventh time, when Mom was only eighteen. But Mom's father was still alive, living in the same house in East LA where she'd grown up. I looked into the fire and said nothing to give away her secret.

The next morning, we all huddled around the smoky fire, swallowing globs of oatmeal. After a clear, cold night, a thin layer of frost clung to the wheatgrass. Sun shards filtered through pinyon pines, and as the light hit the frozen crystals, tiny, shimmering rainbows were released. It reminded me of crisp sunrises I'd seen at Girl Scout camp on Wyoming's Little Granite Creek. I smiled thinking of the names Mama and I had chosen for ourselves there: Medicine Woman and Playful Otter.

"Ayla, baby, why don't you take this down to the creek and fill it with water." Mark handed me a soot-covered pot.

I made my way down the small game trail leading to a pool swathed by willow bushes. As I knelt on the rock bed dipping the pan in the water, I felt someone's eyes on me. I looked up, locking onto the delicate gaze of a doe. She was standing just on the other side of the narrow stream, so close I could have reached out and touched her if I wanted. She wasn't spooked by me. She lowered her velvety head and wrapped her thick black lips around succulent grass shoots. I could hear plant roots rip, and then the gentle gnashing of her teeth.

A memory of who I used to be welled up inside me. Recalling afternoons spent with deer, elk, and moose down by the Snake, I gushed fat tears.

The doe turned her head slightly, looking directly at me.

I felt her words like a tingling on the inside of my forehead. *You are not forgotten. You belong.*

We stood together quietly for a while until there was movement on the hill above us as Mark made his way down the trail. It was just the deer and me, no one else around, and I worried about being so far from the group if Mark tried anything. No one would hear me if I screamed.

Mark froze when he saw the deer, and a sweet, boyish grin emerged from beneath his beard. The deer wasn't uneasy around Mark at all. Her ears barely shifted position, indicating that she trusted him. Living with abuse had made me hypervigilant, attuned to the smallest details. I took the deer's reaction as a sign that I was safe with Mark. The deer, Mark, and I passed several minutes observing one another, until the deer calmly carried on downstream.

"That was neat," Mark said, beaming. He looked up at the streaky clouds starting to build. Squinting one eye, he surveyed the sky, letting out a steady yet faint whistle through his teeth.

"Mares' tails," he said without looking at me. "See 'em? They curl up on one end like a horse's tail."

I nodded. The clouds were thin and wispy against a stout blue sky.

"It's gonna rain in the next couple of days," he continued. "Could be as soon as tomorrow afternoon."

It seemed unlikely that a couple of tiny, turned-up cloud strands could predict an oncoming storm. As we both looked up, I stole a glance at Mark's tanned, bearded face—more bearlike than human—and I shifted slightly into the possibility that he might have something to offer me. Even though I didn't want to let him into my heart, I considered allowing myself to acquire his skill set. I wanted to know everything about surviving in wild conditions.

"Can I ask you something?" I said, eyeing him cautiously.

He nodded.

"What about bears? I always heard you play dead, right?"

"Yup. That's right. You should never be too close to a bear or any predator, but if you happen to startle one, take off your pack and throw it away from you. You don't want them ripping it off you to get at the food. It also distracts them. Don't make direct eye contact with a bear or any predator. It's a sign of aggression. If it charges you, drop down to your knees, cover your head, bend over, and kiss your sorry ass goodbye." He walked off laughing.

The next night, Laura unzipped the tent to go pee, returning just as a deluge of rain droplets pelted the ground.

"Shit!" She reentered our little haven, sealing it shut against the storm. "I started my period of all things. I wasn't expecting it, and I don't have anything."

"Here, I packed supplies just in case." Kelly handed her a stash.

Later, Kelly jostled the tent door open and went out in the steady rain. "It's raining like hell out there," she said. "And guess what? I started my period too. So weird, I wasn't due until next week." Laura and Kelly divvied up the supplies: there wasn't enough to get them through today, and we had two more days left on the trail.

It was still pissing rain the next morning. I slid on my raingear and headed into the trees to pee. I discovered that, although I had just finished my period two weeks earlier, I'd started bleeding again.

"What are we going to do?" asked Laura.

I had an idea to peel off the neon-yellow long johns I was wearing—loaners from Shiray—and got out my pocketknife. I sliced pad-sized rags of fabric off the legs and stacked them into three neat piles until there was nothing left of the pants but the elastic waist.

"Here." I handed Kelly and Laura each a pile. "Since we're all 'on the rag.'"

The hilarity of it took our breath away, and we laughed until we were deep-in-our-bones spent.

Mark called out, "Breakfast!" None of us moved from our sleeping bags.

"Rise and shine," he said, coming over to our tent.

Laura unzipped the door and looked out at Mark standing in the rain. "Are you kidding?"

"We've got miles to go," Mark said. "Time to make like hockey players and get the puck out."

Laura squinted through her glasses at Mark's gleaming white smile. "What are you, a sadist?" Behind Mark's raingeared form we could see that Tom and Max's tent was still shut.

"Nobody else is up. And besides," Laura said, "we're experiencing some kind of mass menstruation event, so maybe we could just take a layover day or something."

"Or hike out," suggested Kelly.

Mark's mouth gaped slightly. "Lots of women backpack on their period. It's not a pass."

Laura's eyes bugged out. "Could you be any more insensitive? Honestly, Mark, you're an absolute Neanderthal."

He broke into a shit-eating grin. "Why, thank you."

Laura turned around, looking between Kelly and me. "Seriously! Am I missing something?"

Mark caught my eye and jerked his head in a *get out here* motion.

I followed him over to his tent. Mom was inside, rolling her Therm-a-Rest.

"What the fuck is going on?" Mark asked.

"We all got our periods last night," I said. "And we have, like, two tampons between us. I had to cut up my long johns into pads so we could get through today."

Mark was silent for a moment, considering this. "They're all using your long underwear?" he asked. "Isn't that strange?"

"No," said Mom. "It's women solving a problem, and unless you want to sacrifice your long underwear next, we need to get these women out of here."

"What about Tom and Max?" Mark sighed heavily. "We can't just tell them we're cutting the trip short because everyone's fucking bleeding."

"These women are way more in shape than those two guys," Mom said. "Kelly and Laura have been smoking them the whole time. I mean, Max and Tom aren't exactly jumping out of their tent singing a musical right now. Trust me, if you tell them we're hiking out early because of 'feminine issues,' they'll load up their packs faster than anyone and be happy about it because they don't have to be the ones to wuss out—they can blame it on the women."

"You think so?" Mark was nearly convinced.

"Patriarchy ain't dead yet, honey. Not by a long shot. It's all well and good for women to be equal on paper, but for a woman to be physically stronger than a man?" Mom pressed her lips together, snorting out a cynical laugh. "That completely subverts the dominant paradigm. You think Tom and Max are ready for that?"

Mark shrugged, his forehead furrowed into deep creases. "I guess I'll go talk to those guys, see if I can sell them on hiking out early." He set off, breathing hard through his nose like a lathered horse.

I studied my mother as she coolly packed her earplugs and travel pillow. I remembered that she'd told me she'd left Sully because she wanted me to see what a strong woman looked like. I didn't imagine that this was what she'd meant. I was struck by how masterfully she had controlled the situation while letting Mark and the other men believe they were calling the shots. She'd played their biases against them and influenced the outcome, but it felt like she'd sacrificed something of herself to do it.

Back at the Super 8 parking lot, Max and Tom made a big show of being understanding and sensitive to women's needs, giving goodbye hugs with a condescending smugness that was maddening. Laura weaved her way through the departing scene, avoiding Mark. When she got to me, she hugged me tightly.

"I'll never forget how you saved us. You're going to be one hell of a guide someday, just like your mom."

Kelly waited until Mom was out of earshot to say goodbye to me. "It's true, you're going to be an amazing woman. You already are," she said and paused before going on. "And, you know, it's okay to be the woman *you* want to be, not the one your parents or anyone else makes you out to be."

I tried not to cry as our little group disbanded. Even though we all exchanged addresses, I knew I'd never see them again. It felt shocking to go from a small, self-contained social group back into mass society filled with pawn shops and McDonald's. Here, there was no understanding of our simple daily routine and the connection we'd forged among the juniper, deer, and sagebrush.

"Fuckin' A," said Mark as we drove back toward Travis and Rainbow's house to dry out the gear. "That trip had *way* too much estrogen. I feel like getting shit-faced and knocking some skulls together."

Mom loaded her pipe while I craned my neck to catch one more glimpse of my tentmates.

We rolled into Travis and Rainbow's to find Ivan in the kitchen, scooping out bowls of vanilla ice cream.

"Major score on the run today," he gushed gleefully. "Safeway was throwing out a bunch of ice cream just as I got there with the bike. I rode home as fast as I could so it wouldn't melt."

Mom, Mark, and I helped Ivan devour the cartons, ignoring the expiration date on the lids. Then we pulled out all the backpacking gear and set it to dry.

Mom and I prepared to head north, back to Jackson. Mom transferred her plane ticket to me, since I didn't want the hassle of dealing with my father, and bought herself a one-way fare on the Greyhound. Mark wouldn't be joining us for another week, since he still had another desert trip to guide.

It was near midnight when we dropped Mom off at the Tucson bus station; degenerates of all sorts were draped across the orange plastic benches.

"Mom, I'll ride the bus," I said, not wanting to put her out.

"Are you kidding? My little girl is not going overnight on a bus by herself," she said, scanning the crowd. "I'm from East LA, man. I got this." She gave me a hug, then laid a big fat kiss on Mark.

Mark looked at Mom all googly and started singing a David Allan Coe song right there in the bus station, his clear tenor echoing off the scuffed floors:

"You don't have to call me darlin', darlin'."

Mom gave him the same mushy smile and picked up the next line of the tune.

I watched them, thinking how wild it was that out of all the people in the world, they had managed to find each other. Although I missed Mama and Sully with a grieving ache, anyone with eyes could see that Mom and Mark were something extraordinary. There among the vagabonds and filth, I decided to give them a chance.

Early the next day, Mark drove me to the airport. After check-in, he took me to the terminal bar and ordered a Bloody Mary.

"Here you go," he said, sliding the drink over to me when the waitress wasn't looking. "Your mom told me you get anxious about flying." He positioned his thick, muscular body so I was blocked from view. "This is Mark's Surefire Fear-of-Flying Cure."

I guzzled it down. I thought about telling him that it wasn't a fear of flying that made me anxious but having to change personalities midair. I switched into my mother's daughter or my father's daughter, depending on whether I was northbound or southbound. I had no memory of ever being my parents' daughter, or even a singular version of myself. My anxiety over this identity shift had progressed over the years until I couldn't fly between them without vomiting or getting headaches. I almost told Mark that I didn't even care if the plane crashed (sometimes I wished it would), but I decided against it. Instead, I opted for another Bloody Mary, which Mark didn't hesitate to order for me.

Eight

Nothin' Left to Lose

While Mom worked the night shift at the hospital, David, now nine, and I were left alone in the tiny one-room cabin Mom rented in Jackson. One evening about a month after my return, I was sitting at the dinette table doing homework as usual. I was attending Jackson Hole High School with the same kids I'd grown up with and was still trying to catch up in my new classes. Even though the kids were much nicer to me than when I'd left three years earlier, and the town was familiar, it was tough adjusting to the tight living arrangement, lack of amenities, and new family system. To manage feelings of anxiety, overwhelm, and depression, I used alcohol and pot, readily supplied to me by my mom and Mark.

David opened the mini refrigerator next to where I sat trying to teach myself statistics. He stared at the few condiments and the leftover carton of greasy Chinese food from the restaurant where Aunt Theresa worked.

"There's nothing to eat," he said, shutting the door.

I pulled a *National Geographic* magazine out of my backpack and turned to the feature story on the famine in Ethiopia. A photo showed a starving boy—the same age as David—being bottle-fed by a rescue aid worker, his near-skeletal frame curled up in her arms. I ripped it out and pinned it to the refrigerator door.

"That kid has nothing to eat," I said.

I had just begun to make David some Top Ramen when the phone rang. No one but Mom ever called us, and it was still hours before her usual time to say good night.

"Sal just came by the hospital," Mom said. "He's a friend of Mark's and needs a place to crash. When he knocks on the door, it's okay, you can let him in."

I looked around the cabin trying to imagine where Sal would sleep. Mom and I alternated sleeping in the double bed (she slept days and I slept nights). David got the pullout sleeper sofa. There was a bathroom the size of an outhouse, with only a toilet and sink, no shower (I showered in the locker room before school or at the gym down the street). The whole cabin was smaller than my father's kitchen. It was half the size of the yurt in Montana where Mark lived full-time and Mom spent her days off. The only place in the cabin where one might throw down a pad and sleeping bag was on the three-by-seven-foot strip of linoleum in the kitchenette.

"How long is he staying?" I asked.

"Only a night or two," Mom said. "He's a trout activist and Save the Earther. Mark's known him for years."

I hung up and turned to David. "Have you met a Save the Earther named Sal?"

"Does he wear a raccoon pelt and buckskin?" David asked.

"That's Solo Lobo," I said.

"Solo Lobo is the one who does poetry and plays the bongo drum," David said.

"God, I hope it's not *that* guy," I said. "Didn't he do a bunch of acid and leap into the fire at the last gathering?"

David twirled his pointer finger in a circle next to his ear. *Crazy.*

I went back to my homework and looked out the tiny cabin window into the dwindling light. Rain droplets struck the windowpane just as a knock landed on the cabin door.

I opened the door to a wiry, bearded guy, presumably Sal.

"Wow, it's really coming down out here," he said. I was relieved to see he was not wearing a pelt or buckskin but cargo pants. They were stained, but at least he was in the right century, and not visibly mentally ill, which you couldn't say about all Save the Earthers.

I opened the door a little wider and sidestepped out of his way.

He took off his large backpack and leaned it against Mama's antique dresser, dripping water onto the door she'd carefully refinished back when we lived in the trailer park with Sully. Lashed to the outside of Sal's pack was a tin cup, like the kind prospectors drink out of in old movies. I tilted my head slightly, noting that this was just the sort of thing that would send Mark on a tangent about how food and kitchen items should be secured in the pack's zippered pockets to streamline the load and, more important, to minimize food scents in bear country. Walk around with stuff dangling off your pack and you were damn near a clueless yuppie in Mark's book. I wondered how well Mark knew Sal.

"Would you like something to drink?" I offered. "We have water."

"How about a little whiskey?" Sal shook the water from his dark curls and wiped his round glasses dry, then pulled a pint of Jack from his back-pack. "But maybe I shouldn't drink with the little fella here." He motioned to David and started to slide the bottle back in place.

"It's okay," I said. "We drink in front of him all the time." I wanted a shot of Jack to smooth out the anxiety starting to buzz in my temples and neck.

"'We'? Are you even old enough to drink?"

"Isn't that kind of an arbitrary question?" I asked. "I mean, who decides when you're old enough to do anything? The government?"

Sal grinned and handed me the bottle. I toasted him and threw back a shot.

"This is a real nice place," Sal said, looking around. "You live here with just your mom?"

"Mark stays here when he's in town, but it's tight with us all in here at the same time." I took another hit and passed the bottle back to Sal.

"Where's Mark living these days?"

"He's been living in Montana since he got out of jail." I thought it was weird Sal didn't know.

Sal pulled a joint out of his chest pocket and looked at me, one eyebrow raised questioningly.

"Fire it up," I said. The Jack Daniel's was doing nothing to squelch my anxiety. My ears were ringing now, and my stomach hurt so much it felt like I had cramps.

"Your mom won't get mad?"

"If Mom was here, she'd be mad you held out so long."

He motioned his head toward David, who was reading in the corner, hidden behind a copy of *Naya Nuki: Shoshoni Girl Who Ran*.

"It's cool. We always smoke around him."

Sal, who was in his midthirties like Mom and Mark, shrugged as he lit the pinner. A tendril of greasy brown hair covered one eye. He took a toke, then handed it over.

I couldn't get the smoke into my lungs fast enough; the coughing and burning meant only one thing: immediate relief.

"That's freedom right there," Sal said as I slumped down onto the worn brown carpet.

I laughed and looked up at the A-frame roof. "Freedom's just another word for nothin' left to lose."

"Not only are you beautiful, but you've got great musical taste," he said. He gazed at me in a way that made me squirm.

"C'mon," I said, "everyone knows that line." Was I imagining that Sal was flirting with me? Maybe I was more wasted than I realized.

"What the hell, man? I can't believe you're still in high school." Sal continued to stare directly at me. The intensity of his attention made me uncomfortable. "There weren't any girls like you when I was in school."

Sal *was* hitting on me. I tried to think of something I could say or do to change the situation without upsetting him or making things weird.

"Yup, I'm in high school, and he's in fourth grade," I said, pointing to my brother, "and we have school tomorrow, so it's our bedtime." I acted casual as I stood up, then yawned and stretched, hoping the exaggerated social cue would serve as boundary enough, since there were no doors or parents to keep him from us. I shut myself in the bathroom and changed into a long flannel nightgown that covered me entirely from neck to ankles. I wished Sal would leave, but I couldn't just kick him out to sleep in the rain after Mom had said he could stay here.

"You can lay your sleeping bag down here in the kitchen," I said when I came out of the bathroom, pointing to the sliver of floor space.

"Oh," Sal said, surprised. "I guess that'll work."

As Sal got settled, I set up David's pullout bed and tucked him in, turned out the light, and climbed into the double bed built into the corner of the cabin. I carefully drew shut the pink canopy curtain around the bed frame. I lay very still, my body stiffened against the blackness. Every ounce of my attention was focused on listening. When I heard Sal begin to snore, I relaxed into sleep.

I came to in a panic hours later as I felt Sal slide into my bed. David made baby snores next to us, just on the other side of the curtain.

"You're so damn gorgeous," Sal said. He wasn't wearing any clothes. He put his hands on my breasts over my nightgown. "I can't help myself." He tugged at the hem of my nightgown until he got it up past my knees.

I scooched away from him so he wouldn't pull it up any farther.

"Get out of my bed." I meant for this to be a growl, but it came out like a whispery flutter, like when you try to scream in a dream and barely anything comes out.

"You feel the connection, too, I know you do," he said.

I moved away from his sticky, unwashed body until there was nowhere to go—I was flattened between Sal's hard-on and the rough, peeled logs of the cabin wall.

"I'm not going to hurt you." His hands were underneath my nightgown now, roving over my legs, grazing my pubic bone, over my stomach, squeezing my breasts.

"No, *please*." My throat felt like it was closing off, like I might choke.

"We're not doing anything." His body was clenched and throbbing. "I'm just touching you. Nothing else." He was on his knees hovering over me, pushing his hard-on into my bent leg. Sweat and saliva dripped from him.

I considered screaming and hitting him to get him off me. There was no one nearby to hear me, except for David, and what was he going to do except freak out? Better to protect him, let him sleep through it. I remembered what Mark had said, next to the creek in New Mexico after we saw the deer: that when you were confronted with a predator, it was best to play dead in order to survive. *This isn't happening right now. Not to me.* I lay still as a corpse and went inward, hiding in the cave deep within myself, its blackness shielding me from the panting and the slobbering. Sal's touch couldn't penetrate the cave.

Somewhere around dawn, Sal slithered out of the cabin, leaving me alone in bed. Once he was gone, I jumped up and locked the door behind him. I wished I could wash his fingerprints off my body. I slid out of my nightgown and changed into clothes, eager to get to the school locker room to shower before class.

Mom came home as I poured David a bowl of granola. "Did Sal stay here last night?" she asked, kicking off her white nursing shoes.

I didn't look at Mom or answer her question about Sal. Instead, I studied the photo on the fridge of the young African boy's hollowed-out body, noting his sagging skin, his hairless, veiny scalp. *That kid has it way worse than me*, I thought as my eyes filled with tears.

"What?" Mom's tired voice sharpened suddenly, taking the tone and cadence of a squirrel on alert when its territory is threatened.

I opened my mouth but couldn't muster the sounds to tell her. There was no combination of words I could string together to breathe this outside of myself.

"What happened, Bridget?" Stern Mom voice. The voice she used when I was little and she would instruct me to tell her immediately if *anything ever happened*. The voice she used when she told me the stories of what her father did to her and how her mother never did anything about it except beat her, as if it were her fault, the voice she used to warn me, starting at age four, about my father, uncles, teachers, priests—*anyone* who might take the thing away from me that had been taken from her. She sounded like Mama from long ago, and I felt relieved that finally she'd returned. Maybe she could fix all this with special parent powers, somehow.

I motioned her outside the front door, so David wouldn't hear us. I didn't know if he'd heard any of it the night before, and I wanted to protect the tiny shred of innocence he might still have.

Mom and I stood on the slanted front porch surrounded by overgrown willow bushes intended to shield the front door from view. There was a break in the rain.

"He touched me."

"How?" Her eyes started to pulse. "Where?"

"Everywhere." A sob slid out. "He touched me *everywhere*," I told her. "He put his mark on every inch of my body."

"Why didn't you say no?" she asked me. As if "no" were enough. As if "no" worked.

"Believe me, I did."

"What else happened? Did you have sex?" Mom asked.

"I don't know," I said. "I've never had sex, so I'm not sure what it's supposed to be like."

"Did he put his penis inside you?"

"I don't think so." I wiped spit and snot from my mouth with the back of my hand.

"What do you mean, you 'don't think so'?" Mom's intensity had increased, but her voice was barely a whisper. "Either he did or he didn't."

"I blacked out . . . like, I left my body. I don't think he did, but I can't remember everything."

There was a moment, a flicker, of excruciating pain around the corners of her eyes and mouth before Mom's face hardened. A shadow crossed over her eyes, turning them gray. She didn't look like Mama, or my mother, at all.

"Well," she said, resigned, "you better get used to it. It's just going to keep happening to you."

She went back into the cabin to finish getting David ready for school. The rain had stopped, but gusts from another oncoming squall spiraled around me. I stood out in the cold Wyoming wind, sheltered by nothing but the storm.

Nine

Life Jackets, Condoms,
and Seat Belts

Near the end of my junior year, a couple of girls from my old Girl Scout troop invited me to join them for milkshakes after school at Billy's Burgers. It was the Friday before Memorial Day weekend—the kickoff to tourist season—and the town square would be packed.

"Tourist boys!" Heather and Kira squealed.

Jackson teens didn't have much in the way of social entertainment aside from keggers in the woods, football games, and pep rallies. Chasing after tourist kids who flooded town in the summer was the pinnacle of excitement.

Heather, Kira, and I put on fresh lip gloss, fluffed up our bangs, and went into the burger joint, taking seats at the counter. A college boy—seasonal help—was cooking and serving the burgers in a white muscle shirt and apron.

"He looks like Tom Cruise," Heather whispered. Kira and I giggled. He was tall, with dark hair and a cocky grin.

"What kind of meat do you have?" Kira asked when he came to take our order.

He dropped his ticket pad and laughed. "Are you flirting with me, little girl?" He wore glasses, but the way he pushed them back with his finger was sexy.

"I bet it's well-done," Kira said.

"Is that the way you like it?" He gave Kira a coy smirk, which made him look even more like Tom Cruise. I wondered if he was going to make a big show of flipping the burgers in the air, perhaps while reciting poetry, like in *Cocktail*.

"What will you have, hottie?" He looked at me, pen poised to write. "I'll get you whatever you want." His slate-blue eyes flashed at me.

"Strawberry milkshake, please."

"Yummy," he said, writing. He brushed his brown hair out of his eyes.

"Me too," said Heather.

When he turned his back to make our order, Heather slapped me on the arm while Kira mouthed, *He likes you.*

"Where are you girls from?" he asked from the grill.

"We're from here," Heather said. She introduced us.

"I'm Colby," he said. "From Salt Lake." He blended our milkshakes and set them in front of us, along with straws pulled from his white apron. He held on to my straw, undid the paper wrapper, and slid it slowly into my drink. "I sure hope I see you again." The way he looked at me gave rise to butterflies in my stomach.

Colby turned to help another customer. Kira and Heather nearly vibrated in their seats with excitement, grinning and mouthing *Omigod* at me.

I sipped the strawberry milkshake, smiling. I could barely contain my giddiness. I froze the scene in my mind, holding on to the simplicity of being a teenager sipping a milkshake, peering over the straw at a cute boy. In my memory, the Beach Boys are piped in, singing "Kokomo."

I spent that summer working as an assistant guide for Mark's backpacking company, running trips in the Gros Ventre Wilderness, Yellowstone, and the Teton, Wind River, and Absaroka Ranges. In between trips one August night, I ran into Colby at the Jackson Hole Cinema's midnight movie.

"You're the yummy strawberry milkshake girl," he said.

It was exhilarating that Colby recognized me. He invited me to hang out with some of his friends after the movie back at his rental at Meadowbrook, an apartment complex where mostly seasonal workers lived.

The party was an older crowd, college kids in town for the summer. There were no decorations or furniture in the house. Instead, mountain bikes leaned up against the walls, and climbing ropes, chocks, and carabiners were laid out where couches and chairs should have been. A couple of guys were doing pull-ups on a rock-climbing hang board mounted above the doorframe.

"You a climber?" Colby asked, handing me a Coors Light.

"No. But I did wake up this morning at seven thousand feet, five miles up Bitch Creek," I said, eyeing the beer. "Do you have anything stronger? Like whiskey?"

"Shit, you *are* a local." Colby grinned at me. He went into the kitchen and came back with a bottle of Jack and a shot glass.

"So," he said, leaning in, "I'm intrigued. Why were you sleeping up Bitch Creek? Are you a guide or something?"

"Assistant backpacking guide."

"Meanwhile, I'm flipping burgers." He shook his head. "How did you get that gig?"

"It's the family business."

I sensed that I had piqued Colby's interest. "What are you doing tomorrow?" he asked. "I'm going to take my canoe down the Snake, and I need another paddler. I've asked everyone here and they all have to work."

"Sure," I said. "I actually have a few days off between trips." Mom had taken my place as Mark's assistant on the Tetons trip, leaving me to watch David.

"Come by tomorrow at lunch and we'll go paddling."

I was filled with anticipation on the mile walk back to the cabin. My first real date in Jackson, and it was on the Snake River.

⁓

The next day, I arrived at Colby's apartment around noon, just as he was lifting his black Lab puppy, Timber, into the back of his rig. His surprised, blank look made me wonder if he remembered asking me out the night before. I hoped we were still going. It hadn't been easy for me to arrange— I'd had to beg Aunt Theresa to watch David.

"You can help me load the canoe," Colby said.

I scrambled to pick up one end of the boat, intent on proving that I was a strong, hard worker.

"Don't drop it," he said as we hoisted the canoe onto the raised truck-bed rack.

His flirty, playful demeanor had been replaced with a gruff edginess I didn't recognize. Perhaps he was hungover, I thought.

"Did people stay late at your party last night?" I asked.

"A couple guys are still crashed out in there," Colby said. "I didn't sleep for shit."

"Well, at least it will be quiet on the river."

He winked at me while taking a long drink from his water bottle, putting me at ease.

We loaded into the cab and drove south of town—past my old cottonwood grove and trailer park, past Hoback Junction, into the coolness of the Snake River Canyon. The smell of cut hay and sun-seared sage wafted into the cab. I noticed the way Colby's forearms flexed as he shifted gears. He ran his wipers, trying to wash away the splattered bodies of winged mayflies that coated the truck's cracked windshield.

"Motherfucker," he yelled when the wipers only smeared the yellow guts, making it harder to see. I started to feel the buzz of anxiety and tried to think of something to say that might calm Colby, but nothing came to mind. I grew quiet, looking out the window at the familiar sights from my childhood.

The truck screeched past a bald eagle eating a flattened racoon carcass on the highway before veering abruptly off the road into the riverside pullout across from Astoria Hot Springs. Colby cut the engine, then reached behind the cab seat and pulled out a homemade plastic bong from inside a brown paper bag. He packed a bud tightly into the bowl and lit it, devouring the thick smoke inside the bubbling tube in one enormous breath. He packed it again and held it out toward me, expectantly.

"Um, do you think we should be getting high before taking the canoe down the river? I mean, isn't that sort of dangerous?" I asked.

Colby rolled his eyes. "Come on . . . I've done this stretch lots of times, don't be such a baby." He looked me over. "How old are you, anyway?"

"Old enough," I said.

Colby was acting so differently. He was a lot less like Tom Cruise in *Cocktail* and more like James Spader in *Pretty in Pink*. Maybe if we got high together, things would change. I took the bong from him.

"That's it," he said as he lit the bong and I inhaled a huge hit. "Here, have some more." He grabbed the bong from me and packed it again.

Stoned to the bejesus, we exited the truck cab. It was only midafternoon, but already, gray-bottomed anvil clouds stacked into thick spires in the not-so-far-off distance, promising afternoon thundershowers, a regular late August phenomenon.

We unloaded Colby's canoe off the truck-bed rack.

"Where are the life jackets?" I asked, thinking of my mom's parenting mantra for teenagers: always wear life jackets, condoms, and seat belts.

"God, nobody wears life jackets on this stretch. It's only mellow Class II." Colby handed me a wooden paddle before shepherding his puppy into the canoe. "Let's go. We don't have all fuckin' day."

I knew in my gut that this was a monumentally bad idea; I felt my insides twist and scream. A family friend had drowned on this very stretch of the Snake while fishing many years earlier, and I could hear my mother's voice in my head saying, *Promise me, Bridget, that you'll always wear a life jacket on the river.* I was definitely not allowed to go on the river without one. It wasn't like she was ever going to find out, though. She didn't know what I was doing most of the time.

I considered walking across the bridge to the Astoria Hot Springs pool office. I could call my aunt to come get me. But then I remembered her car wasn't working.

"Quit lagging already," Colby said.

What were my options, really? Hitchhike back to town? Who knew what sort of psycho might pick me up out here in the middle of the woods. Plus, I really wanted to float the Snake. It had been three years since I'd last seen her.

I got into the front of the canoe as Colby shoved off from shore. He jumped into the stern, where he could steer.

"Dig it in!" Colby said. "Paddle harder! That's not hard enough. We're going to flip for sure if you paddle like that." Small waves lapped over the gunnels as the yapping puppy jumped around in the bilge, causing the canoe to pitch from side to side. My thin cotton tank top and shorts quickly became soaked with cold river water.

"Haven't you ever paddled before? Don't tell me this is your first time in a canoe." Colby's tone was biting.

I didn't answer, afraid I'd start crying if I spoke. As I scanned the familiar shoreline, I spotted a great horned owl hunkered down in a cluster of willows. It was strange to see an owl in the middle of the afternoon. I remembered reading in Mama's books of Native American stories that owls are a sign of deception, dark magic, and also great knowing.

"Let's pull over here," Colby said, annoyed. "I think you need to rest, because you're not paddling worth a shit."

We stopped at a gravel bar on the river-left side, a few miles upstream from East Table Creek, the take-out before entering the Class III Blind

Canyon section. As we pulled the canoe up onto shore, the sun went into hiding behind the thunderheads. I lay on a flat granite boulder still hot from the sun, trying to warm up.

Colby sat on a fallen cottonwood, its enormous roots laid bare, ripped from the gravel by previous high water.

"Come sit by me. I'll warm you up." Colby patted the wide wood of the ancient tree.

I walked unsteadily over river rocks to where he sat and plunked down next to him. I was baffled by how he was acting. When was he going to go back to being the charming heartthrob serving up milkshakes?

"Shit, you're a hot little babe, aren't you?" Colby's arm across my neck felt more like a headlock than an embrace. He brought his head close to mine as if nuzzling me. The heated moisture of his breath entered my ear. He was so close, I could smell the alcohol from the night before, the bong hits we'd done earlier. In one swift motion, he pushed me down onto the fallen tree and laid the weight of his body on top of me.

"Wait," I said. I twisted my hips, trying to thrust him off me, while pushing against his chest with my hands.

"Come on, don't be so weird. Stop pushing me away from you. Just relax."

"Let's get back in the canoe," I suggested. I swung my legs down on either side of the tree, trying to get footing, but they caught only air.

"I don't think so," Colby said. His eyes, no longer blue, were as cold and gray as the sky overhead. As he lay with his full weight on me, he reached down with one hand and yanked my shorts down past my knees.

"I don't want to do this right now." My heart beat rapidly, in sync with the pulse of the river current.

"You've probably never even done it, have you?" Colby smiled. "You're a fucking virgin, aren't you?" He said it like I should be ashamed.

"We don't have a condom," I said. "We'll have to wait."

Colby threw back his head, laughing. "Trust me, we don't need a condom." He held my shoulders down with his hands, impaling my back onto knobby, broken-off bits of branch.

Earlier that summer, while backpacking with Mark in the Gros Ventre Wilderness, our group had been caught near the top of a ridge when a fast-moving lightning storm blew in around us. Mark had turned to me as panicked as I'd ever seen him and yelled, "Run! Back down to timberline." I could feel the air around me gathering into lightning. The hair on my body stood up and terror flashed in me, coursing down my limbs. That day in the Gros Ventre, I saw how terror was a tool that fueled my legs to move faster than they ever had, down off the exposed ridge, back toward tree line to safety.

Pinned under the weight of Colby's body next to the river, I had the same experience: my hair stood up as the bolting force gathered around me. It sparked a terror, only I couldn't run or move; instead, it incinerated my core like wildfire. I wasn't going to make it below timberline. Colby penetrated me and I jolted with pain as if struck by lightning.

Daughter. Here. I heard the Snake talking, reaching me through the tinny thrum in my head. *I am here.*

I turned my head toward her voice. She was bright as the sun, glittering from beneath the water's surface. It had been so long since I'd heard her speak. I floated toward her, hiding inside her brightness. I heard myself crying in the distance, but I was safe with the Snake. It felt peaceful, like being in an underwater cave during a storm.

I am collecting your tears, she said. *Shhh, my girl. I am here with you.*

When I came back to my body, there was blood. I felt it trickling down my leg like a nimble spider. Colby was off me and had gone down to the canoe to train Timber to fetch driftwood he lobbed along the stony beach for her. I sat buckled over on the cottonwood, legs dangling heavy beneath me, still unable to reach the ground. I felt pain between my legs and in my bruised, scraped-up spine.

I dabbed at the blood between my legs with willow sprigs before pulling my soggy shorts up and heading down to the canoe.

When the first colossal crack of thunder rumbled the canyon, it was so deafening it seemed as if the sky had severed. Heavy droplets beat down around the canoe, pinging off leaves, obscuring the current, and ushering in a silence louder than the storm itself.

We paddled into East Table just as the rain kicked up a notch. Hoisting the canoe over our heads, we carried it onto shore toward the shelter of a broad Douglas fir.

"I'm going to hitch back to the truck," Colby shouted over the storm. "Wait here with the dog and the canoe."

Holding Timber by the collar, I collapsed under the thick, sturdy boughs of the tree. If I hadn't been so concerned with looking cool, I would have brought a raincoat or something other than my now soaked cotton clothes to keep me warm. I knew better than to be out here like this, facing hypothermia. The sting of my own stupidity was nearly as bad as the sting between my legs.

After about an hour, the storm subsided. It was only a twenty-minute drive back upstream to Astoria, but Colby still hadn't arrived with the truck. Sunset waned into twilight, and the chill of blanched alpine forest reached deep inside my sinuses and nipped through my rain-and-blood-soaked shorts. I curled my head over my knees, hand hooked through Timber's shaking collar, and listened to the timeless gurgle of the river. I'd resigned myself to the possibility of spending the night cozied up against the solid fir when headlights finally appeared, several hours after Colby had left to get the truck at the river put-in.

"You'll never guess what happened." Colby chuckled as he flung open the driver's door. "Some friends of mine picked me up when I got to the highway. What are the chances? We drove back to town and had some drinks at Spirits of the West. I'm way too wasted to be driving, but I couldn't leave my dog out here. Come here, girl." Timber ran from my arms to her master.

After loading the canoe on the rack, we climbed into the truck's cab. Considering Colby's inebriated state, I figured I'd better heed my mother's advice on the seat belt, only to find it jammed when I tried it.

"Your goddamn seat belt is broken!" I yelled, yanking on the belt repeatedly.

"What is your problem?" Colby asked. "You know, you can just find another ride if you don't like it. I'm not putting up with this bullshit all the way back to town."

I considered briefly what that would look like—finding another ride—and gambled on a no-seat-belt-with-a-drunk-driver scenario over a hypothermic demise in the Wyoming woods.

Please, let me make it home, I silently pleaded with the Snake. *I just want to go home.*

Colby played the Rolling Stones *Hot Rocks* album as we drove back to town. He drummed on the steering wheel and sang along until he dropped me in front of our cabin. I slammed the truck door closed and limped inside. I hoped Colby would just drive away, but I heard his leather Top-Siders crushing the grass behind me. I opened the door to find Theresa fixing up stir-fry for David and my cousin Lana, daiquiri in hand. Her signature scent, Poison by Dior, flooded the cabin.

Colby entered behind me, took one look at Theresa's twenty-three-year-old ass in tight Guess jeans, and accepted her giggly invitation to stay for dinner.

I went into the bathroom to change and clean myself up. All I wanted was a hot shower, but I did the best I could with a cold washcloth in the sink, avoiding looking at myself in the mirror.

I could hear Theresa and Colby's clumsy, drunken flirting from the bathroom.

"Bridget, come eat," Theresa called.

Famished, I sat down at the table and ate without looking up from my plate.

"Would you mind watching the kids while we go to the Shady Lady Saloon?" Theresa smiled at me winningly. "There's a really good band playing tonight, and you don't have an ID anyway." She batted her lashes pleadingly, her fuchsia lipstick on slightly crooked. She was going out no matter what I said.

I looked from her to Colby, too exhausted to feel anything except that I wanted them both to get the hell out of the cabin. I stood up and grabbed a bottle of Wild Turkey off the cupboard shelf.

"Hey," I said, pouring myself a shot. "Have at it."

I was all done with tourist boys.

Ten

The Other Side of the World

After Sal and the harrowing canoe trip with Colby, I avoided seeing anyone. Instead, I looked for places to hide, my favorite being the movie theater, where I could sneak in pints of whiskey and escape into other people's lives. I'd also taken to wearing big, baggy clothes and had grown out my leg and underarm hair, mistakenly thinking that men might leave me alone if I kept my body hidden.

One October night, I stumbled out of the darkened theater after watching *The Milagro Beanfield War*, an enchanting movie directed by Robert Redford filled with Mexican magical realism. Outside, the first puffy snowflakes of winter drifted beneath the yellow veil of lamplight. It had been so long since I'd felt the possibility of magic. I lifted my face, letting the frozen crystals land on my lashes.

Coming out of the theater behind me, someone whispered, "Bridget."

I turned to find Steve, Aunt Theresa's old boyfriend. I hadn't seen him since my eighth-grade graduation three and a half years earlier; I had moved to California that very same day. A year and a half after I'd moved, Mom told me that Steve had suffered a terrible climbing accident in the Tetons. His two best friends had died, and he was the lone survivor of their group. He'd spent a month in the hospital as frostbite claimed most of his toes.

After the accident, he and Theresa split up, which wasn't a surprise. Theresa was always scheming up ways to catapult herself out of low-income housing and food stamps, preferably by landing a rich guy to rescue her. Taking care of an out-of-work ski bum with a mountain of medical debt was not part of her agenda. Theresa packed up Lana (whom Steve had helped raise despite not being Lana's father), leaving Steve and their two-year relationship behind. After that, Steve went from being someone in my family to somebody I no longer saw. Like Sully.

Outside the theater, Steve's cheeks appeared flushed against his blue fleece jacket.

"It *is* you." He hugged me. "What are you doing here?"

"I moved back."

"Who are you with?" Steve asked, looking around through his wire-rimmed glasses. Snowflakes settled onto his thick brown mustache. We were the only two people still standing there; the other moviegoers had hurried out of the wafting snow and into their cars.

"Nobody. You?"

"I couldn't find anyone else who wanted to see a film about water rights. Apparently, I should have asked you."

I let out a weak laugh, swaying slightly. He grinned, and his blue eyes locked onto mine.

"Have you been drinking?" He looked just like Rob Lowe in *St. Elmo's Fire*, reminding me of the crush I'd had on him when I was thirteen and he was twenty-three. When I was fourteen, I'd convinced Steve to buy me a bottle of peach schnapps, only to get wildly sick in the back of his car. Theresa had been furious, although I was never sure if it was because Steve had gotten me drunk or because he'd taken me out alone.

"Me? Drinking?" I laughed.

"Isn't it a school night?"

"I don't really go to school anymore. I mostly ditch." High school interfered with my otherwise adult life, in which I waitressed six nights a week alongside Theresa at Woktastic, the restaurant where she worked. I didn't have time for friends, since I needed to look after David while Mom worked the night shift or visited Mark in Montana on her days off.

"Listen, I live right across the street at Meadowbrook," Steve said. "Do you want to come over? Talk a little?"

I winced at the mention of Meadowbrook. Since Colby, I'd developed a pretty clear understanding that it was dangerous to hang around with older men alone, especially when I'd been drinking. I did a quick calculation: Steve was now twenty-seven, ten years older than me. Not as bad as Sal, who was my mom's age.

It seemed oddly coincidental that I'd bumped into him—a living miracle—at a film about conjuring miracles. I needed someone to talk to, and I was willing to bet that after nearly dying in that accident, Steve could understand better than most my struggle to survive. Framed by sparkling snowfall, Steve seemed harmless, his intentions innocent, his smile kind and gentle. I decided to follow him through the storm.

⤳

Back at Steve's condo, he whipped up two blended margaritas and handed me one.

"How long have you been back from California?"

"Six months." I licked the salt off the glass. "Living with my dad didn't really work out."

"Well, you sure look different," Steve said. "I wouldn't have guessed you'd grow up to be so attractive."

I stiffened.

Steve noticed that my body language had changed. He popped a cassette into the tape deck, something cool and bluesy I'd never heard. "You don't like being called attractive?"

The question was a trap. If I said I did, it meant I was a conceited, conniving slut. Saying I didn't made me ungrateful and undeserving, also a liar and a hypocrite.

I gulped down the margarita as if it were a Slurpee, then sank down into my chunky sweater.

"I get it," he said soothingly. "You just want to be you, right? And you end up being somebody's fantasy."

"Exactly." I sat up in my seat, relieved that Steve was just making conversation and not hitting on me. "Like last summer, I was babysitting Lana when Theresa and some guy came home late from the bar and he wanted to have a threesome."

"Did you?"

"Please. The guy had a perm. Also, he was, like, super old and fully dressed in acid-wash denim. They came home, and Theresa put on this skanky black teddy. That's when this guy, who apparently owns some rafting company in town, said, 'You know, it's always been my fantasy to have sex with two beautiful women who are related.' It was so gross."

Steve covered his mouth to keep from spraying margarita. "That's funny."

"Not really." I fidgeted with my earring, remembering the anxiety I'd felt. "Not when it's happening to you."

Steve's laughter continued, chipping away at my outrage, until I couldn't help but laugh too.

"You're right, it's kinda funny, but in a really fucked-up way," I admitted. "I think I need another drink."

"Ditching school again tomorrow, huh?" He headed for the kitchen.

"I just want to graduate already so I can move to the Virgin Islands and teach windsurfing," I yelled over the whir of the blender.

"I didn't know you windsurfed."

"I don't. But that's not important. My plan is to move as far away as possible, where none of them can find me. After dealing with all their crazy bullshit, learning to windsurf will be the easy part."

Steve returned and handed me a fresh margarita. "Any college plans? You've always been so smart."

"Nah. I'm not really from a college-going family."

"You'd do great. I hate to admit it, but I should've never dropped out. If only my dad wasn't a religion professor, I'd have found another way to rebel."

"I thought he was a minister."

"Yup, a doctor of religion in addition to being a minister and a missionary. I've rebelled against that too." He winked and swirled his margarita.

"Was that why you lived in the Philippines when you were a kid, before you lived in Missouri? Your parents were missionaries?"

Steve nodded. "My grandparents too. My mom's father was held under house arrest in China for years when the Communists took over. My mom was only twelve and had to flee with her younger siblings to the States."

"Where was their mother?"

"Dead." Steve took a long swig of his drink. "They lost everything trying to save people's souls."

"I was sorry to hear about your accident," I said, changing the subject. "How are your feet?"

"Well, for a guy who was told he'd never walk again, I'd say not bad." Steve's smile came off as casual, but I recognized from the tension at the corners of his eyes that he was struggling to keep from wincing.

"Have you been climbing recently?"

"No more climbing for me. I've taken up rafting and kayaking. I just finished a private rafting trip down the Grand Canyon. On the river, everyone wears sandals, and it's trippy how people reacted to my feet—always staring, but hardly anyone asked about them. When someone finally did, I told them it was a crocodile attack." Steve forced a laugh.

"You didn't tell them the truth?"

Steve shook his head. "It brings up too many questions I don't have answers for. I'm not very good at talking about it like it was a spectator sport."

"Will you show me?"

He hesitated a moment before unlacing his sneakers and gently peeling back his socks. All the toes on his right foot and two on his left had been taken by frostbite. What remained was a mess of scar tissue. I thought about what it would look like if you could see the scars I carried inside me.

"Do you think about your friends when you look at your feet?" I asked, meaning his buddies who'd died.

Steve nodded. "It feels weird to still be here when they're not. Hans was supposed to be married right after. That trip was his bachelor party." Steve's face quivered. "I tried so hard to save them. I still can't believe they didn't make it. I could barely look at Hans's fiancée afterwards." His voice was just above a whisper. "Or sit with Tim's parents. He was their only son."

We stared at each other without looking away. The music clicked off, but we didn't move. I understood the sense of disbelief at things going so badly and the despair of barely escaping. Grief rose from my chest, and the tears I'd dammed for too long seeped out. Steve's eyes never left mine, even when his glasses grew foggy from his tears. He lowered himself onto the floor from his chair and slid across the room toward me on his knees, then rested his weathered hands on my clenched fists.

"I get why you want to run away," he said. "Sometimes it seems like the only way to survive is to disappear somewhere and start over."

Unlike everyone else, Steve didn't pretend not to see my pain, and it made me feel safe.

"What I'd give to leave it behind," I said. "The welts my dad put on me. My mom losing her mind. Men taking from me what's not theirs." I was so relieved to no longer hide the turmoil in my life that I leaned over and kissed him.

He pulled back, slid off his glasses, and set them on the scratched coffee table. "Shouldn't you tell your mom where you're at? It's getting pretty late for a school night."

"She doesn't keep track of me. Besides, she's in Montana. Took my brother with her." I kissed him again. "Which means I'm on my own."

"You can sleep here. But that's all that's happening." Steve helped me up and led me to his room. I fell into bed and drifted off to sleep under his down comforter with his strong arms wrapped around me.

Sometime in the night, I woke up to find his face next to mine. I could make out the shape of his nose and his lips beneath his mustache. I felt so cozy and warm, yet at the same time charged by his muscular body draped around mine. I put my lips on his, kissing him gently. He took my face between his hands and softly probed my mouth, sending tremors through me that resulted in an ache between my legs like I'd never felt.

He ran his hand down my side, etching the curve of my waist and hips. Everywhere he touched me felt hot and chilled at the same time. I pressed closer into his chest. I felt I couldn't get close enough to him.

He ran his hand down cautiously between my legs, then paused. "Have you done this before? Had sex?"

I hesitated before saying, "Not by choice."

He moved his hand to smooth the hair off my face. "Oh no," he said quietly. "We can stop. I don't care if we make love. I can just hold you."

I kissed him deeply, desperate at the thought of him stopping. "I want to."

"Is that so?" he said naughtily, then disappeared under the covers. He flicked his tongue over my inner thigh until I felt nothing but blind longing.

"Yes," I cried.

Steve lifted his head from underneath the comforter. "You should be on top." He pulled a condom from the drawer of his bedside table, put it on, and waited for me to make the next move.

I lowered myself onto him slowly, surprised it didn't hurt. It felt slippery and tight at the same time. Steve grabbed my hips and went deeper, prompting me to move faster. Just when I felt close to erupting, he would back off, pressing his hands down on my shoulders, holding me still. Shivers of electricity traveled down my arms, flowing from my skin into his. Nothing existed except the hunger to disappear into him—the intensity of it filled my body and my brain until I was overcome with a rush as we climaxed.

I flopped down onto his chest. "So that's what it's supposed to be like."

"It only gets better from here."

"How is that possible?"

He kissed the top of my head. "The first time's always the worst."

⌒

In the morning, we woke up next to each other, my head nestled on his shoulder. Outside, the world was blanketed in deep drifts of snow. Sunlight streamed through the window, illuminating the reality of our situation.

"What if Theresa finds out?" Steve asked. "Nobody can know about this."

"Ever," I agreed.

"We probably shouldn't see each other again."

"Definitely not."

Steve looked at the clock. "You're going to be late for school." He ripped the covers off me. "Up and at 'em."

Steve's place had a shower, so I didn't have to sneak into the locker room before school. He made me hash browns and eggs for breakfast. As I headed off to school, he handed me a peanut butter sandwich. He'd also made himself one to take along while backcountry skiing Teton Pass with a friend from the restaurant where he worked. I had a mix of emotions as I drove myself to school in my red Ford Festiva that I'd bought using the money I'd earned working for Mark—guilt, excitement, shame, relief, and an overriding fear that I was in deep shit.

Later that day, I left school early and drove over to Steve's place to say hi, in case he was home. He opened the door just as I was knocking.

"I didn't go skiing," he said.

"Why not?"

He pulled me in from the cold, and I shed my boots so I wouldn't track snow across his floor. "Matt couldn't believe I passed up thirty-four inches of fresh. He thought I'd lost my mind."

I stared at a vase of red roses on the living room coffee table.

"They're for you. In case you came back."

"You blew off three feet of powder and bought me roses instead?" I smiled and lifted my hand to touch one of his brown curls. "Holy shit."

We spent the rest of the week in bed. We told stories, had sex, but mostly, we hid out. We didn't want anyone to trample on what we'd discovered: that our wounds, and our bodies, fit together perfectly. Finding this unexpected haven erased everything that was inappropriate: the ten-year age difference, that he used to date my aunt, or that we'd met when I was thirteen.

As I lounged in bed, a book on his shelf captured my attention: *Rivergods*, by Richard Bangs and Christian Kallen. I took it down, and it fell open to a picture of a small Zambian boy obscured by woodsmoke. He was holding up his arms, as if soaring on tendrils of smoke to the spirit world. Beneath this image was a photo of pictographs found in caves along the banks of the Zambezi River.

Steve walked into the bedroom and snuggled deep into the covers next to me. "That's my dream life," he whispered. "To explore rivers like these guys in the book."

"I've always wanted to go to Africa," I told him. I described covering the walls of the closet at my father's house with images from the Serengeti. "I didn't know you could whitewater raft there. Is it like the trips on the Snake?"

"Rafting is pretty new there. The first descent of the Zambezi gorge in Zambia wasn't until the early eighties. It's more like a wilderness expedition than the tours down the Snake."

I turned the worn pages and we looked at each photo with quiet reverence, transfixed.

"The Zambezi chapter is my favorite. The way the whitewater buries the raft is just unbelievable. Plus, there are pods of wild hippos and massive crocodiles waiting below the rapids." Steve touched a photo of three men huddled in a rock lean-to, holding up dried bream. "I'd love to meet these fishermen. Wouldn't it be awesome to see them drying the fish? To eat with them?"

"Look at this one in Ethiopia," I said, flipping through the book. "The Omo River." I ran my fingers over a photo of a Bodi tribesman wearing an enormous decorative red earplug, his head shaved bald save for a shock of beaded fringe in front. "Too bad we can't transport ourselves into this book, like jumping into a chalk drawing in *Mary Poppins*," I said.

"We could just disappear," Steve said, drifting off to sleep, "and find ourselves on the other side of the world."

⌒

Steve and I managed to keep our relationship a secret for months—a feat achieved mostly by my ditching school and his ditching his life to spend our days together. At night, we both showered and ran off to our respective restaurant jobs, where Steve explained to Matt, his coworker and ski buddy, why he'd blown off another powder day, and I tried to act normal around Theresa.

"You've been so happy lately," Theresa said when I rushed in late one Sunday night. "You're glowing. Did you meet a boy at school?" She softly ran her finger down my cheek.

"No." It wasn't a lie.

"By the way, you just got a table. Some guy requested you."

When I peeked out from the kitchen, all I could see was the back of his head covered in matted brown hair.

I fumbled to get a notepad and pen from my apron as I walked over to the table. "Do you know what you want?" I asked before seeing his face.

"What do you recommend?" Sal's voice sucked the air out of the room. "It's a little confusing." The Chinese lanterns overhead seemed to flicker, and the red carpet tilted sideways. What was he doing here, talking to me like a normal person, like he hadn't forced himself on me in my own bed?

"Why are you here?" I meant it to come out hostile and aggressive, but it sounded more like a whimper.

"I ran into Mark in Missoula last week. He told me you're working here now. He sent me over. Said the place has great food," Sal said, smirking. "Maybe you could have a drink with me. You don't look too busy."

"I've got a boyfriend," I said. I wanted to tell him to go fuck himself, but I felt like throwing up. I gripped the edge of the table to keep from falling over. "Get out," I growled. I spun around and hustled through the swinging kitchen doors, straight back to the dishwashing station.

Theresa ran after me. "What was that about?"

We huddled in the corner with the Cambodian dishwasher, who, despite speaking only Khmer, followed every word.

"He's a friend of Mom and Mark's from Save the Earth."

"I thought he smelled funny. Would it kill those people to use deodorant?"

I let out a feeble laugh, but Theresa saw I was about to cry and grabbed me gently by the chin to steady me. "What happened?"

"Mom said he could crash at the cabin a while back, and he came into my bed and molested me. I told Mom, but she and Mark are still friends with him."

"Gross. He's totally too old for you."

"It doesn't matter. I told him I'm taken."

"I knew you had a boyfriend! Who is it?"

"I don't want to talk about it."

"Hey! You two!" yelled the owner from behind the grill. "Why you ignore customer? You run out customer, you no work."

"He's not a customer." Theresa smiled endearingly at our boss. "He wants to be Bridget's boyfriend, but his pee pee is too small." She held her forefinger and thumb close together. Hin laughed, revealing crooked gray teeth, then slammed his palm on the bell, shouting, "Order!" even though we were standing right there.

"Don't worry, Bridgey. I'll buy you a fried ice cream later." Theresa picked up a plate of egg rolls and peeked through the swinging kitchen door. I hid out in the soup station for fifteen minutes while she covered all the tables, walking past Sal as if he weren't there. Eventually, Sal realized that no one in the restaurant was going to serve him, so he got up and left.

I was anxious the rest of my shift, closely watching the door to see if he'd return. I dropped an order of moo shu pork on the carpet and forgot to place an order of wontons. I was so distracted that Theresa said she'd cover for me.

I headed directly to Steve's. He had Bonnie Raitt playing and a fancy bottle of pinot noir left behind by one of his tables during the lunch shift.

"You're back early."

"Theresa sent me home."

Steve looked sideways at me. "What's wrong? Something happened."

I told him about Sal, about my mom and Mark not doing anything before or since to protect me from him. "Can you believe Mark sent him over to see me? Sal should be in fucking jail, not lurking around where I work."

"That's awful, Bridget." I wondered if he might offer to fight Sal or tell him to leave me alone, but he was quiet as he poured me a glass of wine.

"Why would my mom and Mark set me up like that?"

"I wish I knew. Your mom has changed a lot since she was with Sully. I saw her at a party last summer and she was super wasted. I mean, she's always partied, but this was something else. It doesn't seem like she's thinking clearly."

"It's like they care more about protecting wilderness than their own daughter."

Steve didn't deny it, and I saw the sad truth of my words reflected in his eyes. "That can't be easy."

He made me laugh with a story of how his buddy Matt had scored fresh tracks at Thanksgiving Bowl on the pass, then shown up to work in his ski pants and eaten an entire cheesecake in the walk-in freezer.

"Matt asked us to swing by Spirits of the West tomorrow night for a drink. He wants to meet you."

Like Steve, Matt was in his late twenties. The idea of meeting him as a peer made me feel young and fraudulent. And we had yet to come out as a couple to anyone.

"I'm underage," I pointed out.

"Didn't you tell me Theresa gave you her old ID?" Steve asked. "Come on. One drink. No one's gonna find out."

The restaurant was closed on Mondays, so I didn't have to work. I knew that Theresa usually hit the bars on the ski hill looking for rich tourist guys, so she wasn't likely to be at Spirits, a seedy dive joint next to the mini-mart.

I agreed to go, despite the sick feeling in my stomach.

The next night, we walked to the bar, which was less than a block from Steve's place, and slid into a booth across from Matt.

"So this is the girl worth missing the best ski season on record for, huh? I don't know what special powers you have, but apparently they're better than Mother Nature's." Matt gave me a wide grin and shook my hand. His face was tanned except for the white goggle mark around his eyes. I'd learned from Steve that Matt had dropped out of Columbia the year before to move to Jackson Hole. Now his trust fund had run dry, so he waited tables to support his ski habit.

Our drinks arrived, and I coolly sipped a Tom Collins, marveling that Steve and I were really out on the town. As a couple. In public. It was heady and thrilling, until I spotted a mass of blond hair striding into the bar on long legs just like mine.

"Theresa's here," I whispered to Steve. I tried to duck.

"Who's Theresa?" Matt asked.

She noticed us right away but pretended not to as she veered directly to the bar.

"Maybe she won't see us," Steve said.

"Too late."

"Well, she doesn't seem too upset. She's not looking at us."

Matt craned his head, looking around to see who Steve and I were talking about.

"We should go." I pulled on Steve's sleeve.

"But you just got here," said Matt.

"Let's wait and see what happens," Steve said.

I watched Theresa throw back three shots in less than five minutes. Then she swiveled her barstool around and catwalked across the saloon to our booth.

"What the fuck are you two doing here?" she asked, hands on hips.

"Just having a drink with a friend," Steve said evenly.

"Since when are you friends with my niece?" Theresa squared off, ready for a fight.

I could feel Matt's eyes go from me to Steve to Theresa, but I couldn't meet his gaze. Instead, I pressed closer to Steve's side.

"You should try to calm down," Steve said in a lowered voice.

"You pervert," Theresa yelled as loud as she could. "You're a goddamn pedophile." The whole bar turned to look at our table. "You probably fucked my daughter, too, you fucking child molester." She lunged across me, her red fingernails clawing at Steve.

I grabbed Theresa by the shoulders and lifted her up in front of me. Even though she was older than me, I was three inches taller and at least thirty-five pounds heavier. She was hardly bigger than a multiday backpack.

"Shut the hell up," I whispered in her ear, pushing her toward the bathroom.

She wouldn't stop—only hollered and thrashed more—so I threw her through the swinging saloon-style doors into the ladies' room. Women scurried out as I slammed Theresa into an empty stall, locking the door behind us.

"I'm going to have you thrown out," she shouted. "She's underage! She's not allowed to be here!"

"Theresa, shut up."

"She can't be in here!"

I slapped her rouged cheek with my left hand.

Theresa glared at me. "Out of all the guys in Jackson, you had to pick him?"

"It doesn't matter who I pick," I said. "There's no one in this town you haven't slept with."

"Scheming little bitch. You always get everything you want." Tears of betrayal smudged her black eyeliner.

"I didn't plan it. It just happened."

Theresa thought I'd contrived the whole thing to hurt her because that's what she would've done. Ever since we were girls, Theresa coveted whatever I had: parents, clothes, food, toys. My entire life, I'd had a front-row seat to Theresa's suffering. I witnessed how she scratched her way with fierce ruthlessness to get ahead, only to keep backsliding. Forget college, or travel, or the luxury of being sick. She busted her ass for food and rent and then went to the bar at night to numb the misery.

Tipped off by the women who'd fled the ladies' room, the bouncer came and banged on the stall door, asking for my ID.

"I don't have one," I said, freeing the lock. "I'm too young to be here."

I pushed through the swinging doors back into the bar, where Steve was waiting, holding my coat. Matt gave an awkward wave from the booth. The place was silent with all eyes on us as we walked out into the frigid night.

"Now she knows," Steve said, his steaming breath wafting into blackness.

"Everyone knows." I linked my arm through his. Even though my cheeks burned hot with shame, I was relieved that the truth was finally out. We leaned into each other, walking back through the cold night, no longer carrying our burdens alone.

~

The next day, I went by the cabin after school to confess to Mom about Steve and me before she found out another way.

"Theresa called me already. She was absolutely apoplectic," Mom said. "I told her I already knew about it."

"You did?"

She shrugged. "I'm your mother, I know everything," she said, packing a bowl. "I've known ever since I was at Woktastic a couple of months ago having dinner and you looked over my shoulder. Your face lit up like a fucking Christmas tree. I thought to myself, I've lost Bridget to who-ever she's looking at right now." Mom took a toke off her pipe. "I turned around, and there was Steve, getting take-out, also lit up like a fucking Christmas tree."

"Am I in trouble?" I couldn't help but think how my father would dis-cipline me. Probably with a belt, or a shoe. Or a wooden spoon.

Mom snorted while trying to hold in her hit of pot smoke. "Like I told Theresa, I could ground you or tell you not to see Steve, but it won't make a difference. You're going to see him no matter what I say."

"I have to get another job," I said. After the bar fight with Theresa, it would be too awkward to keep working at Woktastic with her. Theresa really needed the job, but it wouldn't be hard for me to find somewhere else to work. One good thing about living in a tourist town: places were always hiring.

"I know just the thing," Mom said. "One of the nurses at the hospital just quit a balloon delivery job. I'll ask her about it."

A few days later, Mom had it all fixed up. I didn't even have to fill out an application. I couldn't wait to tell Steve. I thought he'd be pleased when I told him I was the new birthday balloon delivery girl at the novelty shop Mostly Fun. Instead, his lips collapsed into a straight line.

"You're kidding."

"I thought you'd be happy I'm not working with Theresa at Woktastic."

"Obviously, you can't work there anymore," Steve said. "When's your first delivery?"

"This afternoon at the Elkhorn. The owner, Bill, is turning sixty-eight. I'm supposed to wear this"—I held up a tight leopard-print unitard—"sing 'Happy Birthday,' and drop off some balloons."

"You should cancel," Steve said.

"Dennis, the manager, said if today's trial run goes well, he can work me into a regular rotation with the deliveries, and he might even be able to give me some hours at the store."

"Doing what? Selling vibrators?"

"They have cards and gag gifts too," I said. "I mean, my mom went out of her way to get me this job. Plus, she's being really cool about us being a couple and everything. I don't want to disappoint her by messing it up."

Before Steve could respond, I went into his bathroom to get ready: cat eyes with liquid liner, red lipstick, wild animal hair. "Look sort of sexy/ trashy," Dennis had said. I shimmied into the unitard and faced the mirror. I looked like Sandy in *Grease* after she got the bad-girl makeover.

I felt the adrenaline flood my body. I dismissed it as preperformance jitters. Nothing a joint couldn't smooth out. I rolled a quick pinner, lit it, and went into the living room to show Steve my new look. "Well?" I purred, arching against the hall doorway.

"Whoa." Steve looked stunned. "I've never seen you wear makeup before. I had no idea you could look like that."

I blew him a kiss before heading out into the snow. "Wish me luck."

I didn't want to slip on the ice in the stilettos I'd borrowed from Theresa before our fight, so I drove my Festiva around to the front of the diner even though it was only a block away. The tires crunched over snow along the alley until I was under the restaurant's buzzing neon sign. As I sat trying to calm my nerves, I realized that I hadn't been to the Elkhorn since I was in junior high, when I used to get up at four in the morning to hitch a ride with Sully. It had been only four years, but it seemed lifetimes ago. I wondered if I'd see Sully inside, and what he'd think of me now. He was still living in Jackson, but I'd been back from California for nearly a year and I'd only seen him from afar, sitting in his van at the curb outside the cabin as he dropped off David. He didn't visit or call me. I wasn't his daughter anymore.

Trailing balloons, I teetered across the small slippery parking lot. Inside, my eyes automatically went to the booth Sully and I used to share. Bill, his hair grayer than I remembered, looked up from the register, and for a moment I thought he might recognize me—I imagined him dragging his wooden leg while carrying a hot pot of coffee, smiling. I blinked, and Bill *was* smiling at me, but in a way that was expectant and sheepish, wrenching me back into the reality that I'd been hired to sit on this old guy's lap and sing "Happy Birthday," all breathy like Marilyn Monroe.

I wanted to get it over with, so I started singing, my voice shaky as hell. I was distracted by the cinnamon-bacon smell settling into my ratted hair. I sidled up to Bill, who chuckled as he took a seat at the bar. Waitresses, cooks, and regulars crowded around, all of them laughing and ribbing one another. I kept singing, but it wasn't clear to me if there was sound. My throat felt clamped shut. I couldn't stop looking at Sully's empty booth. I tried to bring myself back, focusing on Bill's faded jeans as I edged onto his good knee. I noticed that the waitresses had frozen, horrified smiles on their faces—had I stopped singing? I wasn't sure. It was possible I hadn't been singing for the last half of the song. The men who had looked at me hungrily when I came in now looked away, embarrassed. If only I could hear something beyond the tinny echo of my own heart pounding, something besides Sully's voice going on about integrity, then I'd have a better grasp on how my performance was going. I was pooled in sweat. I gave Bill the balloons and smiled weakly. I felt like I might fall over or faint. The crowd parted a bit, making room for me to exit.

I walked to the door, then paused. The sound of my heels clacking hung in the air. "Happy birthday," I whispered.

Back in the car, the cinnamon-bacon smell still clung to me, and all I could think of was Sully. I banged my fists on the steering wheel to keep the tears back. It was clear to me I'd gone down a no-good fork in the river. I wanted to go back to the girl I was before. I started the car, intent on returning to Mostly Fun and trading in the unitard for whatever was left of my dignity.

Dennis was waiting for me when I came in the back door. "They just called over here from the Elkhorn," he said.

"Where can I change?" I spotted the dressing room before he could answer.

"They were very disappointed. There was no dance at all. You didn't finish the song. You were supposed to act more sexy—flirt with Bill and really play it up."

I felt ashamed for not being confident enough in my sexuality to do the job and also for thinking I could pull off being a girl who wore a leopard-print unitard and stilettos. Stronger than shame was the determination to return to a version of me I recognized.

"Take it." I tossed the crumpled unitard to Dennis.

"I have to refund their money, so I won't be able to pay you. You understand it was just a trial run."

"I don't want your money," I said and walked out.

It wasn't until I saw Steve sitting on his couch, flipping through an outdoor magazine, that I let the tears go. I crawled onto his lap.

"It was awful."

"I can't believe your mom put you up to it. You realize it's sick to set up your own kid like that, don't you?"

"She was trying to help me."

"By pimping you out?"

For a long time now, the way my mother looked at me appraisingly and talked about my body to Mark and his friends had made me feel uneasy. I didn't know what to say or how to defend myself, so I usually sat in the discomfort and pretended it wasn't happening. I didn't admit even to myself that she crossed boundaries with my sexuality, appropriating it and wielding it as her own. Hearing Steve call my mom a pimp stung, but it was also a relief. Finally, I had a witness. My mother had set me up.

"I can't do this with her anymore," I said.

"You don't have to. Come live with me."

As it was, I rarely stayed at my mom's now, preferring to share Steve's bed rather than hers. I was eighteen, and in a couple of months I'd graduate from high school.

"She's sick, isn't she?" I asked Steve.

"Yes."

I wiped my cheeks dry, accepting both the truth and the remedy. I understood that I had to cut my mother's sickness from me, and that meant detaching from her completely. Unable to free herself of the trauma she'd suffered growing up in an incestuous and violent family, she used drugs and men to quell the pain while the disease kept spreading, claiming another generation.

The woman beneath the trauma—Mama—loved me fiercely, I knew that. Mama would want me to protect myself. Even if it was from her.

I'd made the decision before to leave her behind, as I had with my father. I would leave them both now, and take a fork in the river no one in my family had ever been down.

Eleven

Born Again

In the spring of 1989, high on speed, nicotine, weed, and DJ EZ Rock, I exited California's Highway 178 and pulled into the windblown town of Lake Isabella. A tumbleweed lodged itself into my Ford Festiva's front grille as I pulled in next to a row of SUVs topped with kayaks and mountain bikes. A month earlier, Steve had left Jackson for California's Kern River to attend a weeklong river-guiding school and work the season. As soon as I graduated from high school, I'd packed a bathing suit and a baggie of cross-tops to keep me awake for the fifteen-hour drive from the Rockies to the Sierra Nevadas to be with him. Whitewater rafting would feature as the main activity.

As I cut the engine, I noticed the blue neon sign across the road announcing "ISABELLA MOTEL," only the "TEL" wasn't lit, giving the scene an undeniable Bates quality. I took a moment to steady myself, adding a few drops of Visine for good measure. So far, I'd succeeded in keeping my drug habit mostly hidden from Steve, who, aside from being a moderate drinker, was surprisingly straight. For the road trip, I'd needed something stronger than weed to manage the anxiety I felt about running the rapids of the Kern. A sign I passed when entering the canyon read: "WARNING: 264 lives lost on the Killer Kern since 1964."

This trip marked my first time returning to California since leaving my father's house. I had no plans to visit him, despite being just over a hundred miles from Ventura. This would also be my first time on a river since canoeing down the Snake with Colby. I ate cross-tops like Tic Tacs during the drive, hoping different drugs might lead to different outcomes for me with rivers and California.

As I opened the car door, Steve appeared, wearing yellow quick-dry shorts and river sandals. His brown curls had been straightened by grime and desert heat. His skin was darker than I remembered, whether from dust or sun, I couldn't tell.

"Oh my God, I missed you," he said hugging and kissing me. The desert version of Steve looked different but felt the same. I felt relieved to be reunited. As we walked from the car to the guide house that served as the office and center of the operation, I focused on not twitching, since I could still feel the speed driving my limbs.

I followed Steve through the back door and noticed a closet-sized nook with a pay phone on the wall. Through a doorway to the left was the kitchen, where he filled us plastic cups with a vodka and fruit punch mix. The kitchen opened to a living area, with dingy thrift store furniture strewn around. Steve and I nestled ourselves into a sagging love seat just as a group of five muscled guys burst in, their hair matted, sun-streaked. They went into an adjoining room I figured for an office, since it had a door that closed.

"That's the Forks crew," Steve whispered. "They just came off a three-day Forks of the Kern trip." I'd noticed while poring over maps for my drive that the uppermost section of the Kern was in the Golden Trout Wilderness. Known as the Forks of the Kern, it channeled water drained from Mount Whitney, the highest peak not just in California but in the lower forty-eight states.

"Have you guided it yet?" I asked.

"I wish. I went down as a paddler during guide school in one of the instructors' boats. It's some of the hardest whitewater in the world: fourteen Class IV+ and V rapids in seventeen miles."

I'd rafted down the Class III section of the Snake as a kid with Mama and Sully. The guide had let me row during a flat section between rapids. I was somewhat confident I could manage doing IIIs but unsure about anything above that.

"What's the highest class of rapids?" I asked.

"Class VI. There are a few on the Kern, but they're considered unrunnable because the chance of dying if you swim them is nearly certain. We portage around them."

"Any on the section we're doing?"

"We'll do the Upper Kern Class IV one-day stretch tomorrow. Then we'll do a two-day Lower Kern trip below Lake Isabella, also Class IV with one Class VI portage."

"What's the difference between Class III and IV?" I asked.

"In Class III, there's one big move you have to make in the rapid. Class IV has two or more."

"And V?"

"Serious maneuvering around obstacles with deadly consequences if you blow it."

I nervously sipped my drink, hoping I wouldn't join the 264 other people who'd already lost their lives on this river. Just then, a statuesque woman, over six feet tall, walked into the room. She had a brown pixie cut and wore a rattlesnake-print minidress that left her arms bare, revealing cut biceps and chiseled shoulders.

"Melissa," Steve called, "this is my girlfriend, Bridget."

Melissa waved, and although she remained unsmiling, her steady brown eyes were welcoming and observant.

"Sean in there?" she asked, pointing her chin to the office.

"Yep. Just got back," said Steve.

Melissa walked past us and barged in on the Forks crew as they discussed the upcoming schedule. "What's the deal?" she asked. "Do I need a dick to get on this crew? I've been training my ass off on the Forks the last two seasons. Surely I should be on the schedule by now."

From where we sat, we could see that the men looked stunned. None of them moved.

"What's it gonna take?" Melissa continued, even-toned. "*Is* it a dick thing? Because I can grow one of those if that's what's required."

Everyone's eyes shifted to the guy I assumed was Sean, who was holding a pencil in his long, thick fingers, writing down names. He shook his head and sighed heavily before adding her name to the list.

"Damn. Thank you." Melissa sounded more exasperated than grateful. As she turned to leave, one of the guides muttered, "Squeaky wheel gets the grease." She flipped him off with her eyes as she walked out.

"Fucking dudes with their politics and ego-tripping." She snorted. "It's just rafting. It's supposed to be fun." She turned to go. "See you tomorrow, Bridget."

"Bye," I managed, too astonished by the paragon of a self-possessed woman to form a sentence.

The next morning, I boarded a bus along with five guides and twenty-four clients. All the guides were staying in Lake Isabella for the season, except Dexter, an aspiring producer who made the three-hour drive from Los Angeles on weekends. All seated in the back of the bus, the guides clipped carabiners onto water bottles and sniggered at inside jokes, speaking a boater language I didn't understand.

Dexter said, "So then I yelled, 'Highside,' and they were all gaping, so we got surfed until I dump-trucked. Poor bastards, most of them got Maytagged. Thanks for bagging me, by the way." He looked over at Steve.

"Hey, brother, you know I will always set safety for you. Especially if you give me your Sandies," said Steve.

"What are Sandies?" I asked so quietly that not even Steve heard me. I was too intimidated to repeat the question.

We drove upstream, past the town of Kernville. I noticed that in some places the water was so low you could see the rocks on the bottom, something I'd never seen on the Snake. The two rivers couldn't have looked more different: the Snake flowed a deep jade green, while the Upper Kern shimmered in golds and browns, the white aerated water lending a sheen of lightness. Farther up, Melissa pointed out Upper and Lower Salmon Falls, a thundering succession of Class VI drops stretching half a mile long.

Five miles upstream from the falls, the bus stopped at a dirt turnout marking the put-in spot. Because of the hazardous Fairview Dam just upstream and the experts-only Class V sections below it, we couldn't just put in high up on the river and float down to the take-out, as on the rafting trips I'd done on the Snake as a child. Instead, we had to piece together short sections of whitewater, unloading and reloading the rafts each time before driving to a different section.

Melissa directed the clients to gather under the shade of a stout cottonwood for a safety talk. She then conferred with the other guides as they unloaded gear off the trailer.

"Melissa! Melissa!" Dexter yapped around her like a crazed lapdog. At five feet four, his head barely grazed her breast line. "Can you put Harry Hamlin and Nicollette Sheridan in my boat? Please? I want to pitch them an idea I have for a show."

"Who?" Melissa held up her trip leader clipboard, shielding her eyes. All the clients looked the same in matching life jackets and helmets.

"Them." Dexter pointed toward two model types standing away from everyone else, smoking.

"Fine," she said, "but don't get too hopeful. I've heard Hollywood people eat their young for breakfast." Melissa walked over to give her safety speech.

Steve asked, "Are they famous or something?"

"Are you shitting me? Ever heard of *LA Law*? Or *Knots Landing*?" Dexter said.

Steve shrugged. Aside from college football and Bulls games, he didn't watch TV.

"Wasn't he the guy in *Clash of the Titans*?" I asked.

"He played fucking Perseus! And he was *People* magazine's Sexiest Man Alive." Dexter rolled his eyes at our ignorance, then looked at Nicollette. "She's damn sexy, that's for sure. And totally my type."

"And that's why we call him Dexter the Molester," Steve said, laughing. "You should stay far away from this guy. In fact, get over there and listen to the safety talk." Steve swatted my leg playfully.

I walked over to the group and stood across the circle from Harry and Nicollette, who, though attractive, appeared pale and soft, like uncooked dough. Harry Hamlin may have played Perseus, but Melissa resembled an actual goddess, with deeply tanned skin the color of the canyon and abdominal muscles so chiseled they reflected sunlight. Even so, no one was looking at Melissa as she gave a talk about how we were going to stay alive; instead they watched Harry and Nicollette as they smoked.

"If your boat flips or you fall out," Melissa said, "don't get trapped underneath it. You won't be able to breathe. Also, keep your feet up. One of the most common causes of death in rafting is foot entrapment, which happens when you try to stand in the river. Your foot gets wedged under a rock while the current pushes the rest of you downstream. It's nearly impossible to save someone who is foot entrapped."

The more I listened to Melissa talk about the dangers of rafting—getting your teeth knocked out, having your face slashed open by low-lying branches, being impaled by logs or fishhooks—the more terrified I became. I'd never heard of any of these things happening on the Snake. Hypothermia, sure. Getting hit by hail the size of baseballs, you bet. Since I didn't know how to survive on this river, I clung to every word she said.

Melissa divided us into five groups and sent us to the rafts. I got on Steve's boat, opting to sit close to him in the back so he could grab me if I fell out. We floated in a calm eddy of recirculating current just below the booming Class V rapid called Bombs Away. I was kicking myself for leaving my cross-tops back at the guide house. I'd stashed them deep in my bag, saving them for cross-country driving only. But here I was, facing harrowing conditions, and I was stone-cold straight.

Steve handed out paddles to everyone in our boat. He showed us how to hold them with one hand on the T-grip and drilled us on paddle commands. "Forward" meant we should generate momentum with our whole body, not just our arms. When back paddling, we leveraged the paddle off our hip. "You should have a bruise on your hip at the end of the day," he told us. He taught us how to turn the boat: "Right turn" meant the right side of the boat back-paddled and the left side went forward. Opposite for "left turn." "Stop" meant quit mid-stroke.

Steve guided us out of the eddy, and we immediately threaded through current and rocks to the bottom of what seemed to be our first rapid.

"What's that one called?" I asked.

"That's not a rapid, just some current," Steve said. "An unnamed riffle."

I gripped my paddle tightly and watched as Nicollette Sheridan paddled in the front of Dexter's boat, riding one leg over the bow as if astride a horse. Melissa had expressly warned us to keep both feet in the raft in case it careened into a boulder. Luckily, we only had a few riffles before stopping at a shaded parking lot next to the river.

We loaded the boats onto the trailer, and I helped the guides prepare lunch while the clients milled around, casually taking photos in the direction of Harry and Nicollette.

Dexter began unpacking the food. "Sandies," he said, holding up a bag of cookies in front of me. "These are the best cookies available in the Kern River Valley. I think these go to the guy lacking toes but in possession of great river skills." Dexter tossed a couple of Sandies to Steve.

"What's 'getting Maytagged' mean?" I asked Dexter sheepishly, referring to another mysterious rafting term they'd thrown around in the bus.

"Recirculating in a keeper hole, like the spin cycle of a Maytag washer."

"Does that really happen?"

"Mostly to gapers." Steve laughed. I looked at him, stumped, and he added, "People whose mouths are permanently agape."

"What's the deal with that actress riding bareback in your bow?" Melissa asked Dexter while carving a pineapple into little rafts. "Did you tell her to get her damn leg in the boat?"

"I was afraid to," Dexter said while slicing avocados. "I think she's really interested in my show idea."

"She will not be interested if her fucking leg is broken. You need to rein that shit in," Melissa said.

Never had I seen a woman stand her ground among men so unapologetically or effectively. And certainly not while wearing a bikini. Unlike my mother and aunt, Melissa did not employ her sexuality as currency. She advanced by using direct language and actions, and I immediately decided that this was the kind of woman I wanted to be.

After lunch, we drove to another section of the river and got back on the water, with several bigger rapids ahead. Steve asked me if I wanted to move up to the front, and I agreed to try it. After the success of the morning, I felt slightly more relaxed. I lifted my head and surveyed the banks, noting the sparkling flecks of quartz in the rocks and the willow saplings interspersed with gray pine along the shoreline. A great blue heron took flight from a rock on river right. Its giant, lanky wings folded, then reached as it skimmed the water's surface.

We followed the heron around a bend and found that one of our group's rafts had capsized. Passengers were littered across the river, their hair hanging in wet clumps. I was puzzled since there hadn't been a rapid, only a quickening of current. I could see golden rocks beneath the rush of water and remembered Melissa warning that the shallows were far more dangerous than deeper, channelized current.

It was Dexter's raft that had flipped, and he rode solo atop the overturned craft, threading the uncoiled bowline through a D-ring on the boat's outside perimeter. His plan was to fall backward into the water while holding the rope, using the leverage of his body weight to right the boat.

"All forward," Steve commanded our paddle crew in a tone that was all business.

We went for the closest swimmer, who was floating with his feet up and pointed downstream, just as Melissa had instructed. We pulled up alongside him and Steve grabbed the man by the shoulder lapels of his life jacket, faced him toward the boat, then swiftly pulled him in with one motion.

"The guide flipped it on purpose," the man told us in between coughs, "because that actress wanted him to."

He pointed downstream to where Nicollette and Harry were standing in the current, attempting to walk back to the boat. Dexter was midway through falling backward to right his boat and couldn't see them.

"Heads up!" Steve yelled.

It was too late. The raft came crashing down onto Nicollette, crushing her.

Harry's cry echoed through the canyon. "Nic!"

Dexter felt around under the righted raft but couldn't find her. It was as if she'd disappeared. I wondered if her foot had gotten entrapped and she was still upstream, not under the raft at all. Finally, Dexter got hold of her slender arm and yanked her out from beneath the tube of the raft. He scooped up Harry next, then navigated the boat down by himself using the only remaining paddle.

Melissa circled her index finger in the air above her head and pointed to the left, signaling that we should all catch the eddy and regroup. She'd picked up the other passengers from Dexter's raft, and her boat was now dangerously heavy. She needed to off-load them. Steve positioned behind Dexter, sandwiching him between Melissa and us.

By the time we got to the eddy, Nicollette was crying, slumped in the bow of Dexter's boat. Blood trickled from her knee and scraped shin, and she had a nasty-looking welt on her forehead. "I want off this trip," she said.

Melissa tied up her raft and motioned for Dexter to meet her near Steve's boat. The three of them huddled together near the stern.

"What the fuck, Dex?" Melissa said.

"She begged me to. Everyone said they were up for it." Dexter ran a hand through his thick black hair.

"So you let an actress call the shots on your boat?" Melissa shook her head. "Now you've put me in the shitty position of having to kiss her ass so we don't get handed a lawsuit. You better hope she doesn't get a scar."

"Look at her eyes," said Steve. "She's panicked, for sure."

Nicollette and Harry were escorted up the steep riverbank to the bus. They'd ride down and meet the group at the take-out. The rest of us still had several Class IV rapids to get through.

We came to a section of the river that forked into two channels around an island of thick willow bushes.

"On the left is Tequila Chute," Steve told our boat. "The right side's Pepsi Challenge. We're going right today."

I wanted to know what was down the left side.

"It's a snarled mess of downed trees and strainers. Totally impassable once you're in," Steve said, making a sweeping draw stroke with his paddle, pointing the boat right. "Forward, now."

We paddled hard in unison, down the tongue of a wave train. Our bow smashed through the peak of a huge breaking wave, then screamed down the backside and up through another wave, each one dousing us under sheets of water. I kept paddling, even though I couldn't see, until I heard Steve yell, "Stop."

Our crew hoisted paddles in the air, celebrating. As our channel rejoined the left fork downstream, we glimpsed Tequila Chute from the bottom. Steve was right about the trees strewn like beaver dams in the main current, but he hadn't mentioned the raft-sized boulders that spilled down it like a moraine.

We finished the day with clean lines, boats upright, and no more swimmers. When we boarded the bus, Nicollette sat sulking, Harry's arm slung around her protectively. With his other hand, he held an ice pack from the lunch cooler against her knee.

Back at the guide house, Dexter sprinted inside to get his business cards. As I dug around for dry clothes in my Festiva, I saw him reemerge. I watched as he returned to where the clients' cars were parked, but Nicollette and Harry had already left without saying goodbye. Dexter stood backlit by glaring desert sun, his face etched with disappointment, the card clutched in his hand.

116 The River's Daughter

I awoke the next day on a blue tarp surrounded by cheatgrass. Steve and I had made our bed alongside the row of camper-shelled trucks parked outside the guide house along with most of the other guides, since both bedrooms inside were taken by the operation's managers. The sun hadn't yet risen, and the cool air was faintly scented with pine and dew-covered dust, a smell that would disappear once the sun emerged over the ridgeline. Days here were stripped down to bare-bones earth and water beneath a fire-branded sky.

"Rise and shine." Steve leaned over and kissed me. "We launch on our two-day Lower Kern adventure today."

"I'm not going."

"Why not?"

"Because I don't want to end up trapped under the boat and bloody like Nicollette Sheridan."

"That's what makes it fun."

I threw the sarong we had used for a sheet over my head.

"What are you going to do? Sit here for two days and sweat to death?"

He had a point.

"The first day is super mellow Class III. Nothing big," Steve coaxed. "And it's so nice, camping out next to the river under the stars." He tickled me until I twisted and squirmed, shrieking with laughter.

"Fine, I'll go," I said. "But you better not dump me."

When we got to the guide house, it was vibrating with the energy of half-naked workers packing for the trip. Melissa met Steve and me at the trailer, where gear for the Lower trip was being loaded.

"Sean said there's no room for Bridget to go as a guest," she said.

Yay, I thought. *I'm off the hook.*

"But . . ." Melissa said, raising her eyebrows slightly, "she can go in the training boat with Amy and Caitlin. They're R-2ing."

"That'll work," said Steve.

Melissa walked off toward the repair shed.

"R-2ing?" I asked.

"One raft, two people: R-2. With you on board, it will be R-3."

"Wait, I'm not going in your boat?"

"Don't worry. Amy and Caitlin are NorCal guides—they know how to read and run."

"Have they even been down the Lower before?"

Steve shook his head before explaining that water behaved the same no matter the river, so the best guides didn't memorize rapids or runs but instead recognized features as they approached from upstream. He told me that guides from Northern California were exceptional at reading water because they ran so many different rivers rather than the same section over and over. Their strength was in their ability to adapt. Apparently, many of the world's best guides came from NorCal.

I looked at him skeptically.

"Amy and Caitlin aren't much older than you. You'll have fun with them."

Fine Young Cannibals blasted from the outdoor speakers. "She drives me crazy, ooh ooh." Steve and I joined the guides near boats stacked on the ground in the boatyard. As we prepared to pull the top one down to load it onto the bus headed for the river put-in, we heard giggling and shushing.

Three sets of eyes peered over the bow of the boat.

"Dexter," Melissa said, "climb down out of that love nest and leave those poor trainees alone."

Even though they were clothed—shorts, sandals, tanks—the two young women seemed to be all tan sinewy limbs as the three jumped down to help heave the boat onto the top of the bus.

"Caitlin and Amy, meet Bridget, your third paddler," Melissa said.

Caitlin's smile seemed too bright for the one-horse town of Lake Isabella. She slid a straw cowboy hat onto her sun-bleached hair.

Amy took my hand and gave it a proper shake. "Dig your leg hair." Her dark, wavy hair fell down to her shoulders, glossy and thick. Her light blue eyes were startling in both color and intensity. I wasn't sure if Amy had leg hair or not; it was hard to tell with all the bruises on her shins from river carnage. She popped on a pair of sunglasses before leaping onto the roof of the bus, where she grabbed the bow of the raft as the other guides thrust it toward her. After centering the twelve-foot boat, Amy quickly lashed it down with a couple of taut trucker's hitch knots.

"We're going to have fun," she said.

"Yeah, we are," Caitlin echoed.

"But can we stop it with the Fine Young Cannibals already?" Amy shouted. "Good Lord! Who's DJing?"

On the river, Amy and Caitlin showed me how to secure my foot under the cross tube thwart—really jam it in—so I could lean out over the tube to paddle. Our first obstacle was an unfortunate placement of boulders with only a thin gap between them that didn't look wide enough for the boat.

"Will we fit?" It seemed certain that no matter what we did, we'd get stuck on a rock.

"Finesse, baby." Caitlin smiled.

"Easy, now," Amy cooed from the stern, setting an angle to the left. "Gentle forward."

We'd barely dipped our paddles when Amy softly called, "Easy right turn." From the front left position, I paddled forward, matching my intensity to the sound of her voice. Across from me, Caitlin back-paddled in what looked like a slow-motion sit-up. Our boat slalomed around the big boulders without touching.

"It's not really big power moves on this river," Caitlin said. "It's more slow and gentle."

"Totally," Amy said.

We floated along, taking in the white jimsonweed and freckled sandstone. Steve's raft was far ahead of us in the large flotilla of six boats—I caught only glimpses of him before he'd go around a bend.

As we logged miles downstream, no one queried me on Steve or my past. We were simply three girls floating on a river in the sun. I breathed in the slightly fish-scented headwind made cool by the water and felt the edges of my story begin to erode. Midafternoon, our group came to the biggest rapid of the day, a left turn around a thick bank of trees. What we couldn't see was the hidden ledge hole on the bottom right. Melissa had explained in the safety talk that holes were caused by rocks submerged just under the surface. Current pours over the rock, plunges deep, then recirculates onto itself, flowing back upstream to fill in the space behind the rock. This recirculation of water creates a standing wave that takes the exact shape of the obstacle creating it. If the rock is a triangular boulder, the hole will mirror that. A long, uniform, ledge-like rock jutting into the current from shore creates a ledge hole that's similarly long and uniform.

Caitlin captained us toward the left, staying inside the curve where the centrifugal force wasn't as strong. Between haphazard paddling and tree branches blocking the inside current, we didn't make the move in time and ended up taking a piece of the ledge hole. I sat on the tube next to the hole, the part of the boat that took the brunt of the hit. The force of it knocked my foot loose from under the thwart, sending both my legs upward and folding the tube of the boat. As I began to somersault backward into the hole, I glimpsed the gnashing water I was headed into, thinking it as likely a place to get Maytagged—recirculated—as any. As my fear peaked, Amy leaned over and wrapped her hand around my ankle, yanking me back into the boat.

"Didn't see that coming." Caitlin laughed.

"You okay?" Amy looked me over.

I sat frozen.

"There's only two kinds of rafters," Caitlin said, "those who've swam, and those who will."

This was meant to comfort me, or make me laugh, but it succeeded in neither. Swimming a rapid was a frightening prospect that I planned to avoid absolutely. I didn't grasp the fun of having the terrain continually shifting all around me. I'd had my fill of instability getting through childhood. When I looked around for Steve, I discovered he was already downstream and out of view. He'd missed the whole thing.

Our group stopped for the day at the semipermanent campsite the river company leased from Sequoia National Forest. Melissa gathered everyone together to prep for the next activity: intentionally swimming through the rapid in front of our camp.

"Keep your life jackets cinched up, people. Steve's going to demonstrate how to do the camp swim. Follow him upstream along the footpath and he'll prep you at the launching spot. If nothing else, it'll keep you cool in this wretched heat."

"C'mon, Bridget, it'll be awesome!" Amy said, clipping her water bottle to the raft.

I looked from Amy to Caitlin, my arms stiffly crossed. Caitlin reached for my hand, and her fingers around mine warmed the possibility in me.

"We'll go through together," she said, smiling.

We trudged up the trail, skipping over rocks, tree roots, and brush. I thought of playing next to the Snake River with Justin and the time we fell in and swam downstream in freezing snowmelt. I remembered Mama saying over and over: *If you fall in the river, you will die.*

Through the brush, I glimpsed Steve getting into position at the top of the rapid, laughing with the other guides. How could he be so casual when we were about to die? Hadn't he seen what had happened to Nicollette after she'd been so careless?

"Okay, folks," Steve said to the group. "The idea is to jump out as far as you can from shore, well into the current. What you don't want to do is drag along the shore, clutching rocks and branches. Fear and hesitation will get you injured. When you get out into the main flow, get your feet up and use your hands to maneuver around. Once you've dropped through the rapid, get on your stomach and swim for the eddy, where the other guides are waiting with throw bags. If you don't make it into the eddy, the bag will be thrown to you, releasing a rope. Grab onto the rope so we can pull you to shore. See you downstream."

He hurtled into the current and was whisked out of sight. One by one, passengers followed suit, leaping into the river.

Suddenly, it was my turn. "Are you ready?" Caitlin asked. "On three: jump! One, two . . ." Caitlin plunged into the Kern and looked back at me. "Come on!"

I jumped.

The water, dam-released from Lake Isabella, was much warmer than I'd expected. I got situated onto my back and felt as though a giant hand were holding me up. I could see Caitlin's head bobbing in front of me. I felt the current grab me as I whooshed down the trough of a wave cresting far above my head. I held my breath and went through it, dipped into another trough, up through another wave. I saw boats and people onshore, so I turned over and swam toward them. It took only a few strokes before the current released me into the eddy. I heard laughing and was surprised that it was me.

"That was the funnest thing ever!" I squealed, high on adrenaline. "Let's do it again!"

I ran back up and launched myself into the current, dropping down through the waves and swimming into the eddy again and again until I was the last one doing it in the twilight. The guides went to make dinner, except Steve, who watched me swim the rapid, chuckling at my state of delirious joy.

"You're a natural, you know." I could hear the smile in his voice, although I couldn't make out his features anymore. A bat dipped between us, gliding over the water.

"I was born for this," I said.

Twelve

Guide School

As we pulled into East Table put-in on the Snake River, our guide school instructor, Morgan, addressed the class of twenty-five students from the front of the bus. "Everyone needs to know how it feels to be in water this cold, so we'll be flipping our rafts in the heavy runoff to see how quickly you can pull yourselves and each other onto the bottom of a capsized raft," he said. "As a guide, you have to be able to rescue not only yourself but everyone else too."

We were ten miles downstream from the trailer park where Justin and I had fallen into the Snake as nine-year-olds. Although eleven years had passed, I remembered well the gripping, take-your-breath-away shock of the cold water. At least this time I wore a wet suit and life jacket.

I exited the bus wondering if I'd made the right choice in leaving my college studies behind to pursue a job guiding rivers. For two years, Steve and I had lived together in Missoula, attending classes at the University of Montana. Then Steve landed a gig teaching a weeklong guide school in Jackson for the Snake River Rafting Company and had negotiated a coveted spot for me to attend. Out of the twenty-five students, only five were women. At the end of the course, ten students would be chosen to work for the company. Steve didn't want to be accused of favoritism, so we kept our distance during school. It would be up to Morgan, Steve's co-instructor, to decide whether to hire me.

The morning's storm had subsided, and a rising mist overtook the canyon. A meadowlark trilled close by, joining the steady beat of the Snake. The beauty of late May in Jackson Hole enveloped me, yet I felt tense and anxious. I walked away from the group, worried about the upcoming flip drill. Despite the soothing perfume of pines, this spot unnerved me. As I scanned the shoreline in front of me, the sturdy boughs of a Douglas fir tree came into focus. A hot buzzing rose up my spine, bringing with it a memory of thundering rain and blood rivulets running down my legs. This was the tree where I had waited for Colby to return after he'd raped me and left me for hours.

Suddenly I couldn't breathe. Scenes from that day played out before me: the canoe listing and spinning in turbid water; Colby sneering at my inexperience. The scrape of a downed cottonwood snag on my back as he penetrated me. The shameful wait with his dog, Timber, and the Snake as my witness. My body held the memory in my cells.

You are not lost. The Snake's voice came to me. It had been three years since I'd heard her speak, but she was strong and steady as ever. Being recognized by her felt like coming home.

I walked to the edge of the river as the guide school group unloaded rafts behind me. I put my hands into the cold water, releasing the painful memories through my fingers into her current.

"My hands are your hands," I said. "Let me use them to honor you."

I splashed my tears with water and returned to the tree. "Thank you for holding me that night." I patted its trunk, then wrapped my arms all the way around it.

"I knew you were a tree hugger," Morgan said behind me.

"This one's an old friend." I smiled, forcing myself to be present. "I'm from Jackson."

Morgan looked at me, impressed. "Are your folks still here? There's so many tourists and seasonal people here these days, it seems like all the families got pushed out."

"My family's gone." Sully was in California. Mom and Mark were in Montana with David. Theresa was still around, but we hadn't spoken to each other since our bar fight at Spirits of the West. The only family I could rely on was the Snake.

Morgan and I joined everyone else as they loaded into the two rafts. Steve's group pushed off first and floated ahead, running lead, with Morgan's running sweep.

Once we were in the current, Morgan said, "Local girl, you're up. Pretend we're your clients and tell us about this canyon."

I was determined to make a new story for myself here. I scanned the shore, my eyes landing on a tree I knew well from my childhood.

"See the gray-barked tree with the leaves just starting to poke out?"

"I can't hear you," Morgan said, cupping his ear with his hand.

I cleared my throat to make my voice louder. "That's a cottonwood, the state tree of Wyoming."

"I didn't know that," said Morgan. "What about those trees?"

"The tall, skinny trees that all look the same are lodgepole pines. Their seed cones are coated with a resin that needs extreme heat to melt before the seeds can be released, so they have to be ravaged by fire to regenerate. Plains tribes like the Shoshone, Crow, Blackfeet, Cheyenne, Nez Perce, and Gros Ventre use lodgepole trunks to build tepees and also for sleds—called *travois* by the French trappers."

"Okay, definitely not in the student handbook. How do you know that?" asked Morgan.

"Girl Scout camp," I said, "and guiding backpacking trips. Also, my mom's a Wyoming history fanatic." Mama's library was filled with books about the West: stories of starving children forced to eat one another on the Oregon Trail, field guides on edible plants, and survival guides. As she liked to put it, the entire fucking point was to survive.

"That's just the kind of stuff tourists are interested in," Morgan said, looking around. "I think this is a good spot to swim. It's time to flip this baby."

Morgan showed us how to thread the bowline through the raft's upstream D-ring, as I'd seen Dexter do on the Kern. We all stood on the downstream tube while he pulled the raft over on top of us.

I hit the water, unable to gather air into my lungs through the stabbing cold. I surfaced under the raft, so I reached up and used my hands to find my way out from under the boat.

Help me, I pleaded with the Snake. *Give me strength.*

I found the upstream side of the boat and held on to a handle on the perimeter. I remembered Morgan saying that getting back on top of the raft was a matter of leverage. I gripped the handle with my dominant left hand and, while floating on my stomach, swiftly pulled myself forward and up. I bent my elbow into a strong right angle over the handle, then straightened my arm, kicking hard for momentum.

I landed on top of the boat, stunned to be the first one up.

The day after the flip drill, two students dropped out, both women. The Snake was flowing at a volume of over thirty thousand cubic feet per second (cfs). A cubic foot is around the size of a basketball, and the force of the water, equivalent to thirty thousand balls passing the same point each second, instilled legitimate fear in our group. By comparison, the Upper Kern had been around one thousand cfs the day Nicollette Sheridan was injured. The whitewater on the Kern was rated more technical due to the many obstacles, but the higher-volume Snake was colder, with water temperatures in the midforties. The Snake was fast enough to sweep you a half mile away from the boat in under a minute, and cold enough to kill you in six.

That day, the Snake's most formidable rapid, Lunch Counter, had two solid lateral waves capable of flipping a boat or dumping paddlers. Hours earlier, I'd watched Clint, a college quarterback looking for a cool summer job, puke off the stern before captaining the raft into the rapid's laterals at the wrong angle, sending the entire left side of paddlers swimming. They were retrieved a quarter mile downstream after several minutes and would have to sit out the rest of the day in the bus, warming up. After witnessing Clint's run, I dreaded my turn.

"Local girl, let's see what you got," Morgan said to me as we entered Blind Canyon, just upstream from Lunch Counter.

I made my way to the stern and took my seat on the back left tube, across from Morgan. As we drifted, I dipped my hand into the water and asked the Snake for help. *Show me the way.* I rubbed water onto the back of my neck and my forehead, then put my paddle in the water while scanning the rapid before us.

I saw a small crease in the first lateral wave and felt a tug in my stomach indicating that I should aim the raft at the crease.

"Left turn," I called. Then, when we were lined up, I said, "Stop." All we needed was momentum. "Forward!"

The crew dug in, and we built speed toward the breaking wave. From the stern, I held my paddle in the water, bracing it against my hip like a rudder to maintain the angle. We took the hit squarely and crested toward the top of the lateral before sliding off to the right with the funneling surge. I needed to strengthen my angle to stay perpendicular to the wave train, so I called another left turn, all the while cranking back-paddles from left stern. The boat shifted, and we aligned in the center of the wave train. It was a textbook run.

Morgan looked over at me, beaming. "That's it, sister." He held up his hand for a high five.

After the elation subsided, I slipped my hand back into the Snake. "Thank you," I whispered. I knew she was the reason for my success.

⌒

Things continued to go well for me during guide school, and I got pulled out to work a commercial trip before the week was over.

The morning of my first trip as a guide, I got to the office early to meet my new boss, sign paperwork, and help pack. The owner, Dorian, and his wife, Claire, were there with all the forms. I pretended not to recognize

Dorian, even as my breath caught in my throat. He was the man who'd come home with Theresa wanting to have a threesome when I was babysitting. He'd had something of a makeover since I'd seen him last; he'd lost the perm and the acid wash he'd sported years ago. I felt Dorian watching me through his thick, blue-tinted glasses as I filled in my employment history.

"Do I know you from somewhere?"

I turned my head so my profile wasn't as prominent. Many have commented on how, from the side, my nose looks exactly like Theresa's.

"I don't think so."

"There's something really familiar about you."

"It's a small town," I said. "We've probably seen each other around." *Please don't remember that it was in my aunt's living room at two in the morning, with her in a black lace teddy and me in braces.*

"I swear, we've met," Dorian said, puzzled.

I hoped Dorian's nickname, Dr. Dazed, held true and would keep him from remembering who I was. I slid my paperwork to Claire.

"I'm so glad we'll have a woman this year," she said in a thick Norwegian accent as she patted my pile of forms. She smiled at me, adjusting her topknot. "Too long it's been a club just for boys."

Claire was much younger than Dorian, but I wasn't in a position to judge, considering I'd started dating my aunt's ex when I was still jailbait. She looked like a model with her dewy skin, blond hair, and sparkling green eyes.

"Do you think there will be another woman, perhaps?" Claire asked, seeking my opinion about my guide school classmates.

"I really hope so," I said.

"Well, we are so happy. Right, Dorian?"

Dorian looked at me, head still tilted sideways.

After guide school, Steve went to work the Class IV spring season in Idaho to improve his river résumé and skills, and I rented a room in Jackson where I'd live for the summer, working on the Snake as a first-year guide. Steve hadn't been in Idaho long when I received a call.

"You won't believe it," he said. "I'm working with the guy who manages an American company on the Zambezi River. He's looking for guides to work in Zambia starting in late June."

"Holy shit."

"He offered me a spot. Said they'll fly me over, give me a day wage in both US dollars and kwacha, plus a room at the guide house in Livingstone."

"Did you say yes?"

"I wanted to check with you first. There's room for you to stay with me there. You can save what you make on the Snake and fly over after the summer."

"You know I'm in."

After three years together, we were about to realize our dream of running rivers in Africa.

⁓

I was determined to get to Zambia and picked up extra work in the boathouse and on the river, rarely taking a day off. Besides me, one other woman was hired out of guide school. Claire wanted one of us on each of the two daily schedules, so we were split up, both working separately on all-male crews. We ran five two-hour trips per day on a tight schedule with no breaks, earning twenty-five dollars per trip plus tips from clients. Passengers were bused in every two hours from town, while the guides stayed down in the canyon, gulping down lunch in the van while shuttling boats from the take-out back to the put-in, with no time for full bathroom breaks. There was a pocket of forest at the put-in where we'd pee before gathering our next group—the guys went on one side of the van and I on the other, behind a thick chokecherry bush. Most nights I returned home after a twelve-hour day, rubbed cream onto my cracked, river-scoured feet, and slid into bed sunburned, sore, and happy.

By midsummer, the river's lower flows presented new lines through rapids. Lunch Counter's waves became smaller and less powerful, and Big Kahuna—known as Kahuna to the guides—emerged as the biggest rapid in the canyon. Kahuna was a one-hit wonder with a lone standing wave that when hit dead-on, stopped the boat's momentum and doused the raft in water. It was a bad place for swimmers, since it fed into Lunch Counter, making for a stout swim. Even farther upstream lurked a long, jagged rock slab in the center of the river that resembled the back of the Loch Ness Monster. In fact, it was known as the Snake River Monster, its razor-sharp spine capable of gashing the side of a raft clean open.

I was served up my first river carnage by the monster on a typical late July day. The weather had started out glaringly bright under the high-altitude sun and subsided into rumbling thunderclouds by midafternoon. I slid on my raingear before greeting my third crew of the day, a small group of ten: a young Canadian couple took the bow, followed by two families from Spokane, both with 'tween-age sons. From the start of the trip, their powerful paddling threw me; the lily-dipping crews I typically had took three or four paddle strokes to this crew's one. We lurched through the S-Turns, our first rapid, like a Porsche spinning donuts. When we got to the Snake River Monster, I set an angle to the right, aiming to ride the main current between the monster razor rock and the igneous cliff band on river right.

"Forward," I called.

The boat hurtled across the current.

"Stop!" The momentum was too strong, and we glided straight for the protruding granite.

"Back-paddle!" The boat slowed somewhat but still scraped against the rock band with a deep squeaking followed by a long, lone baritone note laid bare against a rush of soprano current.

Initially, the raft seemed to be holding air reasonably well, despite the inch-long slice in the outer fabric. Yet by the bottom of Wolf Creek Boils, the right bow paddler was riding low, engulfed in a mess of Hypalon.

"Is the boat going to sink?" one of the mothers asked. "How are we going to make it through the rapids like this?"

We spilled out of the S-Turns into the Gauging Straits, not far above Blind Canyon. We couldn't get another raft, or even go ashore to properly repair the tear, without wreaking havoc on the tight two-hour schedule. Besides, we didn't have a repair kit on the river or in the van, as patch jobs were so time-intensive and rare, they were done at the boathouse. The worst of it was, we hadn't yet reached the five Class III rapids that awaited us in Blind Canyon. We had less than two river miles of flat water to pull it together.

My entire crew turned in my direction, worry written on their faces.

"The boat's designed with six separate air chambers," I said, keeping my voice steady and calm, with a cheerful edge, like a flight attendant's. "There are baffles separating the chambers, so if one tube loses air, the rest still hold."

"We're sitting in water up here," said one of the Canadians, shivering. I heard the fear in his voice. One of the moms was near tears as she clutched her youngest son.

The stern, where I sat, was unaffected. It occurred to me that the bow and stern were identical, so we could spin the boat and make the stern the new bow. I unclipped my dry bag filled with straps and carabiners from the back thwart and pointed to the Canadians. "You two bring your paddles and come back here."

Jimmy, a college boy from Utah hired out of the guide school, paddled his raft alongside mine and tapped the top of his head, giving me the signal for *Are you okay?* I tapped my head back at him: *Okay.*

I continued rearranging my crew as we floated. "Everyone switch with the paddler straight across. Now spin in your seats and face the other way. Jeez, I feel like the caller at a square dance." Everyone laughed, easing the tension. "Welcome to the Wild West, folks. You're getting a real treat today. Not everyone shoots Blind Canyon in such a rugged craft. It's almost like explorer John C. Frémont's descent of the Snake in 1843 in the world's first-known rubber raft." I settled into the new stern, which was already awash in Snake River water.

"This is so awesome!" The four young boys in the boat now seemed thrilled with our misfortune.

I remembered reading in the guide school manual about rigging a temporary fix with straps run from the strong tube to the flat one to provide shape and support. I rummaged through my bag but didn't have any straps long enough to be effective. I decided to use my throw bag and some carabiners to weave an intricate web across the stern. I zigzagged the line, cranking tension with trucker's hitch knots. It was an entrapment danger, but since I was alone in the stern, I'd be the only one at risk.

"We'll need to bail continually when not in the rapids," I said, looking at the boys. "We're going to take on a lot of water. You guys up for it?"

The boys cheered while their mothers looked at me with doom in their eyes. I didn't mention that instead of guiding from the left side of the boat, where the flat tube was, I'd now have to guide from the right, requiring me to hold my paddle and steer the raft from the opposite side, not unlike driving a stick shift from the passenger side of a car. This, while being hemmed in by a labyrinth of rope.

The sound of current being squeezed through granite echoed off the cliffs above Blind Canyon. Prep time was over. There was nothing left to do but run it.

"Weight over your feet. Everybody stay in the boat," I said. "Let's all dip our hand in the water now and ask the river for safe passage." No one hesitated to put their hand in. *Show me the way.* I swirled my hand in the water, reaching for her. "Forward," I called.

We climbed the first wave. When the stern hit the crest, it folded precariously, then lunged into the next trough. We undulated as if on a slow-motion bull ride through the wave train. The raft filled with water, and the stern fell away beneath me, essentially becoming part of the river. Keeping my footing was impossible, so I compacted my body into a floating ball while gripping the ropes.

After the waves, the boys began bailing, but there wasn't enough time to clear all the water before Kahuna's frothing wave came into view. I saw a softer place in the curling crest, just left of center, and set an angle to punch through there. We were bogged down by the extra water in the raft. The boys bailed with everything they had while their parents dug with their paddles, but it wasn't enough. We locked onto the current headed dead center, lined up to hit the meat.

"Get down!" I called out. The crew hunkered to the floor. The stern collapsed upon impact, launching me upward. I landed in the drink behind the raft, but within reach of the boat, so I swam hard.

I was close enough for the crew to still hear me, so I yelled from the water, "Back on the job! Bail!"

"She's out! She's out!" one of the moms screamed.

I lunged and grabbed the D-ring of the strong tube and pulled myself into the boat using my flip drill move. "I'm back in," I said. "We're okay. Focus up, now. Lunch Counter. Forward!"

There was no sneak run through Lunch Counter. Clients often asked how the rapid got its name. One story was that when you saw it, you were liable to lose your lunch onto the counter-like rock slabs lining the rapid. Another was that it was the most popular place to eat it.

"Dig it in! Forward!" I crouched down slightly inside the tube as I paddled to hold our angle. We rode the wave train, water sloshing over the gunnels as we heaved over each crest. Triumphantly, we remained in the raft at the bottom.

I jumped into the middle of the boat and everyone dogpiled onto me, cheering and celebrating.

"You're the best crew I've had all summer," I said.

"Our guide taught us well," said one of the dads.

Randy, a senior guide, paddled up alongside us. "Nice rig." Randy was the only other local on our crew—we'd gone to the same church growing up.

"Still fell out, though," Jimmy called over from his nearby raft.

"Yeah, but we didn't know she was out," said one of the boys, gripping the bucket. "If a guide falls out and nobody sees, did they really fall out?"

We made it through the rest of the rapids and got to take-out on time to meet the next group.

"Can you take our picture together?" one of the dads asked Jimmy. "We want a photo with the best guide on the river." My crew squeezed in around me.

"Seriously," the dad said after the photo was done. "The best. Thank you for making that disaster the best part of our trip to Jackson Hole." He slid me a hundred-dollar bill. The couple from Canada handed me a twenty and hugged me goodbye.

"Shit," Jimmy said once they were gone. "Looks like we should start pooling tips. Crocker's cleaning up."

"Without even pimping," I said. Jimmy shamelessly included a bit about tipping in his take-out spiel.

Jimmy smirked. "Just trashing."

"Flip for tips," Randy said as we loaded the rafts. "Carnage brings cash."

Inside the van, we cracked open a bottle of Jack and passed it around.

"You ready to do it again?" asked Randy from the driver's seat.

"Fuckin' A," I said, passing him the bottle. He took a long swig while bracing the steering wheel against his knees.

Randy pulled into our usual spot. We all spilled out to pee before meeting the clients. I dashed behind the chokecherry bush, squatting down next to a blooming scarlet gilia. As I peed, I studied how the flower's tiny, trumpetlike red petals were all open, except two at the top.

"You know, I've always wondered . . ." Jimmy suddenly appeared, startling me. I was midstream and couldn't stand.

"Are your nipples pink, or are they brown?" He moved in closer, his body looming over me. The toes of our river sandals nearly touched. "I'm sort of a connoisseur of breasts. I'm pretty sure you're a B cup, right? I figured that out. But the nipples, that's puzzled me all summer."

Jimmy's body was covered by raingear; he wasn't trying to touch or restrain me. Still, my instinct to escape was overpowering, and I retreated into the cave within myself, frozen and still. It was all so familiar: the flat gray light cast by building thunderheads, the occasional thunk of river rock scraping bottom, a charming college boy from Utah threatening to tread onto my body. For generations, the women of my family had carried the trauma of sexual abuse. Disappearing within for survival's sake was bred into my DNA.

Peripherally, I glimpsed the green water of the Snake. She was my mirror, shimmering back who I was, reminding me I was capable of strength. I remembered the sound of the Snake calling out *SWIM!* And how, as a nine-year-old, I'd managed to swim to shore to save my own life. Like then, I forced my arms and legs to move despite being frozen. I clawed my way out of the cave within until, finally, I surfaced.

"You've got some fucking nerve." I stood up and faced Jimmy, realizing I was actually taller than he was. I would take him if it came down to it. He shifted his eyes sideways, unable to look at me. I put my face inches from his and hissed, "Get out of my way, you son of a bitch," before brushing past him.

Randy was holding the CB radio; he'd called the office. "Looks like you're off the hook, Crocker. It's only four boats on the last trip."

"I'm headin' back to town, then." I radioed the bus at take-out and asked the driver to swing by and pick me up, then quickly gathered my gear. I wasn't going to wait around at the scene of the crime this time.

I was met with cheers as I boarded the client bus. "There she is! Our fearless leader." My crew was still aglow from our run. I smiled even though I was shaking with adrenaline. I high-fived them all before taking a free seat in the back.

We drove through the Snake River Canyon, past East Table and Astoria Hot Springs. I thought about how Jimmy and Colby both saw this mountain town as their outdoor playground and its peaks, rapids, and women as their conquests. It was a story as old as manifest destiny, beginning with the trappers and the pioneers. They took what they wanted without fear or consequence.

The bus passed by the trailer court and the single-wide where I'd once lived with Mama and Daddy. The little tree where Mama took my picture on the first day of school each year had grown taller than the trailer. We came to the sage-covered sledding hill, flanked by sentient cottonwoods, the Snake winding around all of it.

Back at the boathouse, I heard my crew relaying our adventure to Dorian and Claire in the front office as I filled out my time card in the back. I had earned twenty-five dollars in wages for the trip, and nothing but another rock in my gut for the ordeal with Jimmy afterward. I wanted someone else to tell Dorian and Claire about Jimmy coming up on me by the chokecherry bush, but there had been no witnesses besides the Snake and the lodgepole pines. I was the only one who could give voice to what had happened. The buzzing I felt in my limbs was my body's way of preparing me to purge it. If I swallowed the rise of adrenaline now, it would always be *my* story, instead of Jimmy's, and I had been poisoned to the point of allergy from a lifetime of swallowing other people's bad choices.

Dorian came through the door separating the office from the boathouse. "Sounds like a pretty wild trip," he said. "You handled it well. Your clients were thrilled."

"Even though they were scared, they pushed through it." I realized it was the same for me now. I had to push. "I need to talk to you and Claire. Can we go in your office?"

"Sure. I'll get her."

I climbed the stairs to Dorian's office, ignoring the deafening track looping in my head, my mother's voice saying, *You better get used to it. It's just going to keep happening to you.*

I sat before Dorian and Claire and looked up. "Something happened after the trip that was very upsetting," I began.

"Not with the clients," Claire said. "They loved you."

"No, with Jimmy. He came up to me while I was crouched down peeing and asked if my nipples were pink or brown, and said that he figured I was a B cup size. He loomed over me, trying to intimidate me."

"What?" Claire said.

"He probably just has a crush on you," Dorian said.

Claire gave Dorian a slow headshake. "She is out there on her own working with these guys and winning over the passengers. Every day, she's making a way for women on the river. She shouldn't have to deal with bullshit from guys like that."

Dorian closed his lips together; he looked like a moose. It was hard to see where he was looking, since his glasses were so magnified they distorted his eyes.

"We cannot expect her to manage that by herself. She needs us behind her."

"Okay," Dorian said after a long pause. "Do you want us to fire him?"

I looked at Claire and saw how much she believed in me. I was a twenty-year-old woman just starting out in my career, and she was nearly twice my age. Unlike me, she'd lived far beyond this town and this continent, but this ugly business was the same the world over.

"Yes," I said. "I want you to fire him."

"Then he's gone," Dorian said.

Claire stretched her hand across the table and put it on mine. We were doing this together. We would not be intimidated. We would not get used to this kind of behavior, and, empowered by the other, we intended to do something about it.

The next day, there was a note taped onto the guide bulletin board that Jimmy would no longer be on the schedule.

Not long afterward, ripped-out centerfolds appeared taped inside the guide van.

"Are you offended?" Clint, the quarterback, asked me. "Are you gonna go snitch to Dorian and get us all fired?"

I didn't answer.

"That's what I thought, you hairy fucking feminist."

I pulled a joint from my bag, lit it, and said, "I may be a hairy feminist, but at least I didn't give the entire office staff chlamydia." I inhaled and passed the joint to Randy. "Check yourself, bro. Like, at the clinic."

"Dude, she got you there," Randy said, laughing. "It's not just the office staff you gave it to either." He took a hit. "That shit gets around."

About three weeks after Steve left for Zambia, I had received a postcard at the company office. The front had a pride of lions ripping apart a gazelle, with Steve's scratchy handwriting on the back. "The river is so big, we call it the Slambezi. Everything is totally wild here. Miss you. Love, Steve." Since the card's arrival, months had gone by with no word from him. One morning as I was packing a trip, Claire came to tell me he was on the office line.

"I just heard about a job opening on the Lower Zambezi," Steve said. The job was guiding canoe trips through a game preserve. Stan, the guy doing the hiring, was from Jackson and used to work for Dorian. "I told Stan you were coming over and would be interested in the job. He wants Dorian to fax him a letter of recommendation."

"When?"

"He said to contact him right away. He's making the decision in the next couple of days."

I jotted down Stan's fax number and underlined it twice.

"You're going to love it here," Steve said. "It's just like we imagined."

That evening, I approached Dorian after unpacking the trip. We were alone under the glare of fluorescent lights, the rest of the crew already gone.

Before I could say anything, he blurted, "I figured out how I know you. You were babysitting one time when I came home with your sister."

"Aunt," I corrected.

"I remember thinking you were pretty hot for a teenager."

"Please," I said dismissively. "I need you to do something for me."

"Do I have to fire anyone?" He gave me the moose stare.

"Stan's hiring canoe guides on the Lower Zambezi, and I'm applying. I need a letter of recommendation from you."

"Tell Claire and she'll write something up later."

"We have to fax it tonight," I said. "I have his number. He wants it from you, not Claire."

"I've got friends waiting for me at the Cadillac Grille."

If I'd learned anything over the summer, it was that my mom was right: patriarchy wasn't dead yet. Not by a long shot. I'd honed my skills and worked hard to get where I was, proving my guiding abilities time and time again. But there was still the matter of the gatekeepers, and for that I had no alternative but to play whatever card I had, including exploiting a weakness to advance, just as I'd seen my mother do.

As Morgan had taught us in guide school, to get on top of the boat, you needed leverage.

"I wonder," I said, shifting forward. "What would Claire think if she knew how you and I met? That I was the babysitter you tried to lure into a threesome?"

Dorian jerked his head back, then froze.

"I need you to write this for me tonight."

"You're a pain in the ass, you know that?" He moved closer to me. "What should I write? Bridget's the hottest guide we have?"

I stiffened. "Try the best guide you have. On the water and with the clients."

He paused, considering, then shrugged. "That's actually true." He sat down at the keyboard and wrote.

The next morning, a fax was waiting for me: a job offer from Stan to guide the Lower Zambezi River. I thought back to the nights I'd spent in my closet at my father's home in Ventura, looking at images of Africa. I'd promised myself that I would escape so far away they would never find me, and now, it was actually going to happen.

Thirteen

Nyaminyami's Lair

As we descended the trail to the river, the roar of Victoria Falls was so loud that Steve and I quit trying to talk over it. It had been three days since I'd landed in Zambia, and my tongue felt sandpapery from jet lag and dehydration. We'd barely started hiking and already I was weary from carrying my dry bag and water bottles. Steve charged ahead, loaded with gear for our seven-day expedition.

It was late October, and four months had passed since Steve had come to work the Zambezi. In that time, his arms and chest appeared to have doubled in size, and he seemed accustomed to the hundred-degree heat of summertime south of the equator. Around his neck, he wore a talisman of a snakelike creature—Nyaminyami, the river god of the Zambezi—which was strange, since he was an atheist. This new version of Steve felt foreign to me. He was preoccupied and distant in the way he walked with his head down, focused solely on the trail.

I wasn't sure if my skin was drenched from sweat or from the mist of the falls, which was so dense it created a pocket ecosystem of riverine rain forest. The slice of lush garden was distinct from the scrubby mopane woodlands of the canyon rim. I thought of the Class V rapids we'd be running within the hour with a growing sense of anxiety. I was glad to be just a passenger riding in Steve's boat without the responsibilities of guiding.

Steve, who'd been in his own world all morning, looked impatient as I made my way down the trail. "I'm going to catch up to Pete," he said. "He's probably already at the put-in." Pete, the leader for our two-boat trip, had gone down ahead with a crew of local guys.

"How far is it?" I asked.

"Half mile."

I wanted to show him I was as tough as he was. He wasn't the only one whose arms had gotten twice as big over the summer. But I was having trouble acclimating to the oppressive heat.

"You won't see anyone besides the highsiders, bringing down gear." He disappeared behind a tangle of mahogany and fig trees.

Highsiders were local men paid by the rafting company to carry equipment in and out of the gorge. Some of them also rode in the rafts to assist in highsiding, a technique of throwing body weight around in the boat so it would stay upright in the high-volume rapids.

I found a patch of shade and stopped to drink from my water bottle. Even though I could hear the falls, I couldn't see them, only the rainbows created by mist catching the sun. Victoria Falls was one of the Seven Natural Wonders of the World, and named for Queen Victoria in 1855 by British explorer David Livingstone. Locally, it was known as Mosi-oa-Tunya, "the smoke that thunders."

Movement in the shrubs across the trail startled me. Jumping from trees to the ground was a troop of baboons, some carrying babies on their backs. The adults were the size of adult coyotes, their tails flagged up in the air. I had never seen a wild baboon. I scoured the area for a large stick as they made calls that sounded like a catfight. I considered running, but I didn't want them to think I was prey. They moved far more swiftly than I ever could.

Four Zambian men, barefoot and shirtless, appeared behind me on the trail. They shouldered an eighteen-foot raft, tightly rolled lengthwise like a giant caterpillar. Their oversized shorts were cinched tightly around their muscular hips with the same webbing used to rig rafts. I scampered out of the way as the highsiders brushed past me in a whoosh of collective power. One of them spied the baboons and promptly sang out in deep, raspy Nyanja. The other men returned the song in a perfectly pitched round.

> *Nani aletwita bane?* / Who is calling us?
> *Whitewater iletwita.* / Whitewater is calling us.

The baboons retreated into the forest. The men kept singing without breaking stride until the animals were gone. As the highsiders passed me, the one in back whistled to get my attention. He was tall, with an easy, gap-toothed smile.

"Come," he said. "Stay close."

I grabbed my bag and water bottles and followed the men down to the river. They deposited their cargo next to gear splayed out like puzzle pieces across a wide boulder field. I nodded my thanks before they bounded back up the hill to bring down more gear, their labor paid by the load.

From the canyon floor, the top of the falls loomed 350 feet overhead and fell over the lip of the canyon in a shimmering expanse. Having been raised near the Tetons, I was used to stunning landscapes, but the grandeur of the falls brought tears to my eyes. I understood how Livingstone, after paddling up to the falls' edge, wrote, "Scenes so lovely must have been gazed upon by angels in their flight."

The Zambezi was the fourth-largest river in Africa and during spring runoff, held ten times the water that flowed in the Snake. Even at its lowest, as it was now, it had five times the volume of the Snake. The mile-wide waterfall beat onto the river below with a power that reverberated inside my chest. The relentless drumming churned up the musty smell of millions of years of human history, dating back to the Oldowan industry and its earliest human toolmakers, *Homo habilis*. I'd studied this place in my anthropology classes at the University of Montana, and the thrill of being here in the present, adding to the ancient layers of lives it held, was dizzying.

Spread over the black volcanic rocks, around twenty highsiders worked on rigging the boats. One of the two gray rafts—both eighteen feet long and nine feet wide—was being inflated with a double-action hand pump. Whereas we'd primarily run paddleboats on the Snake and Kern, with the guides calling commands to the passengers, oar boats were favored on the Zambezi. A metal rowing frame was tied to the boat's center, and two oars controlled by the guide maneuvered the raft while passengers held on. Oar boats accommodated coolers, cooking stoves, and Dutch ovens. Dry bags filled with tents, sleeping bags, and personal gear were lashed to the frame with straps, the load cinched down like on a packhorse in order to prevent the loss of gear in the case of a flip, which, on the Zambezi, happened daily.

It became clear why the put-in was called the Boiling Pot when I saw the bubbling current where Steve and Pete were tying off the inflated boats. As water from the falls hit the river, it plunged deep, then boiled up, wasting no time forming into rapids. The first one, aptly named Number One by the first crew to raft the Zambezi in 1981, was in full view from shore.

Years earlier, safely tucked in bed, Steve and I had read in *Rivergods* how Richard Bangs, expedition leader on the Zambezi's first descent, flipped in Number One barely ten minutes after launching. One participant left the trip after being severely injured, while others evacuated after near-death swims and a crocodile attack on one of the rafts.

Today, we'd navigate rapids One through Ten, a six-mile stretch considered Class V because of the volume of the river, dangerous hydraulics, and remote location. The same section of river took Bangs and his exploratory crew two days to run because of flipped boats, injured swimmers, and evacuations.

I scrambled over the black boulders—all fallen pieces of the basalt rock gorge—until I reached Steve and Pete.

"Great hike, huh?" Steve said as he rigged safety leashes onto his oars.

"I saw baboons," I said nonchalantly, as if I hadn't been terrified of being ripped apart before the highsiders saved me.

"Cool." Steve's eyes were trained on the quick-release knot he'd tied. The sound of pounding water surrounded us. The river's deep green pools were punctuated by frothy horizon lines as it wound its way down the canyon. I realized then that my baboon encounter was nothing compared to the challenges before us. This was the holy grail of whitewater, the Olympics of rafting. As adrenaline began dumping into my bloodstream, it struck me that Steve's new shield might not be indifference but his game face. He was preparing for battle, girlfriend in tow. The more in the zone he was, the better our chances of survival.

"Hand me those oarlocks, would you?" Pete asked me as he stood in his floating raft. A vegetarian from California, he was here for his second season, though with his short brown hair and pale skin, he looked more like a Rocky Mountains boy to me.

I slid the horseshoe-shaped oarlocks over the bow.

"How was the Snake season? You guided there, right?" Pete asked while squinting at me appraisingly.

"It was high water," I said. "But, obviously, nothing like this."

"You'll have to row a boat down the Zam while you're here," Pete said.

"I haven't rowed oar boats much," I said, feeling queasy at the thought. "I'd like to see the river a few times first." *Like, a few hundred times.*

"Here come the pax." Steve motioned to the clients meandering through the slick boulders. "Pax—short for passengers," he said, giving me a quick smile. "It's a British thing." Zambia's colonial past as Northern Rhodesia was evidenced everywhere, from the official language of English to the left-sided driving and highway markers in kilometers.

"Go ahead and safety talk them," Pete said to Steve. "Then split them up so the hot British chick rides with me."

There were six passengers, all Americans besides Gabi, the hot Brit. "Welcome to the mighty Zambezi," Steve said, addressing the group. I snuck a peek at Gabi, who was traveling alone and appeared to be around my age. Instead of wearing quick-dry synthetic shorts and rash guards like the rest of us, Gabi wore denim cutoffs plus a formfitting midriff gingham top, one ruffled strap sliding off her shoulder. Her brown hair cascaded down her back in voluminous waves. Occasionally, she glanced at Pete, tilting her chin coyly while biting her lower lip. As Steve talked, Dakota, a silver-haired woman from New Mexico, circled around taking photos with expensive-looking equipment. Apparently, she was covering the trip for a book project.

Over the next twenty minutes, Steve ticked off the standard points of a safety talk, including the basics of highsiding. "You will all play an important part in determining if our rafts make it through," he said. "We'll need you to throw your weight around in the boat in order to keep the tubes from riding up and flipping when they hit the big stopper waves. Pete and I will go over highsiding more once we're in the rafts. We'll be practicing as we row upstream along the shoreline eddy to get as close to the falls as we can." Steve equipped everyone with a personal flotation device (PFD) and a helmet.

We loaded up then, three and four pax to a raft. Gabi and a couple from Wisconsin went with Pete, while the photographer, two brothers from New York, and I joined Steve.

We settled onto the bench seat across the front configured from a table that also served as an emergency backboard if someone had to be carried out of the gorge. Onshore, the highsiders gathered round the front of the boat and raised their arms while yelling out to Pete and Steve.

"*Iwe*," they all shouted, hoping to be chosen to join the trip. I'd heard them calling this to one another earlier while rigging.

"What's *iwe* mean?" I asked Steve.

"You," Steve said. "But they use it for lots of things, like how we say 'dude.'"

Each guide would take two highsiders to help weight the rafts, and the four chosen would be paid extra wages for seven days. Cries of "*iwe*" continued, growing in intensity.

"Sunday and Gordon," Steve called out, the names of two of his friends, both of them small in stature. Sunday had a wandering eye and shy demeanor, while Gordon flashed a bright, toothy smile as they hopped over the four of us sitting in front on their way to the stern.

"Jono and Clement," Pete said, choosing his highsiders. Both men were tall, Jono thicker than Clement. They scrambled to the rear of Pete's raft while the rest clicked their tongues in disappointment.

"Untie the raft," Steve said. I jumped out, coiled the line, and pushed the boat off, surrendering us to the water.

The land-bound highsiders waved goodbye as Pete and Steve pulled hard on the oars against the current, trying to move upstream toward the falls to put us underneath the curtain of water. We spun wildly in the aerated current as we got closer to the base of the falls. I couldn't open my eyes through the pelting spray off the cascade, so I listened.

Beneath the thundering of Mosi-oa-Tunya, there was another, deeper tone I couldn't identify. Could this rumble be Nyaminyami, the half-crocodile, half-serpent river god revered by the local Tonga tribe? Like Steve, the highsiders all wore carvings of Nyaminyami around their necks. I listened to the deeper bellow seizing my gut like a minor chord and sensed a being—not benevolent like the Snake, but a foreboding force.

Steve held his oars steady as the Boiling Pot spit us out into the main current that was being squeezed through the 650-foot-wide canyon below, eight times narrower than the falls. Unable to spread out as it had across the falls, the water went deep, scouring ever closer to the earth's core with each successive rainy season. Over the last hundred thousand years, the falls had receded, leaving a zigzagged river corridor that would be our passage. Our rafts were swept into the gorge.

"Get ready to highside," Steve yelled. "You're going to jump forward onto the front tube, knees bent, bellies facing the river. Hold on to the perimeter line if you can. Let's practice. Go!"

The New York brothers and I sprang forward, along with Sunday. The photographer, Dakota, shot photos with her waterproof camera from the stern, with Gordon poised to keep her in the boat.

"Good. Again. Go!" We tackled the bow. "Great. Come back."

Steve took several strong oar strokes, positioning us for the descent into rapid Number One. "For real this time. Get ready," Steve said. "Go!" We hurled ourselves forward, faces punching through the massive, peaking waves. I got so much water up my nose, my brain tingled.

Once through the rapid, I turned to look at Steve, who was sopping wet and smiling. "Nice job," he said. I was awed by his ability to captain in such overwhelming power. Guiding here seemed like being lost at sea in a squall.

Rapid Number Two appeared almost immediately. It wasn't as big as Number One, but leagues above Lunch Counter, the biggest rapid on the Snake, which had caused me daily anxiety. Following Steve's orders, the brothers, Sunday, and I jumped forward, and although the boat didn't flip, I fell out, with no time to grab the perimeter line.

My body tumbled as I was sucked downward. I swam for the top but was pushed deeper. I felt the water temperature drop several degrees cooler. I opened my eyes hoping to catch a glimpse of the surface, but it was too murky and dark. I used my hands to search for the bottom of the raft or an underwater rock overhang. There was nothing but water. I was far below the current, in water so deep that it was utterly still and cold. Most sun rays didn't penetrate this far down. *I must be over twenty feet deep*, I thought.

Perhaps I was caught in an underwater cave, maybe Nyaminyami's lair. I focused on staying calm to preserve what oxygen I had left and trained all my senses on feeling for Nyaminyami's presence. As I floated, far from gravity and air, I wondered if the river god would speak to me in a concerned, parental tone like the Snake. Or was he a fierce monster, as rendered in the medallions worn by Steve and the highsiders? As fear gripped my lungs, I lost interest in finding out.

I felt my PFD begin to rise around my neck, its buoyancy lifting me. Kicking my feet, I propelled myself upward, swimming with everything I had. The gray tubes of the boat came into view, and when I surfaced next to it, I seized the perimeter line with both hands.

By the time Steve gripped my arm, I was already halfway in the boat. "You look like you saw God," he said.

"It was dark. Like the bottom of the earth."

Sunday smiled knowingly. I looked at his necklace. Nyaminyami's fangs protruded from his flat, crocodile-like snout.

"Nyaminyami's house?" I asked.

Sunday nodded.

Behind him, the New York brothers wore astonished looks on their faces. "Shit," one of them said.

"Never let go of the boat," Steve said. "Get ready for Number Three."

I lunged at the bow and grabbed the perimeter line tightly, as did the brothers. This time, we made it through with everyone on board.

"We're coming up to some big rapids now, Four and Five," said Steve as we passed beneath the Victoria Falls Bridge, which connected the countries of Zambia and Zimbabwe. All I could see from above the rapid was the entrance: two mammoth holes created by fallen boulders. Water poured over the rocks and recirculated in a hydraulic that mirrored the shape and size of the boulders. The water flowing between the entrance holes funneled into a channel leading to two more successive holes along the right canyon wall.

Steve threaded the entrance holes, and we dropped down steeply into the edge of the next hole. We were more than halfway through the rapid when Steve yelled, "Go." We highsided, throwing our bodies toward a cresting wave double overhead the boat. Even with the added momentum of our body weight, the raft stalled briefly before we were spit out toward the sheer canyon wall. Sunday moved to the right side of the bow, toward the wall and the water banking off it to form a pillow. The brothers and I followed him as we felt the boat start to rear up, threatening to flip on the surging pillow line. Steve corrected his angle to be more perpendicular to the wall and pulled back hard on the oars. Despite his efforts, it seemed like we were going to smash into the wall. Just as we were about to hit it, the pillow surged again, pushing us away from the wall and returning us to the main current.

As we approached Number Five, the horizon dropped off next to a giant bump right of the rapid's center. White spray rose up ominously from below.

"That's the Rooster Tail," Steve yelled over the roar, pointing to the mound of water indicating a pour-over created by a boulder three times the size of our raft. "You're screwed if you run there."

Indeed, on Bangs's expedition, one of the rafts ran it and lost a passenger. The man recirculated in the backwash of the hole, emerging with four broken ribs and a collapsed lung, and was evacuated by helicopter, something that wasn't an option for us.

Steve set the boat so his right tube was next to the pour-over as we dropped over the horizon. The brothers and I all screamed as we became buried in so much water, I was certain we'd flipped. I closed my eyes and clutched tightly to the perimeter line, hell-bent on staying with the boat, even if it was upside down. I was stunned when it turned out we'd been upright the entire time.

Number Six offered plenty of bang with minimal maneuvering and no mishaps.

"Seven is the big one," Steve said. There was a hardness in his voice, and I turned to see him clenching his jaw, as he did when he was nervous. I tightened my grip on the perimeter line. The river widened, giving way to a boulder field we had to maneuver through. Hit any of the boulders and the boat would easily flip, sending the whole crew swimming the entire half-mile-long rapid, in which they might be lethally injured. Steve finessed us through the maze, then pulled hard to the right, skirting an almost river-wide hole caused by a rock ledge.

Steve shouted, "The Crease," and nodded toward the ledge hole. I looked at it as we went around, my mouth gaping open. Created by underwater topography, a ledge hole is uniform in its recirculation, with no soft spots for a boat to punch through. Hitting a ledge hole stops a boat dead, before turning it sideways and flipping it, sending passengers swimming in a tube of recirculating water with no release. Like foot entrapment, swimming a ledge hole is a main cause of death on rivers. The Crease was certainly a contender for the largest ledge hole on the planet.

Unbelievably, Number Seven wasn't over after the Crease—there was still a quarter-mile gauntlet of enormous waves to get through. "Land of the Giants," said Sunday as we highsided from one tube to another. Somehow, we were upright at the bottom. We all cheered as water bubbled around the raft like champagne.

Celebration quickly gave way to uneasiness as we came upon a commotion on the shore. Pete stood atop a bus-sized boulder, arms held up over his head to form a cross in an unmistakable hand signal: *First aid*. His left leg dangled behind him where he stood. Once he was sure we'd seen him, he crumpled, clutching his left hamstring. Jono and Clement grabbed Pete under the armpits and carried him over the black rocks away from shore. Fifty yards downstream, Pete's raft was tied off and banging around in a colossal, surging eddy, Gabi and the other clients still sitting inside it, tense-lipped and hunched over.

Seeing the distress signal, Steve pumped at the oars, trying to catch the boiling eddy where Pete's boat was tied. Once in the eddy, he de-rigged the first aid kit and asked me to follow him. I couldn't remember what my basic first aid course had recommended for injuries sustained in remote river canyons where there was no possibility of help. I hoped that topic had been covered in whatever class Steve had taken; then I remembered that we'd taken the same course.

Pete motioned to his leg with a nod. "I haven't looked at it yet," he said slowly through clenched teeth as we approached. "I tried, but I almost passed out. It's pretty bad."

"Sit down here and we'll take a look." Steve's voice was calm and soothing. Jono and Clement helped lower Pete onto a flat boulder. I clutched the first aid kit, my eyes widening as I caught sight of the inside of Pete's leg. A severe puncture wound went several inches into his hamstring. The puncture had just missed his femoral artery, which was still intact and pumping blood through the fat-marbled tissue hanging outside his leg.

"What happened?" Steve asked while putting on latex gloves. We needed a clearer picture of what had caused the injury to best know how to treat it.

Pete, Jono, and Clement all replayed the scene, their words at times overlapping: They'd taken a large chunk of the Crease. The impact of

the hit blew out the right oar, and one of the passengers had come flying forward from the stern and slammed Pete onto his oarlock, where his
hamstring was impaled on the metal prong. "Like a hot dog on a stick,"
Pete said. He was knocked overboard, with his head dragging underwater,
attached to the raft only by the oarlock lodged in his leg. He'd kicked his
foot up to release his leg, then swung around in the water and climbed
back in. He fished his oar out of the river (thank God for safety leashes!),
slammed it back in the oarlock, and pulled for shore. He did all of this
while going through the Land of the Giants.

"We've got to evacuate him," Steve said to me and the highsiders. "But
the closest trail isn't until camp."

"How many more rapids?" I asked.

"Three," said Steve. "But we have to portage Number Nine." Pete
could barely lie on a rock, much less row several more miles and hike
around a rapid.

"There is a game trail here," said Jono. "It goes to Mukuni Village.
Clement and I can carry him out and find transport to the hospital."

"Let's dress his wound," said Steve. "I heard the town of Livingstone
dumps raw sewage into the river upstream. We've got to sterilize it the
best we can. It could be a while before Pete gets to a hospital or doctor."

Steve suggested we clean out Pete's leg with Betadine. We held Pete
down and jammed long cotton swabs deep into his hamstring while he
screamed and thrashed around on the rock. Once the inside of his hamstring was coated orange, we put the hanging-out parts back together with
butterfly closures and layers of gauze before taping it shut.

It reminded me of a similar accident in Jackson when I was twelve.
Sully had sliced open his thigh with a chainsaw while we were getting
firewood on Togwotee Pass. Mama, using her nursing skills, field-dressed
his wound with the shirt she was wearing and threw him in the back of
the van. "We've got to get Daddy to town before he bleeds out," she'd
said. She drove the van and trailer wearing her maroon bra. We arrived at
the hospital just as Daddy complained of being light-headed from losing
blood.

"What a bummer." Pete shook his head. "I was so in there with Gabi. She came on a trip last year and I blew it by not making a move. This year, I blow it before we even get to camp."

Jono and Clement promised to arrange for a replacement guide to be sent down to Songwe campsite (above Number Eleven) to guide Pete's raft for the rest of the trip. The only problem remaining was how to get Pete's boat from here to Songwe.

"Bridget will have to row it down," Pete said.

Poor thing, he's delirious, I thought.

"You up for it?" Steve asked me.

"No-o-o." I drew the word into three syllables for emphasis. "What about one of the highsiders?"

"They don't have much rowing experience," Pete said. "You're a guide."

"What if we put Sunday and Gordon with you, since they know the river?" Steve said. "They can tell you the lines, and you can guide the boat. I'll take the pax, so you won't have to worry about them if you flip."

"You're serious."

"You really only have to worry about Number Eight and catching the eddy above Nine. It's Class VI, so we portage the rafts and everyone around it."

"What about Ten?"

"Straightforward wave train."

I was by no means prepared to navigate high-volume Class V my first week in Zambia. The highest water I'd ever guided was the Class III Snake at thirty thousand cfs. The Zambezi flows averaged 100,000 cfs, making it the biggest whitewater river in the world by volume, and me rowing a boat down it was like a novice hiker taking on Everest without training or a map.

"If you're not up for it, we can hike everyone out," said Pete. His face was waxy and pale; he was grimacing with pain.

I flashed on Mama's face, the determined look she'd had when she got behind the wheel of the van on Togwotee Pass, Sully quickly bleeding out in the back. "Hold on, kids," she'd said to David and me. "Mama's gonna drive like hell."

I took a deep breath. "I'll do it."

Jono and Clement carried Pete across the unstable rocks. I wasn't sure who was in more danger, him or me. While Steve told the pax our plan, I walked downstream, trying to convince myself that the roar inside my head was simply the sound of Number Seven upstream. I put my hands in the rushing eddy current, out of view from where the others were waiting, and I made an offering to Nyaminyami. "My hands are your hands," I whispered, looking deep down into the still blackness. "Use them to honor you." I could almost see Nyaminyami slithering on the river floor, keeping watch as I sprinkled water on the back of my neck, touched some onto my third eye for clarity, and cinched up my life jacket.

When I returned to the group, Steve had hold of his oars and was floating freely in the eddy with the passengers. They all smiled at me optimistically as I approached them. Sunday held our raft's coiled bowline while I sprang off a rock and landed on the front tube, nearly losing my balance. Gordon looked at me with a mix of pity and terror. I paused to steady myself, then walked, perfectly balanced, to my cooler-seat in the center. Gripping the man-sized oars, I nodded to Sunday, and he pushed the boat free, scrambling to the stern. As we drifted toward Number Eight, our fate was now up to Nyaminyami.

The silence in the raft was finally broken when the highsiders began shouting back and forth in Nyanja, deep tones punctuated by forceful, sharp words.

"What?" I asked.

"Oh, this rapid . . . it is sometimes tricky," Sunday answered. I wasn't sure if he was looking at me or the rapid because of his lazy eye. I waited for more elaborate instructions, but the men dammed their words and watched me closely.

I called out a few practice commands and cranked some double-oar turns, spinning the boat hastily in the flat water above the drop. As the distant roar got louder, Sunday and Gordon moved to the front of the boat. Suddenly, it was noisy as hell and all I could see in front of me was the horizon line, which Steve's boat quickly disappeared over.

"Is that where I want to enter?" I nodded toward Steve's entrance. Gordon waved to the right, as if brushing off a mosquito, indicating that I should enter farther right than Steve had. I set a stronger angle, hustled to the right, and searched for a sign that I was in the correct position. I saw the tongue, a clear V-like formation, followed by a series of glassy entrance waves that stacked larger and larger until I couldn't see beyond them. The tongue indicated a channel between a ledge hole on the left and a rock shelf on the right. I aimed for the crest of the first wave and pushed forward hard with the oars, building momentum to break through the wave train and whatever it led to that I still couldn't see. After the first couple of rollers, I spied the finale: a crashing wall of white backwash gnashing onto itself twice as high as the boat.

"Go!" I yelled. Instantly, the highsiders leapt forward, their arms linked in unison, an added measure to keep them in the boat. It was surprisingly quiet inside the guts of the rapid, like a slow, distant dream happening in another time. The oars got ripped from my hands as we took the blow; I grabbed them back as we stalled out at the top of the hole. I gave a final shove forward, and we caught the green downstream current, free and clear of the rapid.

Spurting water from their noses, the highsiders burst into laughter and each gave me an enthusiastic thumbs-up.

Steve waved his finger in a round-'em-up circle near his head, signaling that it was time to catch the eddy above Number Nine. If I missed this move, we'd end up running a Class VI rapid so big it had never been descended and was deemed unrunnable.

Gordon gave me the eddy-out signal again in case I hadn't seen Steve. He and Sunday stood tensely in the bow.

I set up with a downstream ferry angle to pull in, with my stern pointed at the right shore, which was a stronger move, as I could leverage my legs off the frame to pull back on the oars. Seeing my position, Sunday leapt over me to the back of the boat. I cranked out solid oar strokes while he uncoiled the stern line and prepared to throw it to Steve onshore should I blow the move.

I felt the boat shift from the downstream current into the calm eddy water near shore and nearly collapsed with relief. We pulled the boat out of the water, and our small crew carried the two rafts around the rapid. I glanced at Number Nine from shore long enough to see that it was a vortex of hydraulics capable of devouring a raft and pushing a swimmer so deep, they might never reemerge.

We put the rafts back into the flat water below Number Nine. I pulled into the current and floated down a calm stretch. As we rounded a bend, I heard the rumble of another rapid. "This is Number Ten," Steve called from his boat. "Hey diddle diddle, right down the middle."

The waves were big, but all I had to do was keep the boat straight. The wave train petered out where the Songwe River entered the gorge, our take-out for the day. The shore crew of highsiders already had a fire going, and we were greeted by the spicy aroma of samosas upon landing. I tried to hide the fact that I was shaking as I untied the rig and passed day bags off the bow.

I dipped my hands in the water next to the boat and said thank you to Nyaminyami. As I did, a cormorant flew overhead, cruising close to the raft. Sunday and Gordon traded hushed words in Nyanja while looking at the bird.

"What is it?"

"The cormorant is a bad omen," Sunday said. "Somebody is going to die or get hurt."

My first thought was that I was glad it wouldn't be while I was rowing. And then I thought of Pete.

Fourteen

Ghost Boat

Sweat-drenched highsiders carried blue barrels of food down the Songwe trail in an uninterrupted line from canyon rim to floor. Keeping the boats light through the difficult Boiling Pot section was preferred to running them overloaded with all the heavy gear and food for the entire seven-day trip. For that reason, the shore crew had brought most of the gear to our first night's camp for packing on the rafts. This was the last time we'd have access to supplies until we reached our take-out some sixty miles downstream at the Matetsi River confluence on the Zimbabwean side of the river.

I found Steve sorting through food under a thatched lean-to onshore. Giddy with adrenaline, I wrapped my arms around him from behind, kissing the top of his shoulder. He stiffened and shook off my embrace, replacing it with a quick pat on the arm. I'd hoped my willingness to take over Pete's boat would earn me some accolades. I began to worry that something deeper was going on beyond the stress of running the trip, especially since our sexual connection had been minimal since I'd arrived in Zambia.

"Nice job rowing," he said, then sighed. "Since Pete's not here I have to organize everything." He raked his hand through his hair. "You could help by showing the pax how to set up the tents."

"You bet." I began helping the clients pick out their sites. As I snapped together tentpoles, I watched Steve closely from across the camp.

It was near twilight when Jono and Clement arrived with Pete's replacement: a tall Zambian guide who entered the thatched kitchen with a bright red life jacket and gear bag slung over his shoulder. He raised his chiseled arms and wiggled his hips, singing "Na ni ni ni ni" in a catchy rhythm before breaking out a charismatic smile.

"Zeke!" Steve gave the handsome guide a heartfelt high five, then dropped his voice to a joking, conspiratorial tone. "So, *you're* Pete now. You're going to be our new trip leader?"

Zeke let out a deep laugh, then, feigning seriousness, said, "Boss said you're the trip leader now. You're supposed to row both boats yourself. They sent me down to tell you."

They pounded each other on the back before Steve addressed the group. "Zeke's just back from working in the States. He's been with the company here on the Zambezi for several years, starting out as a highsider and working his way up to a guide."

Steve joined me at the beer cooler.

"What a relief," I said. "I was worried I might have to keep rowing. Zeke seems great."

"He's perfect," Steve said. "Solid boatman, great English. He's my favorite person to work with ever. The dude's hilarious." He looked over at Zeke sitting with the highsiders. "Plus, have you seen the size of his waist? He's unbelievably fit." Steve walked away from me to join in the carousing. I suddenly felt jealous of Zeke.

Gabi, Pete's foiled love interest, came up to the cooler then in a fresh skirt, hair brushed to gleaming.

"How are you liking the trip so far?" I asked her.

"Brilliant," she said. "But you had quite a go of it, didn't you? Thrown into the hot seat like that. Well done." She clinked her beer bottle against mine. "Careful or they'll hire you on."

I smiled, not mentioning that I already had a job lined up guiding canoe safaris on the Lower Zambezi. I hated the thought of Steve and me being separated again so soon. We had only a few more days to bridge the distance between us, and I felt panicked that we wouldn't get there. I looked over at him, hoping to catch his eye, but he and Zeke were laughing and animated as they talked.

"Too bad Pete had to leave," I said. "You two seemed to hit it off."

"He's not exactly my type." Gabi confided to me her recent exploits in Botswana. She'd spent the last few months traveling from South Africa up the continent and had racked up a number of local lovers. She nodded toward Zeke. "I'd sure like to get a personal tour with *him*." I wanted to ask Gabi if she was using condoms, since during the early nineties, an estimated one in five Zambian adults was infected with HIV. While I considered how to bring it up, she brushed past me, eyes locked on Zeke.

After the group had eaten dinner and the dishes were done, I lay by the fire and looked at the stars. I hoped Steve would join me, but he was still discussing logistics with Zeke. The crescent moon was luminous, and the Southern Cross glinted as it descended behind the canyon wall. I was surprised to see Orion, belt and bow snug against the foreign sky of the Southern Hemisphere. I thought of my mother looking at the constellation from where she now lived in Montana. Did she wonder about me? I pictured my father weaving through traffic in his Porsche, oblivious to the stars overhead. I'd come to the other side of the world to escape, yet here I was, trying to conjure them.

Dakota, the silver-haired travel photographer from New Mexico, lay down next to me in the sand. "Do you see that? Aquarius!" She pointed to what looked like a jeweled tent in the middle of the sky.

"Wow, I've never seen it. It's my sign. And my mom's too."

Dakota smiled. "Your mom must be proud of you, running rivers on the other side of the world."

"I wouldn't know," I said. "We're not close."

Dakota reminded me of my mom: rugged with a don't-fuck-with-me demeanor. The difference was, Dakota was her own woman, independent of a man. I was awestruck that she was traveling alone, working on assignment for a book.

"How long have you been a travel photographer?" I asked.

"Longer than you've been alive. I've seen nearly every country," she said. "Like you, I'm not close to my family. My job keeps me distant."

Across the fire from where we lay, the highsiders were unwinding, sharing a cigarette while joking in Nyanja. I struck up a conversation with Jono and Sunday, asking them the Nyanja words for "thank you" (*zikomo*) and "hello" (*muli bwanji*). Jono complimented me on my pronunciation. "You don't choke on the sounds like other *mzungus*," he said.

"*Mzungus?*"

"*Mzungu* means 'wanderer' in Bantu languages," Dakota said. "But mostly, it's used to mean 'Whites' or 'foreigners.'"

Clement and Gordon began to drum on the bail buckets then, while Sunday joined them singing. They harmonized beautifully, sounding to me like Ladysmith Black Mambazo.

I gave up waiting for Steve to join me around the campfire. He was still sorting food in coolers by lamplight. As I headed to bed alone, I spied Gabi and Zeke silhouetted against Gabi's tent, limbs entwined in an embrace. For months, I'd imagined Steve holding me under the African sky, our passion fueled by the lengthy absence. Perhaps it had been naive to think that love born in the heart of Wyoming winter could withstand the Zambian heat.

The next morning, I woke to highsiders arriving with more gear, yelling at one another in deep, raspy tones. Steve's sleeping bag was gone, which was strange, since I'd never heard him come in. I quickly changed into river garb and headed for the kitchen. On my way, I crossed paths with one of the highsiders. I recognized his tall frame and gap-toothed grin—he was the one who'd beckoned me to follow him after the baboon encounter. I noticed that his eyes were red and puffy and he had a horrible runny nose.

"*Muli bwanji*," I said, trying out my new Nyanja skills.

He stopped in his tracks, then chuckled. "*Bwino, bwanji.*"

I didn't know how the exchange went next, so I stuck out my hand and said, "I'm Bridget, Steve's girlfriend."

"Gilbert, madam." Looking at the ground, he touched his left hand to the crook of his right elbow, giving me a dead fish handshake.

"Are you sick?" I asked.

"Yes, madam."

"Please, call me Bridget." I smiled. "I have medicine to help your cold."

I went back to the tent and dug out some Benadryl I'd packed in the States.

"*Zikomo.*" Gilbert lightly clapped his hands together, then raced off to carry more gear.

After several hours of rigging gear, our crew loaded into the rafts and headed downstream. With Zeke taking over rowing, I was free to ride in the front of Steve's boat. There were no mishaps until Number Eighteen, which featured a giant center hole more than double overhead the boat. Steve pushed to build momentum enough to break through, but as the boat smashed into the hole, it stopped us dead. We gyrated and surfed in the surging reversal for several minutes. I clung to the bow while water pounded into my sinuses. When we finally emerged upright, I dislodged my lower legs from under the metal boxes rigged in the raft's center. They had bashed against my legs repeatedly in the violent surf, leaving welts on my shins.

"Kisses from Nyaminyami," Sunday said.

I'd imagined Nyaminyami to be a compassionate, paternal river god. Instead, he reminded me of my actual father. I recalled that the last time I'd had welts on my legs, my father had put them there. I'd gone to the farthest corner of the globe to escape this kind of abuse, but here I was, still getting my ass kicked.

I showed the welts to Steve.

"Shit," he said. "Good thing it didn't break the skin."

After more whitewater, we set up camp on a large sandy beach on the river-left side known as Bobo and started cranking out dinner: lasagna cooked in dutch ovens with coals from the fire. The clients were impressed, since they'd expected freeze-dried food. There was plenty for everyone, but the highsiders didn't want any after Zeke spit it out. Instead, they cooked up a separate pot of *nshima*, the local fare of white corn flour cooked into a pasty Cream of Wheat consistency. With their hands, they rolled the steaming *nshima* into balls and scooped up stir-fried onions and tomatoes coated with oil. They invited me to try some and gasped as I reached into the aluminum cookpot with my dominant left hand.

"It is all right to eat from your left hand with us," Jono said. "We know that you have washed, but do not do that elsewhere." He set me straight: right hand was for eating, left for wiping your ass.

That night, Steve and I fought while setting up the tent.

"Let's sleep out under the stars," Steve suggested. "More romantic."

I snorted. "You don't seem to be all that interested in romance. You barely notice I'm here."

"What's that supposed to mean?"

"All you do is work and crack jokes with Zeke," I said. "It's like I'm invisible."

"Do you have any sense of the pressure I'm under?"

"You're not too busy to go off with Zeke."

"What are you talking about? We're working." Steve glared at me. "There's a lot of shit to take care of. What do you think we're doing?"

I weighed his response. Maybe I was exaggerating his interest in Zeke. Or maybe I was chasing a ghost, holding on to a fantasy of how we'd been before.

"Forget it," I said. "I just want us to be close."

"That's funny, because you sure know how to kill a mood."

Steve threw his sleeping pad on the sand, laid down his bag, and got inside it, signaling that the discussion was over. I set up the tent, worried about scorpions and malaria-carrying mosquitoes. Neither of us said good night.

I woke us both by screaming in the early morning grayness. My left calf had seized up as if somebody had taken a nail gun to it.

"What happened?" Steve stood naked outside the tent door, trying to shake off sleep.

I clutched my calf while emitting agonized yowls. Steve grabbed me under the arms and yanked me onto the sand. He looked at my calf using his head lamp and found only a little red dot in the center, like a baby blood blister. He dove inside the tent headfirst, crawling around while he scrutinized my sleeping bag and pad and the corners of the tent. Then he paused and started chuckling.

"It's a scorpion, see?" He pointed to the insect scuttling around inside and began laughing maniacally. "You wanted to sleep in the tent."

"I don't see what's so funny," I said. "It's going to be a bitch to carry out my rigid, stinking corpse and fly it home." I remained as still as possible so the poison would course through my body more slowly and waited to die.

"Only the clear ones have enough poison to kill a person. The bigger and blacker they are, the less venom they have."

Even so, I remained still, whimpering slightly. Steve pulled on his river shorts and wandered off to start the coffee.

After a while, Zeke came over with a cup of black tea and milk for me and asked to see my leg, which was swollen and tight. He comforted me by saying he'd been stung by lots of scorpions.

"It will hurt for a couple of days' time, then you will be restored," he said. He distracted me by talking about his girlfriend in his village of Mukuni. She was *the one*, he told me; she was strong, a hard worker, and from the same tribe. The only problem, he confessed, was that she couldn't relate to the place he'd just returned from guiding. She couldn't imagine Colorado and its coin-op laundromats with rows of washing machines. He'd tried to explain snow to her by saying it was like the ice you put in drinks, but she'd never had a drink with ice in it. Even though she couldn't understand the world Zeke had just seen, he wanted to marry her. He was saving the money he made guiding to buy some cows for the dowry. It would take a couple of years.

"Maybe by then I will forget Colorado."

I wondered what Zeke was doing with Gabi if he planned to marry someone else, but I recalled learning in my world cultures class that monogamy was not the norm in most cultures. I wondered briefly if Steve had carried on with other women while we'd been apart but dismissed the idea. I had no reason to doubt his loyalty.

Zeke started to return to the kitchen, then turned back and mentioned that there were a few more Class V rapids downstream. After that, the river flattened out and our main concern would be crocodiles and hippos attacking the boats.

"Seriously?"

"We've had boats attacked down here before," he said. "That's how the old boss broke his back. A hippo came up underneath and destroyed the raft. Even the metal rowing frame was broken to pieces." He paused for emphasis. "Sometimes Nyaminyami needs sacrifices. He does not like us coming here. That is why I wear this." Zeke pointed to the medallion he wore around his neck, the figure of Nyaminyami with his crocodile head and coiled snake body. Carved from an ivory hippo tooth, the talisman gleamed against Zeke's dark skin. "If he sees me swimming with this on, he might let me go by." Zeke slid on his Ray-Bans and sprang off toward the kitchen.

We set off in the rafts and stopped after lunch to scout Open Season rapid, a nasty-looking Class V drop with jagged rocks visible just below the surface. Zeke told us about a client who'd shattered her pelvis when the raft took the drop in the wrong place and slammed onto the rocks. Her screams had echoed through the canyon until she eventually passed out from the pain. It had taken days to evacuate her. Zeke succeeded in scaring the shit out of most of the clients, who opted to walk the rapid and get picked up below. Without the extra weight, the empty rafts floated through the rapid easily, causing those who walked to regret their decision.

On the fourth day of the trip was Chibango, a Class VI waterfall. Everyone had to portage, and we spent hours unloading all the gear and carrying the entire kit—rafts, frames, and coolers—three hundred yards over scorching black basalt. Initially, I was trying to keep up with the highsiders, who lapped the *mzungus* several times despite not wearing shoes. I wanted Steve to notice how much weight I could carry, how hard a worker I was. Zeke emerged as the strongest of the group, which wasn't surprising considering his long history as a highsider. He seemed determined to prove to the younger highsiders that he hadn't gone soft living the *mzungu* life in Colorado.

Once rerigged, we floated toward our reward: Ghostrider, a rollercoaster Class IV wave train.

"Who wants to get wet?" Steve asked. I grinned at him from the bow, and he shot me a sexy smile in return, giving me hope that we might salvage things.

The pax and I hung off the front of the boat, waving our arms above our heads, whooping while flying down into the deep green troughs between wave crests. I watched Zeke's boat go through and noticed how Gabi casually touched his massive biceps at the bottom of the rapid.

After camping for the night below Ghostrider, we packed up and made our way down a long, quiet pool through sparse woodlands. The river jagged severely to the left and the canyon constricted, appearing more gorge-like. Before us was a horizon line with white mist frothing up, signaling a serious rapid: Deep Throat. Everyone got out to scout. As we surveyed the narrow slot, bounded on the right side by a rock wall, Steve gave us a history of the rapid. On the first descent of the Zambezi, nobody in Richard Bangs's group had wanted to portage it—they'd just portaged Chibango and cleaned up several flips in Ghostrider. They decided to ghost-boat a few of the rafts and, surprisingly, the empty boats made it through Deep Throat upright. One guide decided to run it with his crew and they got pushed against the rock wall.

"The boat flipped right there." Steve pointed to a huge boiling current bouncing off the wall. "One of the passengers went so deep, he didn't surface for three minutes. When he did, he was unconscious, with blood streaming out both ears. That's how it got the name Deep Throat."

Stone-cold silence from the group.

"C'mon," I said. "Three minutes?"

"That's what I heard." Steve raised his eyebrows.

The river lore prompted more walking from the clients, and Zeke decided to ghost-boat it. While Zeke walked downstream, Steve and I launched his empty raft into the green current above the rapid; it dropped in and got thrashed around by the pillow on the wall, teetering for several minutes while conflicting currents fought for the raft. Finally, between surges, the raft was released downstream. As it approached, Zeke jumped headfirst into the river from atop an overhanging ledge and swam toward the boat. I couldn't help but think of crocodiles in the water and prayed he wouldn't get attacked by one. When he reached the boat, he quickly pulled himself inside and untied the lashed-down oars, then rowed to shore and waited calmly in the eddy.

"That went pretty well," Steve said.

"Except now the crocs know we're here," I said.

"Okay, I'll walk down and you launch the raft," Steve said. "I'll give you a signal."

Once Steve was in place, I shoved the boat out into the current. Like Zeke's boat, it blipped through the meat, but it was kicked out hard to river left. The raft came so close to the left shore that Steve was able to jump on board without having to swim.

It was heartening to see that Nyaminyami wasn't always a mean bastard.

On day six, we stopped at a village of thatched houses. "Smugglers Camp," Steve said knowingly to Zeke, who flashed a smile.

Snot-encrusted little kids without pants yelled out to one another, "*Mzungus, mzungus*," as they rushed the boat. We got off the rafts, sunscreen-slathered, in our shoes and large mirrored sunglasses. The kids huddled together in a tight group, holding hands and staring. One of them yelled out, "How are *you*?" in a singsong voice. Then they were all giggling and singing rounds of "How are *you*? How are *you*?" without signs of tiring. One kid held his pointer finger and thumb out like the hands of a clock and called out, "The hour," which sounded like "the howah." I didn't know why.

Steve and Zeke emptied the coolers of extra food. Zeke carried some onions and carrots over to the oldest man in the village, stepping past toddlers with distended bellies and women hanging laundry to dry. The man welcomed Zeke into his home: a sunbaked, red-clay circular structure covered by thatching. Zeke motioned me inside. Bream fish were pitched on skewers all around a smoking fire, slow-cooking, exactly like in the photo in *Rivergods*. Zeke offered the elderly man the vegetables, and in exchange, the man stuffed a large black trash bag with marijuana. When the bag threatened to burst, Zeke waved his hands that it was enough, but the man kept pushing more of what he called *dagga* into the bag. Finally, Zeke took it away from him, clapping his hands while hunching over to show respect.

While Zeke and I traded for weed, Steve and the highsiders distracted the clients on the other side of the village, bartering with barbed fishhooks for carved wooden stools and bowls made by the village men. Some of the clients tried to exchange US dollars for intricate woven laundry baskets, but the local women clicked their tongues; the baskets were far more valuable to them than the crumpled green paper.

Zeke and I loaded the bag of *dagga* into an empty cooler. A man spoke to Zeke in Nyanja, and Zeke motioned him toward me.

"He has a sore on his arm," Zeke said. "Do you have any cream to fix it?"

I treated the man's oozing wound and quickly found myself administering first aid to a long line of people: gauze and Neosporin for maggot-covered sores, antibiotics for the green mucus flowing from many eyes and noses, aspirin for malaria migraines. I didn't know what to do for the guy who had a tennis-ball-sized tumor on his neck, so I gave him some anti-inflammatories and told him to get to a doctor, though the closest hospital was several days away by foot. I was overwhelmed by all the ailments, but even more so by the power contained in my basic first aid kit, which—aside from the antibiotics prescribed by a doctor for my travels—was composed mostly of things Americans could buy on any street corner.

A few hours later, when we untied our boats and floated away from the village, I opted to ride in Zeke's boat for the afternoon. Onshore, the kids chased alongside us as we traveled downstream, yelling "the howah" over and over.

"What are they saying?" I asked Zeke.

"It is the hour for change," he said. "Zambia needs a new leader. President Kaunda is one of the richest men in the world, but the babies are starving. You saw it yourself in the village."

Kenneth Kaunda had led the fight to overthrow White minority rule in Northern Rhodesia, delivering his country to independence in 1964 without bloodshed, a first in the history of the African continent. But after thirty-one years of resource mismanagement, food shortages, and radical unemployment, Kaunda's countrymen had finally had enough.

"He liberated Zambians," Zeke said, as he rowed past pods of wiggly-eared hippos. "For that he received our loyalty. But now he has forgotten us."

We stopped to camp on the Zimbabwe side of the river, across from a decrepit shack flanked by scrawny acacia trees, at a place known as Hippo Camp. Swilling gin and tonics from our Therm-a-Rest power loungers, we watched a seven-foot crocodile swim back and forth between hippo pods. A dugout canoe from across the river sliced through the green water, approaching us, and we gasped as a wild-haired Zambian came into view, his wiry form standing precariously in the center of the boat. He landed on the beach, offering us precious gems for sale. I traded him a fishhook for a rough-cut amethyst, my birthstone (and my mother's), before he paddled back across the river, once again braving the food-chain gauntlet.

Since it was our last night, the highsiders broke out the *chibuku*, locally made grain alcohol. After a few rounds, Zeke pulled Steve and me aside.

"So, guys," Zeke said. "Gabi and I have been sleeping together on this trip." He paused to light a joint, then passed it to me. "We didn't have condoms. I'm worried, you know, about AIDS."

"Jesus, Zeke." Steve's voice rose sharply. "There are condoms in the first aid kit, man. Use them—that's what they're for."

Since Steve and I hadn't had sex on the trip, I also had a stash of condoms. I regretted not giving some to Gabi or Zeke at Songwe camp when I first saw the spark between them, but it hadn't been my business. My thoughts went to the girl in Mukuni Village that Zeke planned to marry. The AIDS pandemic had a death grip on the African continent. In the years to come, I would lose nearly a quarter of my Zambian friends to the disease, including Zeke.

The next day, we reached the Matetsi River and the take-out on the Zimbabwe side. We loaded everything onto our waiting lorry and passenger Land Rovers and began the long return drive through baobab forests and past tourist hotels before reaching the town of Victoria Falls. We dropped off the clients and said our goodbyes. The crew of guides and highsiders carried on in the Rovers across the Victoria Falls Bridge, back into Zambia and its potholed roads. In full view of each other, separated only by a river, the two countries couldn't have been more different. Zimbabwe had food, hard currency, air-conditioning, a booming tourist economy. Zambia resembled an apocalyptic movie set after civilization collapses.

We crossed the border and were immediately engulfed by fly-covered little kids shouting "the howah" while holding up piece-of-the-pie clock fingers. I returned their salute, watching as they ran barefoot alongside the Rover, their small legs pumping hard to keep up. When Steve, Zeke, and I returned to the guide house, Pete was there, his leg elevated, looking at a *Penthouse* magazine. He told us that he hadn't made it in time to cross the border before it closed for the night at six; he'd spent the night delirious with pain before he was able to get to the hospital the next morning. He described the young, beautiful *mzungu* doctor who'd stitched him up. She was genuinely dumbfounded that he hadn't bled to death.

"She said the only reason I didn't go septic with infection is because of the cleaning job you did at the river," Pete said to Steve. "Thank you."

"Turns out Zeke was the perfect replacement for you," Steve said, his words thick with innuendo.

"You got in there with Gabi, didn't you?" Pete said. "I knew it!"

Zeke smiled sheepishly, then abruptly left to see his girlfriend in Mukuni.

Pete lit up the largest joint I'd ever seen. "Time's a wastin', let's start tastin'," he said and inhaled the entire thing without passing. Then he lit another one and asked, "Who wants to get high?"

Steve and Pete rounded up a couple more *mzungu* guides and we all walked the few blocks into downtown Livingstone for dinner. We had kwacha, the local currency, to burn. In the US, we had been dirtbag river guides, but in Zambia, we were richer than Rockefellers.

The streets were packed with women carrying bundles of wood and heavily filled baskets on their heads, babies tied on their backs. One woman balanced a full-size mattress atop her neatly plaited hair. Men held hands in friendship as they strolled unencumbered in the evening light. From the moment we stepped outside our compound, we became the main attraction—everyone was staring at us and yelling out excitedly, "*Mzungus, mzungus.*" Watching how the women held their babies close and the men walked with their hands linked made me ache for connection. I looked at Steve and tried in vain to get his attention.

Only Steve didn't look back.

Fifteen

Bruised

After running the Class V section of the Zambezi with Steve, I hitch-hiked to Zambia's capital of Lusaka, where the company manager lived. I was anxious to meet with Stan, who'd hired me via fax to guide canoe trips on the Lower Zambezi. I was determined to prove myself in the guiding world independent of Steve, especially since things had become so strained between us and I wasn't sure of our future together.

I stayed in Stan's compound outside the city, where he lived with his "houseboy"—a slight, graying Zambian man named Justice, who slept in a shed out back. My plan was to spend one day prepping for the job before heading to the remote lakeside town of Siavonga, where I'd be based. Although Stan claimed to be from Jackson, not once did he say "rig," "you bet," or "ain't." His polo shirt and well-groomed beard told me that, at most, he'd summered there as a kid or logged seasons guiding on the Snake during college. In our meeting, Stan told me I'd be reporting directly to Gary, the operations manager in Siavonga.

"The operation isn't what it should be," Stan said. "We're hoping you can jump in and run a guide school for Gary and the local staff there. Gary is great at building safari camps from nothing, but he has no river-running experience. That's where you come in." The school would cover topics from reading water to dealing with Western clients.

"You've seen the operation in Livingstone," Stan said. "Siavonga also has an incredible opportunity to be a real destination. The safari potential is as good as it gets."

I nodded, interjecting the occasional "Right" and "Sure," grandstanding about how I'd been working wilderness trips since I was a teenager. My bravado was intended to deflect from the fact that I knew nothing about developing an operation in a foreign country, especially one that, until a month ago, I had experienced only through books and magazines. This was my opportunity to break into international guiding, which would allow me to write my ticket anywhere in the world. It was a job I couldn't afford to lose.

Justice dropped me at the bus station in the company Mercedes-Benz. Because of the cholera epidemic sweeping the city, scores of people were sprawled out on the sidewalks, moaning and lying in pools of vomit. Walking from the car to the bus, I covered my mouth and nose to avoid gagging, while gripping my purple duffel bag tightly. As I stepped over a moaning elderly man, I realized what a privilege it was to have received a cholera vaccine before leaving the States. I felt guilty stepping over him and just walking away without doing anything to help ease his pain. Should I leave him my water bottle and some Advil? Or maybe my shoes? I paused and looked back at Justice, who waved me on with both hands, his brow firmly furrowed. *Go on*, he motioned. *Don't let cholera stop you.*

On the bus for Siavonga, I was crammed on a bench seat with two Zambian women and their three children. I volunteered to hold one of the little ones on my lap. We were lucky to have a seat—the aisle was packed with standing passengers, and people were riding on the roof, crowded in among the luggage. The bus never stopped during the half day's journey, and the young girl peed on me, crying tears of shame as her urine soaked my lap and ran down my leg. I smiled and told her it was okay and cleaned us up with travel baby wipes that I'd brought from the States. She remained mortified and silent. I was the only *mzungu* on the bus, and behind me, the curious, gentle hands of strangers stroked my blond hair. The bus sputtered upward, over buckled asphalt and potholes, into the highlands above the man-made Lake Kariba, where my new life awaited.

I'd read that when engineers began building the Kariba Dam to harness the power of the Zambezi River in the mid-1950s, the local Tonga tribe had laughed and told them that the dam wouldn't last. Nyaminyami, the half-crocodile, half-serpent river god of the Zambezi, would break through it for sure. Nyaminyami, who lived in the Batoka Gorge below Victoria Falls (Mosi-oa-Tunya), wouldn't stand being separated from his wife, Kitapo, who lived much farther downstream, on the Lower Zambezi near Mozambique. The engineers ignored the warning and were shocked when, less than two years later, a bizarre thousand-year flood decimated the nearly completed structure. Convinced it was a fluke, the engineers constructed a second, greatly fortified dam. The second dam was swiftly destroyed by another random flood.

"See?" said the Tonga. "Nyaminyami is angry with you. You cannot keep him from his wife." But the engineers finally figured out a way to harness the river, filling up the reservoir and drowning the Tonga's land. Nyaminyami's people were forced to leave.

Outside my bus window, shantytowns made of tarps and wood scraps housed the Tonga now, far from water and fish. Women wearing threadbare *chitenges* sat in patches of shade; shoeless men and boys roamed along the roadside, looking for a hustle or handout. It was easy to see how the toll of losing their land and livelihood had affected the Tonga—their homes were so starkly different from the tidy, well-built villages near Livingstone. Late in the afternoon, the bus lurched to a stop on a patch of bare earth at the top of a hill. In addition to urine, I was coated in layers of fine reddish-brown dust. I passed off the girl to her mother and smoothed my clothes and hair, attempting to make myself presentable to meet my new boss.

I spotted a dingy white Land Rover and, next to it, a White guy with mullet-cut brown hair slicked back like Errol Flynn. Gary wore beige knee-high socks and rawhide desert boots paired with khaki shorts so short and tight his balls were in danger of falling out. Taking a long drag from his unfiltered cigarette, he looked me over as I approached him.

"How do you like the country so far?" His accent was measured and civilized, yet with a cultivated roughness.

"It's pretty different from the States."

He loaded my bag into the Rover. "It's quite nice once you get out into the bush," he said as he opened the passenger door for me, which was on the left. "Zambia is so run-down. It's a pity. It was really something when there were more Whites living here—when it was Northern Rhodesia proper."

Although I found his comment disconcerting, I nodded. I didn't want to let on that I was so naive, I hadn't considered that there were White Africans living in Zambia. We drove along the torn-up tarmac as the Rover lurched and rattled.

"Are you from Zambia?" I asked.

"God, no. Zimbabwe. Been there?"

"Just the Victoria Falls area, across the river from Livingstone."

"It's nice. Clean. With an infrastructure that bloody works." We rounded into a driveway marked by a falling-down sign for Eagle's Rest. The Rover shuddered to a standstill. Before us, the red-ochre sunset shimmered off Lake Kariba and tinged the Matusadona Mountains a radiant orange.

"I imagine you are anxious to unload your kit," Gary said. "I will have someone show you to your room." He turned toward the collapsing reception building and, over the gentle hum of cicadas, yelled, "Mary!"

A beautiful young Zambian woman appeared. Her bright pink *chitenge* skirt was rolled down tightly around her thin waist, and her hair was neatly braided into a miraculous floral design. She looked about my age, twenty.

"Yes, *bwana*?" Mary asked timidly.

"Show the madam to her room and don't bother her. She's tired from her journey."

Mary smiled shyly at me.

"Please call me Bridget," I said.

I'd be sharing Gary's lakeside chalet—a basic bachelor pad with a camp stove and boxes of dried oxtail soup stacked on the counter.

"You are to sleep there." She pointed to a small room with a mosquito-net-covered twin bed. Mary then walked into Gary's room across the hall from mine, doing her best to appear invisible while gathering his dirty laundry off the floor.

I wrinkled my nose, looking at the stretched-out white briefs in her hand. "He can't wash his own underwear?"

Mary laughed. "The *bwana* is without a wife. Maybe soon you will be doing his wash." She raised her eyebrows suggestively.

"Ew."

Mary slapped her hand on her thigh and pointed at me, giggling. I'd been working almost exclusively with men ever since becoming a guide. Laughing with a woman felt good.

"Mary!" Gary yelled from across the yard, making us laugh harder.

"Goodbye, sister," Mary said, running out the door.

"*Tiza onana*," I called after her, using the Nyanja I'd picked up in Livingstone. See you later.

After a cold sponge bath, I crawled under the mosquito net and slept nearly twelve hours until morning.

I awoke to Gary standing over my bed. "Having a bit of a lie-in, are we?" Through the mesh netting, I smelled the stench of cigarettes seeping out from his sweaty pores.

"We will go to the bush camp today," Gary said. "The boys and I will be loading the kit into the Rover, if Your Majesty would like to join us."

Skipping breakfast, I threw on a one-piece suit, river shorts, and sandals and made my way down the gravel trail to the car park.

"Ah, here comes the madam now," Gary said to the training guides, then to me, "Your pupils, Leonard and Military. Hopefully, you can turn them into decent guides. I will be coming along too, of course, although I am sure this rowing business will come quite naturally to me."

I reached out my hand to Military, the taller of the two men, who had a long, thin scar above his right cheek. "*Muli bwanji.*"

He returned my smile, as did the shorter, stockier man, Leonard, who had thick scar tissue just visible above the neckline of his tank top that looked like a stab wound.

"You speak munt, hey?" Gary asked me, as we all loaded into the Rover.

"Pardon?" I'd never heard the word "munt." In my peripheral vision, I saw Leonard and Military stiffen in the back seat, and understood that the word had the power of a punch.

"What is it the munts speak around here?"

I was taken aback that Gary, an African, was asking me such a basic question about the region where he lived. I'd read in the Lonely Planet guidebook that there were seventy-two different languages in Zambia. The Zambians I'd met in Livingstone could speak eight or nine in addition to Nyanja and English, the official languages.

"We were speaking Nyanja," I said, turning to face Leonard and Military. "But you are Tonga, right?"

"Yes, madam."

"Please, call me Bridget." Leonard and Military shifted uncomfortably in their seats.

It was a twenty-minute drive to the put-in below the dam. We unloaded the gear, and I began our guide school by instructing the men on how to properly inflate the raft.

"You want to make sure to inflate the six air chambers so they're balanced." I showed them how to alternate pumping different sections of the boat so one didn't overpower another. "If the chambers have unequal pressure, they can burst the baffle inside."

Leonard tilted his head. Military crossed his arms.

"The baffles are like eardrums that separate the air chambers. If the boat gets punctured, the baffles make it so that only a portion of the boat deflates, instead of the whole raft." I thought of the wild ride I'd had through Blind Canyon after slicing the boat near the Snake River Monster.

Then I thought of what happened afterward, when that slimeball Jimmy ambushed me.

I straightened my frame and cast the memories from my mind. There was no room for vulnerability now; proving to these men that I was strong and capable was crucial to my success. Not only was I a woman, I was damn near a teenager. By now, I'd learned that my gender and my age were two strikes I had to overcome to be considered a leader.

"You have to check the tubes, like this." I slapped my palm hard onto the Hypalon fabric as if playing a bass beat on a drum.

Leonard's head lifted and Military uncrossed his arms. Gary lit a cigarette and took a long drag while closing his eyes.

"In the heat, the air can expand and cause the raft to explode. You can tell it's too full because it feels and sounds tight when you hit it." I smiled. "Good for drumming but not for rafting." Leonard gave me a bright smile. We were making progress.

I turned my head toward Gary. "Another thing that can make the raft explode is smoking too close to the boat," I said. "The fabric and adhesives are super flammable."

"Bugger." Gary chucked his burning cigarette onto the dirt.

Once the raft was pumped and rigged, we got underway, heading downstream to the riverside camp that Gary and the local staff had built. Pods of hippos surfaced in the eddies, snorting and spouting water out their noses as we passed.

"Dangerous, those ones." Gary nodded to the pink and gray beasts. "Kill more people each year than any other animal in Africa. They run on the bottom of the river and sneak up right underneath your boat before you know it."

The hum of insects enveloped us as we crept along with the languid current. I demonstrated how to push the boat forward by alternating oars in quick succession, as if pedaling a bicycle with your arms.

"You wanna try it?" I asked Leonard, who jumped to take the oars. He maneuvered the boat naturally, working with the current to move the raft.

"That's it," I said. "You've really got the hang of it."

Gary went next, sitting commandingly atop the dirty cooler.

"Have you rowed before?" I asked.

"Not properly," he said. "I was, however, required to do some training when I was a mercenary in the Rhodesian War. I have a mind to go to Livingstone and guide the Boiling Pot. Quite honestly, the only reason I am working out here in the bush with these bloody animals is so I can get on with the company proper."

I hoped that by "animals," Gary meant hippos and crocodiles. I stole glances at the two Zambian men; their eyes were downcast and their shoulders slumped. Like when my father had practically called Jai a monkey in our kitchen, I didn't know how to respond, and it made me feel nauseated.

"Stan tells me your boyfriend is a tremendous oarsman," Gary continued. "Pity he couldn't make it down to do the guide school for us. He has quite a lot of experience, from what I understand."

My breathing was ragged. "Steve was one of my guide school instructors on the Snake River in Wyoming," I said, carrying on like everything was normal, even though I felt that a trapdoor had opened beneath me.

"Is that how you two met, then?" Gary overpowered the oars, causing the boat to lurch and spin on the surface of the water instead of smoothly following the water's lead as Leonard had done.

"No. We knew each other before."

Gary looked at me quizzically, pushing for more.

"He was a friend of the family." I turned my head toward shore to take in the shrunken jackalberry and winter thorn trees growing along the side of the river.

Gary continued to slice the oars jerkily on the surface as a hot breeze kicked up from downstream. I wanted to give him some pointers so he'd stop manhandling the oars, but I wasn't sure what my role was, or how my suggestions would be received. Was I supposed to teach him what I knew about guiding or defer to him? I watched him jerk on the oars as if he were riding a mechanical bull until I couldn't stomach it anymore.

"Try to feel the current by dipping the oars all the way in the water," I said. "That's it. Now, just hold them there in the water. Is one side stronger?"

"Yes, the right," he said, surprised.

"That's where the main current is. Push a bit with the left oar only, so the boat moves into the stronger current."

"Aha," Gary said. "Steve taught you well."

"It was the Snake River who taught me that trick," I said. "Leonard, you were doing that naturally. You have a real knack for reading water."

"Thank you, madam." He lifted his eyes.

"Look, if we're going to be friends, you've got to stop it with the madam stuff, okay? It's Bridget."

Leonard smiled, raising his eyebrows in acknowledgment.

"Playing the teacher's pet, are we, Leonard?" Gary drew his lips into a flat, disapproving line.

I caught Leonard's eye and gave him a nearly imperceptible headshake with my eyes widened. *Can you believe this guy?* Leonard brought his face to the brink of smiling, allowing only his eyes to sparkle. *Kafunta. Crazy.* Our silent communication escaped Gary entirely.

We pulled into camp, which was situated on the edge of thick miombo woodland, and tied up the raft for the night. Facing the river was a newly built semipermanent thatched structure intended for dining. The heavy wooden table was already set for afternoon tea service. Military and Leonard hurried off with the cooler to join the other Zambian staff behind the screened-off kitchen, while Gary pulled out a chair for me to sit in.

"Thank you."

"Pleasure."

There was a lovely view of a sand-and-reed-covered island in the middle of the river. Hippos grunted from across the way, their backs glistening in the equatorial sun. An African skimmer swooped down, taking a drink from the river with its enormous red and black beak. It was magical, being there, in the place I'd imagined so vividly all those years ago.

"Moses!" Gary's angry tone jerked my attention from the sparkling island.

A stately man appeared from behind the screen. He was as solid as a mukwa tree.

"Haven't I told you that the tea must also be poured?"

"Yes, *bwana*." Moses walked over to the table.

"Bloody hell. Run by savages, I tell you." Gary shook his head and smiled at me as though I were sympathetic to his plight.

"Tea, madam?"

I wasn't in the habit of having hot afternoon tea in hundred-degree weather, but I smiled at Moses politely. "*Zikomo*," I said. Thank you. Moses nervously poured, shaking the pot as Gary sucked air through his teeth from across the table. After Moses set the pot down, I extended my hand to him. "We haven't been properly introduced. Please call me Bridget."

Avoiding my gaze, Moses touched his left hand to his right inside forearm while shaking mine in greeting, reminding me of Gilbert, who had given me the same submissive handshake in Livingstone.

"That will be all," Gary said. Moses went back behind the reed screen into the kitchen.

Gary looked over his teacup and saucer at me. "You mustn't let them have that kind of power." His fingers smoothed over his thin mustache. "You must insist that they call you madam, otherwise they'll get ideas."

"I'm uncomfortable being called madam," I said. "These men are older than me. If anything, I should defer to them."

Gary winced. "That's the way things are done here. If you want to get on, you'll need to accept it."

From the river-bound island, a slow grumbling wafted up to the table, sounding like gruff panting. I strained to listen, trying to decipher the noise. Gary jumped for the binoculars.

"Lions," he said, his face quickly transformed into glee.

A tingling rushed through me as I listened to their guttural pants. I was in Africa! Not just gazing at glossy *National Geographic* cutouts, but really here with the vibration of lion calls rumbling in my chest. I had kept the promise I'd made as a teenager to escape. The power of it moved me to tears.

Overwhelmed with gratitude, I whispered, "*Zikomo.*"

"Why do you keep speaking that gibberish?" Gary asked. "Speak English, the staff needs to learn it. But you mustn't use big words. They cannot understand you. You must talk to them like they are children. They *are* children, really."

I'd traveled to the other side of the world only to be back in my father's kitchen. All that was different was geography.

I stood, turned away from Gary, and walked behind the screen into the kitchen, where the Zambian men labored over dinner.

Military held a sun-faded chocolate pudding box inches from his face, trying to work out how to prepare it.

"Is it soup or is it meat?" Leonard asked. Military shrugged, genuinely mystified, before handing me the box.

"It's a sweet." I read the directions written in English on the back of the long-expired cardboard box, and step by step we went through their first attempt at making *mzungu* food. I had never before considered pudding to be so baffling and bizarre.

As the pudding gelled, Military, Moses, Leonard, and I sat on the coolers drinking, while Gary smoked a cigarette in the lounge alone.

"Is it hard for you to understand me when I speak?" I asked them, thinking about what Gary had said.

"You have a strange accent," Military said, putting his cup down, "and you talk different."

"How so?"

"It is like you feel respect," Leonard said, jumping in. "You just talk. Gary, he only yells." He paused, deciding if he should continue. "We Zambians, we cannot be treated like Zimbabweans. We are free; no Whites tell us what to do. I cannot leave because I must feed my family. But I am bruised."

Military and Moses looked at me, nodding.

"We came to work for your company because we heard it was fair, but we are seeing that it is not," Military said.

"Stan, the big *bwana*, he is an American like you," said Leonard.

"Maybe you can talk to him for us? Tell him what is happening," Moses added.

"Yes. When I go to Lusaka next, I'll speak to Stan." My resolve was fueled by guilt and regret over not protecting Jai years ago. Here was my chance to make it right.

⸺❧⸺

Weeks passed, and I continued the awkward dance with Gary and the Zambians: not confronting Gary forthright, but using diversion and the space between cultures as a shield. Then one morning, I was strangely awakened at the chalet.

"Bleedget. Psst. Bleedget." I blinked as Mary came into focus. She was crouched down in the bushes outside my window.

"There is a *mzungu* man on the telephone wanting to speak to you," she whispered, in order not to wake Gary across the hall.

"*Zikomo*, Mary." I arose, slid into sandals, and shuffled quietly into the shifting grayness of daybreak. Outside, the lake was calm and glassy, mirroring changing hues of burnt orange and fuchsia clouds overhead. Roosters announced the dawn, competing with the trill of red-winged pratincoles. We startled a flock of guinea fowl perusing the gravel pathway. Mary held my hand on the way to the reception, only letting go to pass me the phone.

"Hey, Bridge." Hearing Steve's voice brought me to tears.

"Don't cry. I'm coming to see you today."

"Really?"

Mary saw me smiling and quietly clapped her hands.

"I'm at Stan's in Lusaka. I have some big news to tell you. I'll be there in a few hours. Tell Gary, okay?"

I hung up, and Mary and I danced around, spinning on the polished floor.

Returning to the chalet, I found Gary boiling water for tea.

"Steve just called from Lusaka. He's coming on the early bus."

"Brilliant. He can join us at Manchinchi Bay tonight for the *braai*. I think you Americans call it a barbecue." Gary lit a cigarette. "I will clear out of here and let you two lovebirds have the chalet."

The morning crept along until finally it was time to collect Steve. I drove the Rover into town, my first time behind the wheel in Africa. I reminded myself out loud to drive on the left side of the road. Not that it mattered, since the few cars I passed were swerving all over, trying to dodge potholes, chickens, and women carrying head baskets.

The bus had already arrived when I got to the terminal—a mysterious African anomaly considering that nothing was ever on time, much less early. I drove up next to Steve, who was wearing a bright yellow-and-brown *chitenge* shirt. The midday sun glinted off his glasses as he rocked gently to relieve pressure on his feet. It felt like more than just a few weeks had passed since we'd last seen each other in Livingstone.

I opened the driver's door and stepped out onto the rust-colored clay. Steve wrapped his arms around me, kissing my cheek, then my lips. We let go of each other at the same time and worked together to get his overnight bag into the Rover.

"So what's the big news?" I asked, peeling onto the highway.

"Stan offered me the manager's position in Livingstone. That's why I was in Lusaka."

"What did you tell him?" I wouldn't have thought it was possible, but I was sweatier than before. The original plan had been for Steve and me to go back to the US after one season. Did this mean Steve and I were breaking up?

"I told him I was interested in doing it. It would be for two seasons, coming over in June and leaving in January. It comes with the big manager's house and a car." Steve paused, gauging my reaction. "It's a really good way for me to get in with the company and do other rivers like the Bío-Bío in Chile or the Çoruh in Turkey. What do you think?"

"I'm excited for you." I forced a smile.

"I want you to come too."

"To do what? Follow you around, driving shuttle?" My throat was tight. I'd already deferred my return to college to come to Zambia with Steve, and so far, that hadn't panned out as I'd expected.

"You could guide."

"I'm only a first-year guide. Right now, the Boiling Pot is way over my head."

"You could totally guide it. Hell, you *did* guide it," Steve said. "You could do some sort of project with the locals. Or travel around. What do you want to do?"

The truth was, I still hadn't figured that out. My future plan and main goal had always been to get as far away from my family as possible, somewhere they couldn't find me. Zambia had seemed perfect for that.

"What would you be doing if you weren't here? Do you really think it would be half as cool as this?" He was giving me the sales pitch. "You don't see that every day back home," he said, pointing to a group of boys playing with a soccer ball made of twine and a plastic bag.

I knew that Steve deserved this job. He'd worked so hard to get back on track with his outdoor career after his climbing accident. Still, I was resistant. Everything was going exactly the way we'd planned, but it didn't feel the way I'd imagined it would. Steve had been in Zambia several months longer than me, and maybe I was just going through a tough learning curve. I wanted to believe that we would find our rhythm here. I didn't want to be on my own in the world, without him. He was all I had that felt like family.

"Fuck it. We've come this far," I said. "There's no going back now."

"Damn." His face lit up. "You got guts, girl. I love that about you."

Looking out the window, I noticed how easy it would be to drive the Rover off course and plummet from the shoulderless road into the steep ditch alongside the highway. As I was thinking it, we passed a rusted, upside-down car in the ditch, grass growing up through the smashed-out windows. Whatever misgivings I had were overtaken by the sudden rush I felt at betting everything on the dream we'd created. I hit the brakes hard and stopped the rig in the middle of the road. A fierce sun shimmered through the acacia trees. Steve reached across the cab and kissed me long and hard, just like he used to.

Sixteen

Pool Party

We rolled into the chalet, which Mary had cleaned to gleaming, leaving plucked verbena flowers in a plastic bottle on the bedside table.

"I've brought you a present," Steve said.

We sat under the mosquito net on the bed. He kissed me softly before handing me a tiny paper bag. Coiled inside was a gleaming Nyaminyami necklace.

"It's gorgeous," I said. "Real silver. Like for a queen."

"My queen," Steve said, hugging me.

I wasn't sure what had caused the sudden change from being cool and distant, but it felt so good to be close again, I didn't care. I started unbuttoning his shirt. His hands were on my shoulders, my neck and breasts. Sudden rapping at the door made us freeze.

I spied a brown mullet through the front window.

"It's fucking Gary." I sighed.

Steve put his shirt back on, opened the door.

"Hey, man." Steve put out his hand. "Appreciate you letting Bridget drive in to pick me up."

"Not a bother a'tall. Glad you will be joining us for a few days."

"We have a lot to talk about. Looks like I'll be the new manager in Livingstone next season. Stan says he wants us to put some trips together."

"Cheers. Shall we discuss it over gin and tonics at Manchinchi?"

~⌒~

It was midafternoon when we pulled into the Manchinchi tourist lodge in Siavonga, but our hosts were already well into happy hour. Steve and I were welcomed warmly by Gary's friends: a group of three White Zambian men—one of whom was the manager of the lodge—and their three college-aged sons home from school on holiday. They'd just finished a competitive game of squash and soon wandered off to freshen up for the *braai*, leaving Gary, Steve, and me to fend for ourselves at the poolside bar. Steve and Gary dove straight into business, discussing logistics and marketing ideas for the two operations until dusk collapsed into darkness and our hosts, freshly scrubbed, returned one by one, like the stars popping up overhead.

As I took in the skyline, a warm breeze grazed my neck, perfuming the air with the scent of grilling meat and the distant acrid smell of burning garbage. The only woman at the gathering, I lightly swirled the gin and tonic in my hand while walking the perimeter of the pool, trying to relax into the forced luxuriousness of my surroundings. From a distance, I surveyed the eight White guys I was with as they teamed up for a competitive game of darts. Behind them, a line of Black Zambian men stood at attention in starched white suits, red linen napkins hanging on their outstretched forearms.

The evening progressed, as did the drinking, and I was soon paired with one of the college boys for a round of darts. While waiting for my turn, I worked in vain to catch the eye of one of the waiters, to exchange a smile or nod. I was equally unsuccessful in capturing Steve's attention; he'd been cozied up with Gary at the bar for most of the night.

Nigel, the manager of Manchinchi, filled my hand with another drink and sat down next to me, along with his red-faced buddy Doug.

"Here's one for you," Nigel said. "What do you call one of those rusted-out cars you see on the side of the road?"

"What?" I asked.

"A car in munt condition." The men's cackling sounded like a busted-down engine trying to start. I'd come to understand that "munt" was the N-word in this part of the world. I looked again to the Black Zambians standing next to us, within earshot; they didn't blink or even flinch. Outrage settled into a low, steady hum in my head.

"She's not laughing, Nigel," said Doug.

I moved my drink to the side and leaned in closely, so they were sure to hear me. "I'm not laughing because I don't think you're very funny."

Nigel turned a shade of purple I'd never seen on a human being. "You fucking Americans." Spit flew out of his mouth and landed on me. "You think you can come over here and tell us what to do with our Blacks. You went over to your continent and slaughtered the natives. At least we haven't killed them all off, have we?"

Unlike Gary, Nigel wasn't my boss, and I didn't have to bite my tongue to spare my job. I'd also had enough gin and tonics to not give a shit about offending him.

"Let's get one thing straight, Nigel," I said, squaring off. "I wasn't personally involved in killing any Native Americans, but right now, you are responsible for killing these men's spirits." I pointed to the waiters standing like statues behind them. For the first time all evening, the waiters broke their invisible wall to look at me.

Nigel and Doug were stunned and silent. I saw rage begin to bubble from every oversized pore on Doug's face. Swiftly, he picked me up and tried to force me over his shoulder. I flailed my legs and arms and scratched at his red, leathery neck, thrashing around like a mountain lion in a gunnysack. I looked for Steve, who was still standing in the back of the bar, deeply engrossed with Gary.

"You're a real fireplug, aren't you?" Doug paraded me around while his friends laughed and cheered. "I think you have a little Scottish in you."

He was drunk and swaying. Timing the sways, I kicked and fought my way off his shoulder, falling onto the cement next to the pool.

"I'm American, you racist piece of shit." I was surprised to hear myself claim American heritage so proudly. I'd left the country disgusted by patriarchy, intent on finding a better culture elsewhere. Yet now I found that the familiar American trope of liberty and justice for all was the first thing I reached for, holding it up like a talisman.

I hustled toward the open back gate, away from the men. Doug came up fast behind me, grabbing at my shirt, trying to rip it off me. I knew all too well how this would end if I didn't fight with everything I had. I threw elbows at his swollen beer belly and stomped on his *veldskoen* boots—like the ones Gary wore.

Where was Steve?

Everything was happening so quickly, I couldn't stop fighting to look for him. Doug was at least a hundred pounds heavier than I was. From behind, he wrangled my arms to my sides. I kicked at his shins and knees as he hoisted me above his head and hurled me into the swimming pool. I sank to the bottom, and when I surfaced, it was to the cruel laughter of Doug and his buddies. I dragged myself out of the over-chlorinated water, dripping as I walked away. Burning tears filled my eyes. I steadied myself by looking straight ahead into the face of a nearby Tonga waiter, whose blank stare had softened into a look of sympathy. He saw my humiliation, and his nod of recognition penetrated the tough-girl facade I used to protect myself from feeling powerless. I stormed out across the car park and down the highway back toward Eagle's Rest, soaking-ass wet.

Eventually, Steve pulled up alongside me in the Rover, driving slowly as I plodded along in the blackness.

"Get in, Bridge."

"Fuck off." I kept walking.

"What the hell kind of stunt was that you pulled back there?"

"Stunt?"

"What were you thinking, putting me in that situation, outnumbered like that?"

"*You* were outnumbered?"

"Will you get in?"

"Go fuck yourself."

"Listen, I didn't know what was happening until I saw you go in the pool. I would've done something."

"I don't believe you." I turned to face him. "I learned a few things tonight, Steve. For one, you don't have my back."

"That's not true. I've always been there for you."

"Bull-fucking-shit."

"You're drunk."

"At least I'm not a coward like you." I walked to the passenger side of the Rover and got in.

Back at Eagle's Rest, I peeled myself off the dampened seat and headed straight for the chalet. I showered and changed, then yanked my duffel out from underneath the twin bed.

"What are you doing?" Steve asked.

I ignored him and began stuffing my clothes into the bag.

"Classic Bridget, huh?"

"What's that supposed to mean?" I shoved my life jacket into the duffel along with my journal and river sandals.

"Anytime things get to be too much for you, you run away."

"I'm not staying here."

"Why not?"

"Basic fucking survival."

"Really? Is that what your dad would call it? Or your mom?"

"This has nothing to do with them."

"Oh no? It sure seems familiar."

"What are you, a shrink? You have no idea what it's like to be me, Mr. Missouri Fucking White Bread. I've got nobody to fall back on—not even you. You sure proved that tonight."

Steve laughed. "Like those guys were going to hurt you with Gary and me there," he said. "Come on, you're overreacting. You know that if you were really in trouble, I'd be there for you." He sat down on the bed next to me and patted my knee.

I zipped the duffel shut and tried to steady my quivering chin. I hated him right then, but I had nowhere else to go.

"How could you just sit there and do nothing?" I began to cry.

"Look, you can't light everything on fire every time you get mad. You saw tonight how dangerous that is. You're going to get yourself and others really hurt."

"I can't stay here," I said, wiping snot with the back of my hand. "I'm going to Lusaka to talk to Stan."

"I still have some business to finish with Gary," Steve said, "but we could leave together on the afternoon bus."

Gary didn't come back until the next morning, and I hid out in the chalet while Steve went to talk to him.

"Tell Gary I have food poisoning," I said to Steve before he left, "from that shitty lodge his friends run." I went deep under the covers and back to sleep.

I was awakened by a continuous pounding on the door. "I'm coming," I shouted, but the pounding persisted.

It was Mary, who'd turned up to clean the chalet. "You are sick?" She looked at me with concern as she entered the room.

"I'm not feeling very well," I said, trying to look weak. "We're going to Lusaka this afternoon."

She noticed my packed duffel. "You are not coming back?"

"I don't think so." I smiled to soften the blow.

"You are leaving us?"

"To talk to Stan."

"You will speak to him for us?"

"I promise I will."

"And your husband?" Mary, Leonard, and Military all insisted on calling Steve my husband even though they knew we weren't married.

"He will be the big boss in Livingstone next year. Maybe that will help us."

"Oh, but I will be missing you!" She grabbed my hand and held it between both of hers. "Very much, my sister."

When it was time to leave for the bus, Mary helped me carry the giant duffel down to the Rover, where Military and Leonard sat waiting on a log.

"My very good students and guides," I said. "*Tiza onana.*"

"Please give our regards to Stan's family," Leonard said, then shook my hand, left hand touching his right elbow in a show of respect for me.

Gary drove us to the bus station, chatting with Steve in the front of the Rover while I remained quiet in the back. I pressed my fingers to the window, silently saying goodbye to the boys playing soccer, the women carrying wood on their heads, the erratic chickens and rusted-out cars on the sides of the road.

Our bus was waiting when we arrived at the dusty patch of a station.

"Well, goodbye then." Gary pushed out his dry hand toward me.

"Bye," I said, barely looking at him. I knew I should thank him, but I didn't.

Steve and I boarded the bus, and people shifted to give us a seat together. Chickens in wooden cages were stacked in the aisle next to us.

"I'll take you to Stan's office," Steve said once we got going. "But you should talk to him about Gary without me." Steve didn't want to jeopardize his good standing or otherwise interfere with his new position. "You understand, right?"

I turned away from him and looked out onto scrubby grasslands and shanty houses the rest of the way to Lusaka.

~

We arrived, dusty and dehydrated, at Stan's fluorescent-lit building suite just as he was leaving for the day. Steve greeted Stan with a hearty handshake, then settled down to read a tattered magazine as Stan and I walked down the hall to his office. Stan motioned me into a blue chair across from him.

"How are things in Siavonga?" he asked.

"We need to talk." My voice was shaking slightly. I slowed my breathing by thinking of Leonard, Military, Moses, and Mary. "I had a hard time working there."

Stan had posters from the Zambian Ministry of Tourism tacked onto his walls: one of Victoria Falls, another of a surfacing hippo. They both said "Zambia, the Real Africa," written in the shape of the sun.

"Why's that?" Stan leaned back in his executive chair.

"Well, it's Gary." I looked down at my fingernails.

"What do you mean?"

"He's racist. He treats the Zambian staff really poorly."

Stan gave me a patronizing smile. "You've been here how long? Two months, maybe three? I think you're finding that things are done differently here than they are back in the States."

"I understand that, but this is extreme. He says that they're animals and must be treated like children. The Zambians asked me to talk to you."

"They didn't say anything when I was down there last. Listen, the Blacks here are different from American Blacks. I've been in this country for nine years, and I remember feeling the way you do now when I first got here. You'll get used to it. The fact is, Gary does a stand-up job down there. It's not easy to create a program from nothing as he has out in the middle of the bush. I can't afford to lose him."

But I am bruised . . . I wanted to scream Leonard's words at Stan, but I knew it would only make things worse.

"Maybe this is more than you can handle," Stan said, when I didn't respond. "At the end of the day, you gave it a go, and it didn't work out. I'll pay for your bus fare back to Livingstone, and we'll just leave it at that."

Don't cry, don't cry, don't fucking cry.

I returned with Steve to Livingstone, feeling powerless and humiliated. I was ashamed at having failed my Tonga friends.

Several months later, I was poolside at the five-star Musi-o-Tunya Inter-Continental Hotel, where I whiled away most of my days waiting for Steve to return from running the Boiling Pot. The rafting company's White guides had access to the pool, bar, and squash courts, since that was where all the clients watched the whitewater highlights video at day's end. Although I wasn't technically an employee of the company, I was White and the "wife" of one of the guides, who was soon to be *bwana*. I was automatically extended full facility privileges.

Frequently, I was the only guest at the hotel. To stave off my restlessness, I swam laps and read books. I consumed the work of Doris Lessing, poring over the pages of *The Grass Is Singing*. Lessing's British family had settled in Southern Rhodesia (later Zimbabwe) when she was five. Before coming to Zambia, I'd been ignorant about the colonial lifestyle; I hadn't even realized that there were White people in Africa! Lessing described English-born settlers who were "brought up with vague ideas about equality. They were shocked, for the first week or so, by the way natives were treated. They were revolted a hundred times a day by the casual way they were spoken of, as if they were so many cattle; or by a blow, or a look. They had been prepared to treat them as human beings. But they could not stand out against the society they were joining." Reading Lessing, I looked for ways to confront the society I'd found myself in. I tried to figure out how I might exist as "madam" and as an ally.

On one such lonely pool day, I was delighted to find a young woman about my age with her toddler. It was sweltering out, but the woman—dressed in flowing garb and a hijab—didn't go into the water, which meant her son couldn't go in the water either. I dove into the pool and swam a few feet away from where she was sitting on the concrete, her pedicured toes delicately tapping the edge of the pool.

"Come in," I said, flashing a smile.

"I do not have the proper attire."

I looked around the empty pool deck and shrugged. "I won't tell."

She smiled. "I already tried wading in, but the pool attendant ordered me out."

"Who? Eric?" I'd spent loads of time with Eric, who kept me well supplied with french fries, towels, and gin and tonics.

I motioned for her to pass the boy to me in the water. He went back and forth between us happily—me in the water and her on the edge.

Eric came round to check my drink level and I smiled winningly at him.

"Why can't she come in the pool, my friend?" I raised my eyebrows up and down in the pretty-please way Zambians do when they want something.

"She must have a proper costume," Eric said, unsmiling.

"Why?"

"It is the rule. It makes the other guests feel shy that she is not properly attired."

"Other guests?" I looked around at the empty pool deck. "You mean me? I don't mind."

"Also, a thread from her clothing could come loose and get caught in the drain or destroy the pumps. It is the rule, madam."

"But she cannot wear a costume because of her religion." I looked at the woman, a foreigner like me. "Right?"

She nodded.

"So?" I looked at Eric expectantly.

"Madam, I cannot. I will lose my position."

"It is no problem," the woman said in a hushed tone. "Do not bother over me."

But I was indignant. "I will speak to the manager," I said, getting out of the pool.

"No, please," the woman said.

"It is not right," I pressed on, drying off. I had half a mind to march into the manager's office in my bikini, but I paused to throw on a cover-up and sandals.

"It's okay, really," the woman called behind me.

I ignored her protests and went directly to Mr. Kwenda's door. I knocked and, without waiting for a response, opened it and sat down across from him.

"Yes, madam?" He shifted in his chair.

After I explained the situation, he denied my request to allow my new friend into the pool without a proper swimming costume. "It is against the rules," he said.

"Why can't the rules be changed?"

He sighed heavily. "Why do Americans always think they can come here and change the rules?" He was spitting slightly. I was surprised to see him so angry, but I soon realized that Mr. Kwenda was truly baffled—he sought to understand what cultural force was at work that would have me presume to storm in and make a policy change on something I found undesirable.

I searched my knowledge of my own culture before settling on a passage from *To Kill a Mockingbird*. "In my country, if you think a law is unjust," I said, "you can write petitions, organize the community, and hire a lawyer to argue your case in court. If you work hard, you can get the law changed."

"And this works? Laws get changed?"

"Often, yes. It works. And we are taught that it is very important to always stand up when something is unjust."

"Oh-uh-oh," he said in a singsong way. "I now see why." He softened somewhat, and I thought that he might cave and change the rule. "This is how it is in my country," he said. "We have had the same president for twenty-eight years. He is very rich, while Zambians are very poor. You yourself can see the queue of people trying to carry cooking oil over the border from Zimbabwe just down the road—only a few meters from where you are sitting at the pool." He sucked his teeth. "Nothing changes here. There is no fighting to get unjust laws changed. We accept things the way they are. We must accept it, or we go mad." He paused before entreating me to see his perspective. "You see, then, why the rules cannot be altered for you or your friend."

Mr. Kwenda's defeated countenance brought to mind all the losses I'd been forced to accept because of injustices beyond my control. But this—a simple matter of letting a woman go in a pool—was not difficult: it was not eradicating rape culture or the intergenerational abuse I grew up in. Keeping this sweet mother out of the pool because of her religion was utterly pointless.

I was so determined to see justice done—just for bloody once—that I pulled out my big American entitlement card and threatened him like a capitalist.

"The majority of patrons you have at this hotel are from our company's trips. It's the only reason your doors stay open. If the woman isn't allowed to go in the pool, I'll start a boycott of this place like you won't believe. I am the new manager's wife," I added, "and please believe me when I say, I will starve this hotel into nothing."

Ten minutes later, Eric brought the young woman a towel and invited her into the pool.

"No, thank you," she said, "I am content here."

I stared at her.

"Also, I cannot swim."

She smiled shyly and looked away. I understood at that moment the meaning of the saying "Geography is destiny." Essentially, you were what your culture said you were.

I charged another gin and tonic to my account and drank it alone at the bar before catching a lift to the guide house back in town. I returned to my enormous gated compound with water that ran out of the tap and cushioned, imported furniture—an opulent house that, each day, felt more and more like a golden cage.

As I rolled a joint in a corner of the garden tended by my grounds-keeper, a vague awareness began to form: I had no business trying to save anyone or change anything when I was incapable of saving or changing myself.

Seventeen

Damage Control

Agusting wind barreled up the canyon of the Lower Salmon River in Idaho, so strong it filled my tent like a sail, ripped its stakes from the ground, and sent it tumbling down the beach, away from camp. I ran to retrieve it, my hair wildly whipping my face in the gale, and resecured it by pounding on the stakes with a sizable rock. A fellow guide, Danny, ran toward me wanting to help. As I smashed in the last stake, lightning lit the sky overhead.

I jumped backward, and Danny ran into me with such force that we fell together onto the sand. He was on top of me; brown tendrils of his dampened hair curled onto my forehead. Even as fat rain landed on the sand around us, we continued lying there, both of us inhaling fresh sage and pine ushered in by the storm.

"You're the woman of my dreams," he murmured.

"Be serious," I said. As corny as it was, no one had ever said that to me, not even Steve, who was across the world in Zambia, settling into his manager's job and the house that came with it. Steve faxed me with updates on the preparations for my arrival; I'd be returning to Livingstone in three months, after I finished the season in Idaho. His bi-weekly faxes and calls were all business, filled with logistics and lengthy lists of things for me to bring over for the operation, nothing about me being dreamy.

"I am *very* serious." Danny smiled.

I'd never noticed before how deep his dimples were, or that his green eyes were the same shade as my favorite swimming hole on the Snake.

After the rainstorm, Danny and I attempted to return to the casual friendship we'd had before. But the electricity of the storm seemed to have sparked something in us. Everything pulled me toward him, from the way we played Indigo Girls songs together by the campfire, harmonizing our voices around his guitar, to the thrill I'd feel when I sensed his deep-set eyes on me and turned to find him watching me, his grin warm and steady.

Steve had trained Danny to be a river guide in Idaho the year before, while I'd been on the Snake. Danny was twenty, a year younger than me, and Steve had been charmed by his small-town Idaho roots and prep school education and had treated him like a younger brother. In fact, they looked like brothers. After we'd returned from our first Zambia season, Steve and I had both signed on to work for the Idaho company, which ran raft trips on the Lochsa River, the Lower Salmon, and the Snake in Hells Canyon. I planned to work in Idaho until September, but Steve had worked only the spring training season before leaving to set up the Zambezi operation.

As I'd driven Steve from the Lochsa to the airport, he told me that the previous summer, while I'd been in Jackson, he'd had a fling with Steph, a guide I was scheduled to work with in Idaho through the upcoming summer and early fall.

"It was nothing," Steve said. "A drunken hookup that's ancient history."

"So why tell me?" I asked as I pulled into the airport drop-off lane. "You hid it this long. Now suddenly you're dumping this on me right before you leave?"

"I wanted you to hear it from me, so you're not blindsided," he said. "In case she starts talking shit." He opened the car door, then leaned back over to hug me. "Don't worry about it. Listen," he said, steadying my chin as if I were a toddler, "you know I love you."

I drove away without saying I loved him back. For months, I'd ruminated over why Steve had become distant and cold toward me in Africa, why he'd taken to treating me like his annoying kid sister instead of someone he loved. In all my reasoning, I hadn't seriously considered that he might have cheated on me. Now that I knew, I was so hurt and disillusioned that I called my mom from a pay phone, something I hadn't done since moving to Zambia. The answering machine picked up. Mark's voice said they were both out guiding and would return in a week. I left a shaky message with the name and number of the company boathouse where I was staying between trips.

I was so angry at Steve, and also at myself for my gullibility, that I spent the entire four-hour drive from Missoula back to the boathouse screaming Melissa Etheridge lyrics out the window as I drove along the Lochsa River. "Does she love you like the way I love you?" I hurled my venom toward the Lochsa, where it happened, blaming the river for its complicity. But even though I was furious, there was no showdown between Steph and me when I got back to the boathouse. She never mentioned anything, and neither did I, but I could see regret in her eyes whenever she looked at me. Eventually, I let it go—another episode of *As the Oarlock Turns*, what we called it when fit, tan, half-naked guides fell into one another's sleeping bags while out on the river for weeks and months at a time.

Unlike what had happened with Steve and Steph, the beginning of my affair with Danny was neither drunken nor a hookup. After the rainstorm trip, Danny and I were bunked next to each other in the boathouse, unable to sleep with the current between us. "Come outside," he whispered. I followed him. As we made love the first time, the star-filled sky felt both vast and close.

I knew he was meant for me, not just because of the quakes of electricity we felt when we touched but also because we could go from talking in Northern Rockies accents littered with "ain'ts" and "you bets" to quoting Simon and Garfunkel lyrics or T. S. Eliot just as easily. What developed between us in the months after Steve left for Zambia could not be brushed off in the airport drop-off lane or mended with hasty apologies. It was substantial and would require a major rearrangement, something I didn't want to do via fax.

"I have to tell Steve to his face," I whispered to Danny one morning, our bodies entwined under zipped-together sleeping bags.

"If you go, you'll never come back." Danny traced a crooked line with his forefinger down my sternum, extending it past my rib cage. The Salmon River rushed just beyond our feet, only a few miles upstream from its confluence with the Snake.

"I owe it to Steve," I said, kissing him softly. "I promise I'll come back."

"You don't owe him a damn thing." He'd heard Steph's version of her failed river romance with Steve, had been there to pick up the pieces when she had found out about me, Steve's girlfriend of several years, *after* she'd slept with him.

What Danny didn't know was how Steve had rescued me when I was seventeen, saving me from emotional, physical, and sexual abuse. How he'd opened the world to me, introduced me to an exciting life of guiding rivers. Without him, I'd likely be strung out, institutionalized, or dead, definitely not lounging next to the river tangled up with Danny. Misguided as it was, my gratitude and loyalty to Steve ran deep.

"Let's talk about it more after my Snake trip." I sat up and slid into my bathing suit top.

For most of the summer, Danny and I had been scheduled together, but we'd be apart this week, with him staying on the Salmon while I moved to the Snake in Hells Canyon—a change that had been prompted by my mom. After hearing my phone message, she'd signed herself up on a Hells Canyon trip with the company, requesting me as her guide.

"I hope you have fun," Danny said, stroking my back. "I wish I could meet your mom. I bet she's tough and smart and beautiful like you."

"She's all those things," I said, then hesitated before continuing. "But I'm not like her." It wasn't yet daybreak, and across the river, scant patches of ponderosa pines stood out against a lavender-gray sky. The clients would be up soon, wanting coffee and breakfast. I shimmied into my river shorts and threw on a fleece jacket.

Danny laughed. "That's what everyone says about their parents. It's inescapable."

I didn't tell him that since I was fourteen, my sole purpose had been to escape. I feared that if he ever found out what I was running from, I wouldn't be his dream woman anymore.

Just below Hells Canyon Dam, fellow guides Lonnie, Donna, Arnie, and I had mostly finished rigging our fleet of four sixteen-foot self-bailing rafts when the bus full of clients arrived. At the prospect of seeing my mom again, I felt more nervous than I ever had in the Boiling Pot eddy of the Zambezi. This would be the most time we'd spent together since I'd moved in with Steve my senior year of high school four years earlier.

When I saw her, my breath caught in my chest. Even though I'd done my best to detach from her emotionally, I still loved her with every cell I had. I waved at her with both arms as she exited the bus. She looked good—strong and toned from backpacking. Her signature wild perm had been replaced with a long bob, which framed her tan face. She smiled and waved to me as she exited the bus alone. The fifteen other clients on the trip were all coworkers, part of a corporate team-building group from Nevada.

Lonnie, our trip leader, ran a veiny hand through his mullet as he walked over to the clients to deliver the safety talk for our four-day trip through Hells Canyon. This remote section of the Snake, designated by Congress as part of the Wild and Scenic Rivers System, served as the border between Idaho and Oregon and was nearly two hundred miles from the boathouse or any other vestige of civilization. Between rattlesnakes, Class IV whitewater, and average temperatures in the midnineties, Hells Canyon had unlimited potential for wreckage, so a lot went into the safety talk. I had plenty of time to finish rigging my boat before going over to catch the bulk of Lonnie's spiel.

"We have a large metal box to deal with toilet waste, affectionately known as the groover." Lonnie flashed a nicotine-stained smile. "Please, folks, only number two in the groover, no number one." Lonnie tugged his sliding shorts back up over his butt. "In this heat, methane gas from the pee expands and could explode. Trust me, we don't want the groover to blow up." He'd once told me about a trip where the groover had exploded, coating the guide on board in excrement. "If you just have to pee," Lonnie continued, "go in the water, that's the Forest Service policy for this stretch of river. That way, it doesn't start to smell like a cat box in the arid desert canyon."

My eyes followed my mom as she broke away from the group in the middle of Lonnie's talk. Since finding out that she was coming on the trip, I'd worried about how she might behave and how that would affect me in my workplace. We hadn't even pushed off yet and I already questioned the sanity of having her on the trip. I chastised myself for calling her and giving her a way back into my life.

I wanted to follow my mom, but Lonnie was about to introduce Donna, Arnie, and me to the group. From there, we'd go straight into putting life jackets and helmets on people and loading their personal gear on the rafts. It was showtime, and I had a job to do. By the time Lonnie started splitting the clients into boats, my mom still wasn't back. I went down to the water again and welcomed my three clients into my raft, all the while scanning the hillside to locate Mom, who'd now gone missing. Lonnie and the other guides, Donna and Arnie, were seated in their boats, hands on the oars, ready to launch into the downstream current. I briefly considered pushing offshore and leaving Mom behind.

At forty-five, Lonnie was the company's oldest guide. He once told me he liked working with me because I was always rigged and ready to go and could stay in the downstream current, even in an afternoon headwind. This was high praise from a guy who lacked any patience for rookies, let alone female ones. Getting on Lonnie's bad side meant constant admonishment on the river. I had no intention of falling out of his favor.

But now, as I waded into the water next to Lonnie's boat, I felt a grow-ing sense of dread. "Give me a minute," I said.

"You bet, kiddo." Lonnie winked at me. "Whatever you need." He took out a bag of tobacco from his pocket and started hand-rolling a cigarette.

I sprinted toward a black basalt rock outcropping above the launch ramp, where I expected to find my mother hiding from the downstream wind in order to light her travel bong. I had scrambled two-thirds of the way up the hill when she popped out from behind the rock and began shuffling down the trail.

"There you are," I said. "You snuck off before I could say hi." I hugged her awkwardly, both of us off-kilter and straddling rocks in the trail.

"I had to pee," she said.

I could tell she was full of it. Her face had shifted; it was now smooth and lifeless, like a stroke victim's, in that blank way it always was after she got high.

"We're supposed to pee in the river," I said, engaging in her charade with forced cheerfulness.

Mom stopped mid-stride. "That's disrespectful to the river. You know better than that." Mark and Mom's policy on backpacking trips was that all peeing must take place at least one hundred yards from any water source.

"It's a Forest Service rule," I said. "The company could lose their permit if they don't follow it." I knew she wouldn't listen. After all, she had a bumper sticker on her truck that read, "STOP THE FOREST SERVICE, SAVE OUR WILD COUNTRY."

"We didn't raise you to be like this," she said.

I wondered which "we" she was referring to. There had been so many configurations of parents involved in my upbringing.

"They're waiting for us in the rafts," I said, turning back toward the water. I hoped she wouldn't follow me, that I could leave her at the put-in, where she could still find a way back to town. Our take-out wasn't until Heller Bar, seventy-nine river miles away, just past the confluence with the Salmon River. A lot of shit could go down between here and there.

Mom and I rejoined the clients, who were splashing around in the seventy-degree water, floating on their backs in the eddy to stay cool. My anxiety was crushing—it must have been palpable because Lonnie caught my eye and smiled, which he rarely did. We pushed off, and our flotilla joined the downstream flow, moving toward Cliff Mountain, the first of three minor rapids we'd run before camping just above the Class IV Wild Sheep.

I escaped into the water, using the two oars as extensions of my arms to meet the changing force of the current. I focused on what the Snake was saying, hiding myself in the comfort of her voice, letting her whispers shield me. We were nearly seven hundred miles downstream from where I'd grown up and guided my first season, yet the river still recognized me. I kept my sights on Lonnie ahead, putting my boat right behind his. I pushed to stay ahead of Donna's and Arnie's rafts because it was something I could control.

"How did a little girl like you ever get into guiding?" asked one of my clients. It was a question every female guide got on the first day of every trip, and one to which I had a canned response: *My parents are guides. It's the family business.* But with my mom on the boat, I was hesitant to use that line. After her earlier comment, it seemed she didn't approve of the type of guide I'd become. I didn't want to risk being reprimanded in front of my clients.

"I started guiding on this river. I was raised upstream from here," I said.

"In Jackson," Mom said.

"By my mom, Eliza." I introduced her to the group.

"You must be so proud," said one client, Joyce.

Mom hesitated before saying, "Yeah." The sarcasm was scarcely detectable.

Joyce picked up on the tone and flashed me a sympathetic smile. "Well, I can't imagine how difficult it is to row this heavy boat. She makes it look easy."

"That's why I named her Bridget," my mom said. "It means 'the strong.' Strength will get you through anything."

"That's true," Joyce said.

Lonnie gave the circling eddy-out sign as we neared Wild Sheep. Instead of running the biggest rapid of the trip this late in the afternoon, we'd camp above and scout it after rigging in the morning.

I couldn't wait to get off the boat, away from my mother. My nerves were shot from being hypervigilant, watching every word and nuance, waiting for the bomb to drop. I handed over her dry bag and watched her walk as far away from the group as the beach allowed to set up her camp.

"How's it going?" Lonnie asked me as we assembled the kitchen.

"Made it through day one," I said.

"Day's not over yet," Arnie piped in, dropping the heavy commissary box in the sand with a thud. His shaggy brown hair poked skyward in the electric heat.

"She seems real cool, your mom," said Donna.

That was exactly what kids in Jackson used to say in high school, after I'd returned from California. My mom supplied us with liquor and pot, saying that she'd rather we get it from her than risk driving all over hell's half acre and getting busted.

Honestly, I liked my mom better *before* she turned cool. I preferred the version of her that cautioned me about drugs and people who did them over the version who invited drug-addicted, lecherous vagrants into our home to be alone with her children. But I wasn't going to say that to Donna or anyone else.

Lonnie got out the dutch oven. He was the master of baking pineapple upside-down cake using a cast-iron pot and charcoal briquettes. I'd been apprenticing with him for some time but hadn't been turned loose yet.

"Can I make the PUD?" I asked.

Lonnie nodded. "You're ready."

I got to work mixing the batter and lighting the briquettes. After I arranged the coals on top of the dutch oven, I left the cake to bake while I went over to help make the rest of dinner. Clients gathered around the happy hour table, pouring themselves glasses of boxed wine to wash down brie and crackers. Lonnie mixed gin and tonics in coffee mugs for the guides, which we kept on the down-low, since we didn't have enough to share.

My mom arrived at the camp kitchen as I smelled the PUD for the third time and watched as I pulled the lid off and checked it. I'd first seen dutch oven cooking when she introduced it to my Girl Scout troop, back when we lived in the trailer park. I hauled the DO over to the table and prepared to flip it onto a plate, the final step. The solid cast-iron pot was quite heavy, and it took focus and commitment to flip it onto the plate. The guides, along with my mom, all gathered around as I prepared to make the big move. Wanting to shake the sting of her earlier disapproval, I was determined to impress her with my camp cooking skills. Quickly, I turned the DO over, then gently lifted it to find a perfectly toasty-brown, unbroken PUD.

"Would you look at that?" Lonnie said.

"Wow." Donna clapped her hands.

"I can't believe all the food you bring on these trips," Mom said. "On our backpacking trips, we only carry what we need. We don't have all this waste." Her eyes surveyed the five-course meal we'd worked for hours to create. I wondered what it would take to win her approval.

"You do backpacking trips?" Arnie asked.

"My husband and I are outfitters. We guide multiday trips in wilderness areas."

"Well, you're our guest tonight." Arnie handed Mom a plate. "Too bad Danny's not here. His brownies are irresistible. Bridget definitely thinks so."

I shot Arnie a look, wanting him to keep his mouth shut. But Arnie was Steve's best friend in Idaho, and since I'd started seeing Danny, Arnie had begun waiting for me outside the groover and other locations where I'd be taken off guard to ask if I'd told Steve yet.

"Who's Danny?" Mom said as Arnie dished up her plate.

"Another guide," I said, trying to sound nonchalant. "I'm going to get some dishwater."

"I'll come with you," Mom said.

When we got down to the river, I filled two metal chicky pails with water, then turned to go back. My mom stood in my path with a look that said *Out with it.*

"Danny's someone I'm seeing."

"What about Steve?"

"He's in Zambia."

"Did you break up?"

"Not exactly."

"Does Steve know about Danny?"

I shook my head.

My mom set her plate down on the sand. "I'm concerned about your morals, Bridget. That's a real lack of integrity."

I overcame the urge to dump the water from the pails over her head. "*My* morals?" I was shaking mad at the hypocrisy.

"Mark and I already have some real issues with your behavior and the choices you're making. And now this. It's worrisome." She drew her brow together in concern.

I pictured her as a spider, weaving a web. This was a trap. I'd watched her do this kind of crazy-making before, and I wasn't going to get caught up in it, especially while I was working and there was an audience.

"I've got dishes to do." I walked past her, heading to the kitchen.

When I got back, Lonnie turned on the propane blaster and motioned for me to set a pail onto the flame. "Everything okay?" he asked.

"Fantastic," I said, forcing a smile.

"Looks like you need a safety meeting." "Safety meeting" was guide code for getting high.

"You bet," I said. "I'm very unsafe right now."

We finished the dishes just before twilight; then Lonnie and I snuck off, down the trail toward Wild Sheep. As we reached the edge of camp, Mom appeared from the willows. "Where are you guys going?"

"Safety meeting," said Lonnie.

"Can I come?"

Lonnie looked over at me and shrugged. "What do you think?"

Maybe the tension between us would ease if we got stoned. Smoking weed seemed about the only thing we still had in common.

"I guess."

Mom's teeth gleamed like pearls in the gray light as she joined us on the trail, and for a moment, she reminded me of my mama. As we climbed onto the black boulders overlooking Wild Sheep, the Snake drummed loudly next to us, tumbling over the obstacles in her path. According to the Shoshone tribe, the Snake was created by accident. While traveling north of the Tetons, trickster Coyote was messing around and accidentally spilled a basket of fish and water belonging to a woman who lived on top of a mountain in Yellowstone country. Coyote tried to stop the spill by running ahead of it, piling rocks up high to block the water, but it couldn't be stopped, and it gained enough momentum to break through four dams he built. Coyote ran far ahead to a place where there were two very high hills and built a dam so high that he sat on top of it and whistled, certain it would stop the flow. The water filled the tall dam, then crushed it using all the rocks from Coyote's past failed attempts. These rocks are what carved out Hells Canyon.

After that, Coyote gave up trying to stop the water's flow. The water rushed on to the Pacific Ocean, taking all the big fish that had been dumped out of the woman's basket. That's why there are only small fish in Yellowstone country. Salmon and sturgeon have never been able to get back up because of the waterfalls.

I studied Lonnie as he lit a joint, then exhaled. "Did salmon run up this far from the ocean before the four dams downstream were built?" I asked him.

"I hear they used to," said Lonnie as he passed the joint to Mom. "This was as far upstream as they made it."

"When I'm old," Mom said, "I plan on strapping dynamite to my wheelchair and rolling myself onto Glen Canyon Dam on the Colorado. I'd like to blow that motherfucker up."

Lonnie laughed. "That would shake things up."

We finished the joint and returned to the group. Around the campfire, someone had pulled out a guitar, and a flask was making the rounds.

Mom and I stood next to a silver-haired man with a kind face, who introduced himself as Roy before handing me the flask.

"Cheers," I said, tossing it back. The thick licorice sweetness caught me off guard. "Who the hell drinks Jägermeister out of a flask?"

"You're probably a whiskey girl," Roy said.

"Bet your ass."

"We've got some of that too."

"So what is it you guys do?" Lonnie asked, settling onto a boulder near the fire.

"We work at a nuclear facility," said Roy, "manufacturing nuclear devices."

Mom stiffened. "You mean weapons?"

"You could call them that, yeah."

Mom's long fingers were clenched into fists. "This is something you're proud of?"

"The company takes real good care of us," Roy said.

"And how about you?" Mom rocked forward on her feet. "How are *you* taking care of *us*? Engineering the destruction of the planet?"

"We employ every precaution to make sure what we do is safe and benefits the public."

"What a load of horseshit." Mom glared at Roy.

"Mom." I said it like a warning.

"Oh, you're going to defend these slime bags?" She stepped back, away from the group, and stared at me.

"Let's just all try to get along," I said. "We're on vacation, right?"

"That's right," said Roy, passing me a bottle of whiskey he'd pulled out.

"I don't know what's happened to you, Bridget," my mother said. "You've sold out, working down here, catering to these people."

I took a long, slow swig from the whiskey bottle, then twisted the cap back on, deliberate and measured. "Drop it, Mom."

"Fuck this shit," she said before storming across the sand.

"Holy hell," Roy said. His buddy next to him let out a low whistle.

"Sorry about that," I said. "She gets a little fired up. Now you know why I prefer whiskey."

Across the circle, Lonnie caught my eye, and I knew he saw the shame I'd been trying to hide. I averted my eyes and threw down another shot. Whiskey, weed, and running rivers were the only things that brought me any relief from my family or past. If they ever stopped working, I'd be screwed.

I stayed up for hours doing damage control, drinking with the nuclear boys, long after the other guides had gone to bed. Afterward, I stumbled over to where Mom was camped and slid into my sleeping bag.

"Aren't you going to take your hair out of the braid?" Mom whispered.

I didn't answer.

"Here, let me brush it for you." She reached out to touch my hair.

"No thanks." I shrank back.

"Remember how I used to do your hair when you were little?" she asked.

"No. I don't," I lied. I couldn't trust my mother to do anything but detonate, blowing everything all to hell. Tears flooded my eyes. I closed my lids to try and dam them, but still they spilled out.

Eighteen

Confluence

"You're going to have to do something about your mother," Lonnie said to me as we scouted Wild Sheep the next morning.

We were downstream from the group, geared up like gladiators in our river armor of life jackets, river knives, helmets, and throw bags. Donna and Arnie were still rigging their boats at camp.

"What do you mean?" I asked.

Resolve settled into the deep lines on Lonnie's face. "We can't have her alienating the other guests." He lit a cigarette roach he'd pulled out of his shorts pocket.

"Believe me, if it was possible to do something about my mother, I would have done it by now."

"Was she always like this?"

I shook my head. "She had a complete personality change when she was thirty-five. Just woke up one morning as someone else."

I told Lonnie how once, when I was ten, Mama and I had been in the produce section of the grocery store when we encountered a toddler throwing a fit. His mother reacted by screaming at him. The other shoppers watched uncomfortably but did nothing. The hysterical mother was about to hit the kid when Mama gently put her hand on the woman's shoulder. "Honey," she said to the woman in her distinctive gravelly voice, "it seems like you're having a hard time right now. Let me help you, okay?" The frazzled woman crumpled and cried in Mama's arms. Mama handed the fussy boy a banana, calmed the frantic mother, and sent them on their way.

Before she changed personalities, Mama had been extraordinarily polite, and had raised me to be that way too. But the current version of her sought confrontation—being right trumped being kind.

"Could it be a chemical imbalance?" Lonnie asked.

I was dumbstruck. That had never occurred to me.

"Regardless," Lonnie said, "you've got to rein her in. Look, I know this isn't easy for you, but it's your job. We have to keep the group happy. They paid to see the canyon, not get sucker punched by your mother, who, like it or not, represents you. And you, my dear, represent us."

At the bottom of Hells Canyon—the deepest canyon in North America—I was being tasked with running an intervention on my mom. I had no hope that it would go well. I decided to do it later that day, after we set up camp, on the afternoon hike at camp to Suicide Point. That way, I wouldn't be trapped on the raft with her all day afterward.

I walked back from scouting the rapid and untied the raft's bowline from a juniper tree onshore.

"Is it big?" Mom asked as I settled onto my cooler seat and gripped the oars. "You look terrified."

"You're pretty much screwed if you go too far right."

We left the calm shelter of the eddy and drifted into the current. The anxiety clenching my throat clicked into alignment with the pulse of the oncoming rapid. The nervousness was no longer a burden but the frequency necessary to connect to the water. I shifted into another dimension, the one where there was no mom, no clients, no self. My focus on the sound was so intense and constant that I became the vibration; I was no longer observing it but channeling the hum into my cells.

The boat slid down the glassy tongue of the rapid, and I knew by the tone of the waves where the boat had to be. As if I were hitting the notes of a scale, I maneuvered through the crest, angled past rocks, and dropped the boat down between the goalpost rocks for a smooth run.

"Way to go!" Mom turned around, her white-blond hair plastered down with water. Her freckled nose crinkled, and I felt giddy, like I'd spent the afternoon dancing to ABBA and eating her homemade chocolate chip cookies. For a moment below Wild Sheep, there was joy.

That afternoon, when we reached the highest part of Suicide Point, Arnie turned everybody around to return to the safety of camp.

"I'll run sweep," I said, hanging back with Mom.

"See you down there," Arnie said, giving me a half smile.

Mom waited for the other clients to get far enough away before packing a bowl and offering it to me. I pulled a lighter out of my pocket, sat down on a rock, and fired up. Might as well get good and stoned. I inhaled as far down into my lungs as I could and passed it back to her.

"So, Mom . . ." I began, exhaling. "Maybe you could try to chill out a little around the other clients. You know, not call them out on all their shit. It puts me in an awkward position."

She took a huge hit, snorted, exhaled. She turned the pipe over and tapped it on a rock, discarding the ashes, and then put the pipe in her shorts pocket as she stood up.

"You're ashamed of me," she said in a wounded, little girl voice. "You're ashamed of me and now you want to shut me up."

"It's not that," I said, my insides pinching. "I am getting paid on this trip to be their guide. We can't be rude to them. You get it, right?"

"The only thing I get is that you are ashamed of your own mother." She began to tremble. "I don't even recognize you anymore. You've turned into somebody else's version of you."

"You're one to talk." I stood up to my full height, which shadowed her. Our bodies were built exactly the same, only mine had three extra inches of arms and legs. "You have your head shoved so far up Mark's ass you can't even see straight."

"And your head isn't twisted up Steve's?" She looked at me, mouth open wide. "Or is it Danny's now?"

I started walking down the trail. Away from her. "I'm nothing like you," I yelled back to her.

"You keep throwing your family away, girl, and one day we're not going to be here when you need us."

"Maybe you should have told yourself that, like, seven years ago," I yelled. "You're the one who threw us away like fucking trash." My words echoed off the canyon walls.

"You still blame me for leaving Sully?" She laughed. "Get some new material already. That was lifetimes ago, honey."

I stared at her, unable to respond.

"People are allowed to change," she said. "One thing I can promise you is that I will keep changing, and you don't have to like it."

The idea that she would change even more provoked in me a terror so pure, I felt dizzy. I leaned against a rock wall to steady myself. I wasn't willing to accept her being a shape-shifter. I just wanted her to be Mama. *My* mama.

"I don't like all the disaster that comes in the wake of your changes," I said.

"You're so fucking dramatic." She rolled her eyes. "What disaster?"

"Everything that happened after you decided to blow up our family: Losing Sully and getting the shit beat out of me in California. Getting dragged around to protests and worrying that you'd be hauled off to jail like Mark. Or how about being left alone with pervy old guys who molested me?"

"What are you talking about? What guys?"

"Sal."

"You never told me about that."

"I told you the morning after it happened."

She looked at me reproachfully. "This is the first you've mentioned it."

Her response was maddening enough to make somebody hurl themselves right off Suicide Point.

I looked down at camp, saw Lonnie getting out the DO and Arnie and Donna pulling food from the coolers to start dinner. I only had to survive through tomorrow; then we'd be to take-out by lunch the following day. My mom and the other clients would leave. I'd see Danny again.

"I'm done trying to hash this out with you," I said. "I've got to help make dinner."

I turned to walk down the trail. Mom didn't follow me. She didn't come back until hours later, stumbling in the near darkness. Arnie handed her a plate of dinner he'd saved, but she wouldn't take it, just walked right past us down the beach to her camp.

～

For the remaining two days of the trip, Mom was silent. She spoke no words to me or anyone else, but her fury said volumes. Her mouth remained twisted in a flat-lined grimace, while her eyes stared dully ahead. Her silence was as uncomfortable to be around as her tirades had been.

Lonnie quit speaking to me also. When I caught him looking at me, his eyes darted away, filled with a mix of pity and repulsion, as you might view a doomed animal that you felt sorry for but didn't want to get too close to. The Snake alone held me in balance. When I was near her, I had a sense of who I really was. I listened to her gurgling lullaby and dripped tears onto the sand, imagining Danny singing in his grainy tenor, shaking a curl from his eyes as his fingers formed chords on his guitar.

Twenty miles from the take-out at Heller Bar, we stopped briefly at the confluence with the Salmon River. I noticed that something in my mother's face had lifted.

"Take my picture." She handed me her camera. My mom was the family photographer. Rarely did she have her own photo taken.

I looked at her quizzically.

"I used to imagine this spot. When I was a girl in East LA, I would dream about disappearing deep in Hells Canyon, where no one could find me and I could be free in the wilderness."

For just a moment, we each set down our burden of being right. We staged the photo with her standing on a wide expanse of white sand, arms opened to both the Snake and the Salmon Rivers. She faced me with the same shy, unsteady smile of her childhood photos, her lips parted as if she were exhaling rather than smiling. Her long, tanned legs were strong and slender, rooted firmly in the earth. I looked through the viewfinder to center the frame, noticing as I clicked the shutter that her indigo eyes were alight with joy.

I handed her back the camera, and we both picked up our disappointment and outrage, carrying them with us down the river for the remainder of the trip.

Toward the end of the summer, Danny and I had a couple of days off together between trips, so he suggested we head to his folks' house north of Coeur d'Alene.

"I want to show you where I grew up."

We made the two-hour drive on his motorcycle, skipping along the highway in the afternoon's tangerine glow. As we drove through Moscow, Idaho, Danny veered off the highway, toward the university.

"Let's show you off." We pulled in front of a fraternity house.

"Do you know anyone here?" I asked. I was thrown, since Danny had gone to college on the West Coast.

"Not yet." He took my hand and led me to the front door, then rang the bell.

A couple of tall frat boys with sandy blond hair appeared. Danny did some secret handshake with them, and they all started laughing and slapping one another on the back.

"This is my girlfriend, Bridget," he said, placing an arm around my shoulder.

Being introduced as his girlfriend made my cheeks burn. I felt dishonest and didn't know how to respond. Luckily, we only stayed for a few minutes. While Danny chatted with the guys, I pretended to be interested in the decor of pinup girl beer posters and worn-out plaid couches.

Back at the motorcycle, Danny kissed me before putting on my helmet. "I liked calling you my girlfriend," he said.

We rode through brown high-desert landscape until it subsided into the lush, old-growth cedars and Engelmann spruce of the Idaho panhandle. When Danny eased to a stop in front of a lakefront estate with multiple wings and a circular driveway, I thought he was kidding. Surely he didn't know the people who lived inside the mansion. I spied a pool and a pool house, with a private dock on the lake.

"Is this your house?" I asked.

"Maybe you don't like me anymore," he said as we took off our helmets.

I tilted my head sideways. "Because you're rich?"

"Yeah."

"You're kidding, right?" But he wasn't. In the way he couldn't look at me, only the ground, I recognized shame.

"I definitely like you." I smiled at him. "I don't give a shit if you're rich or not."

We went inside to meet his parents, who had afternoon cocktails and hors d'oeuvres waiting for us.

"Here they are." His mom nearly squealed as she hugged him, then me. "Danny has told us so many wonderful things about you, but he did not mention what a gorgeous smile you have."

"Thank you." I was surprised that Danny had talked to his parents about me already. Steve had waited two years to tell his family we were together.

"We've been waiting all summer to get some time with the two of you," she said.

We sat on the deck overlooking the lake. His parents were lovely. The way Danny kept looking over at me, it was clear how much he adored me and was proud of me. It was a relief not to be scurrying around trying to keep our relationship underground. The only thing we had to hide was my plane ticket to Zambia in two weeks, and Steve.

That weekend, Danny and I drove around in the powerboat, water-skiing in the mornings before the wind hit the lake. In the afternoons, we holed up in his room, talking about literature and music. We'd dine with his parents, afterward sneaking off to the water, making love while floating on the gently rolling dock under a jeweled sky.

"Stay with me," Danny whispered in my ear as we awoke on the last morning. We'd spent the night sleeping on the dock, and the lake was ablaze with the colors of sunrise. "Don't go back to Africa. I love you."

It was the first time either of us had said "love." I buried my face in his chest.

"Are you crying?"

I lifted my head to look at him. "I've got to."

"Didn't you hear me? I love you." His low voice was tender and earnest.

"I heard." Shafts of light hit the lake as the sun rose, revealing rocks and fish beneath the surface.

He sat up, pushing me off his chest. "Say it."

"I can't."

"Bullshit."

"You know how I feel."

"Say it."

We sat face-to-face, Danny cross-legged, my legs wrapped around his waist. He leaned his forehead against mine, then reached to untangle my long hair with his fingers, smoothing it around us like a curtain. In Danny's eyes, I saw the woman the river had raised me to be. The dock creaked as a wave rolled toward shore. The feeling of surrender swept through me, just as it had when we'd collided during the lightning storm on the river.

"I love you," I said, finally, just as a pair of Canada geese honked overhead, the cool air rustling through their beating wings.

Nineteen

Chibango

I was picturing Danny's green eyes as I dropped my duffel in the foyer of the manager's house in Livingstone, Zambia, with its peeling yellow walls and barred windows. The smell of burning mosquito coils and floor polish caught in my throat, adding to the nausea I felt after twenty-four hours of travel. But as I stood there, my stupor finally lifted, and I realized how groundless my sense of integrity was. Had I really flown halfway around the world with a changeable return ticket to tell Steve to his face that I was in love with someone else? What was I thinking? Danny was right: I should have handled it over the phone.

As I waited in the empty house, Doreen and Angela burst through the warped wooden door, their smiles almost as big as the enormous hand-woven basket they'd made for me as a returning gift. Doreen, our housekeeper, and Angela, the guide house maid, were my two best friends from the previous season.

"Sister, why are you crying?" Angela asked. She set down the basket and touched my cheek as tears forged down my face.

"I'm leaving Steve," I said.

Doreen grabbed my duffel loaded with helmets and first aid supplies needed for the rafting operation. I'd promised Steve during our fax exchanges over the summer that I'd bring them, along with plenty more gear—rafts, frames, oars—all still at airport customs. Doreen carried my duffel into the master bedroom, while Angela struck a match for the teakettle.

"You are needing to rest," said Angela resolutely. "That is all. Sit down."

Doreen sidled her tiny frame onto the armrest of my chair, petting my blond arm hair—"fur," she called it. Her delicate features were twisted into a puzzled expression. "I think I am not understanding you," Doreen said. "Bleedget, why is it you are leaving?"

"I'm tired of following him around." I sniffed. "I need to get a life of my own." I didn't tell them about Danny.

"But Steve is not hitting you," said Angela. "He has a very good job. And he does not care that you have no babies, although you have been together for some time." Angela shook her head at me. "This is a good man."

"Yes, he's a good man," I said. But he wasn't the right man for me. Not anymore.

I wiped my face dry. "How are things here?" I asked. "How is everybody?"

"You have heard about Bendu?" Doreen asked, exchanging glances with Angela. I'd lived with Bendu in the guide house after he and Zeke had returned from guide training in the States.

"No, what?"

"He got the Skinny," Angela said, meaning AIDS. "He passed."

"Some months ago now," Doreen said.

It was odd that Steve hadn't mentioned it over the phone. Maybe he hadn't wanted to churn up memories of what we'd been through with my own HIV diagnosis. I considered telling Angela and Doreen that my doctor had called not long after Steve and I returned from our first season in Zambia, saying I had HIV and was going to die of AIDS. My doctor theorized that I'd contracted it from doing first aid in the Zambian villages along the river without protective equipment. I underwent a string of medical tests while Steve stood by me. During the weeks we waited for conclusive results, he and I made plans as if I were infected with an incurable disease, a scourge we'd already seen kill many of our Zambian friends. He bought me fancy pajamas we couldn't afford so I'd look good in the hospital bed, dying. The results of my final test came in days before he told me about Steph and boarded a plane for Zambia: I was negative. It had all been a mistake, a misdiagnosis. The doctor was wrong.

My HIV scare wasn't a story I could fit into a cup of tea, not when I'd just heard of our friend's death from what the Zambians called "the Skinny" because you wasted away until you disappeared.

"I'm so sorry," I said, reaching out to hold their hands. I was stunned and sad to hear about Bendu, and also: it had almost been me.

Angela and Doreen left just before Steve turned up at the house. He rushed to where I sat alone in the living room and wrapped me in a hug.

"What's the matter?" he asked, stroking my arm.

"I heard about Bendu."

"I wanted to tell you," Steve said. "But I thought you should find out in person, not over the phone."

"I waited to tell you something in person also." My only hope of pulling off this breakup was to act quickly and get out before he reeled me back in with guilt. "I had an affair with Danny," I said.

Steve pulled his hand from my arm. A sharp look of disbelief contorted his features, and his rosy cheeks blanched of color.

"Is this about the thing with Steph? I told you it was nothing." He ran a hand through his thinning curls.

"No. It's different."

Steve stood up from the couch and began pacing over the red cement floor. "When did it start?"

"June," I said. It was almost October. Nearly four months had passed since I'd last seen Steve.

"It's over though, right? You ended it." Steve looked at me hopefully.

"It's not that easy." I wanted to go over and comfort him, even as I intended to leave.

"How could you?" Steve kicked over the coffee table. It was the first time I'd seen him raise his voice or turn his anger outward. My anxiety rose, a reaction from the years I'd spent with my father. Steve felt me tense up and replaced his anger with sorrow. "After everything we've just been through."

Here was the guilt: I'd cheated on Steve after he'd vowed to take care of me while I died. I'd even worn the pajamas Steve had given me the first time Danny and I made love—he'd fingered the pearl buttons, unfastened them slowly, one by one, until they'd slid off my shoulders onto the ground. What kind of a shitty, heartless person does that?

"It's not like I set out to have an affair," I said. "I wasn't trying to get back at you for sleeping with Steph, even though I was mad about the chickenshit way you told me. We both know things happen on the river. At least I had the courage to come over here and face you, not scurry away."

"You think you're being courageous right now?" Steve let out a laugh. "That it takes courage to sneak around all summer with your boyfriend's buddy, parading it in front of everyone?"

"It wasn't like that."

"That slimy scumbag. I was good to him. I took him in."

"Danny felt bad about it."

"Well, then he shouldn't have fucked my girlfriend," Steve said. "Does he even know about us? About you? You probably didn't tell him anything, huh? You probably let him think you were some cool wilderness girl from Jackson Hole from a respectable family. What a joke." He let out a snort. "You didn't tell him what their friends did to you, what they would have kept doing to you if I hadn't saved you."

"Shut up."

Steve smiled then, walked over, and put his face close to mine. "A trustfunder like him, good family, frat boy. You think he's gonna stick around once he finds out how damaged you really are?" Steve laughed. "You're not exactly a debutante."

The thought came to me, *Now. Leave now.*

"No one will ever see you the same way once they know all the sick shit that's happened to you." Steve sat down again and put his arm around me. "Trust me, when Danny finds out, he'll dump you like trash. That's the sort of piece of shit he is."

In my mind, he was right: I wasn't entitled to the fiery love Danny and I shared, or to be treated well. Hadn't my father shown me at sixteen that I deserved to be punished, chiding me: *You're a slut just like your mother?* Hadn't my mom told me, when I went to her with Sal's greasy handprints all over me: *Get used to it, it's going to keep happening?* Get used to having my own desires and ambitions taken from me, get comfortable having my voice ignored, the autonomy of my body cast aside.

"Do you love him?" Steve asked.

I didn't say yes. I didn't say anything.

"You can't leave," Steve said. "You said you'd come with me to Africa if I took the manager's position. You promised me. I need you."

For too long, Steve and I had mistaken being in need for being in love. I pried the top off a warm Mosi Lager, wishing it was whiskey, and washed down the ache while unpacking my duffel. Living with the discomfort of denying my feelings felt like home. I'd grown up in four different families, and I'd learned to survive by stripping away parts of myself until I was a mirror, reflecting back someone else's version of me. This was how I was with Steve too—as long as I squelched my own desires and was who he wanted me to be, he would never leave.

With Danny, I'd found a man who was in love with the joyful woman I'd been on the river, but I believed what Steve said, that it was only a matter of time until he knew the truth. Besides, I had a very long history of running to safety. Steve was home base; he would always take care of me. That was the best a broken-down, trailer-park girl like me could hope for. I sent Danny a postcard from Victoria Falls, letting him know I wouldn't be returning. Imagining him receiving the card gutted me.

Over the next months, I devoted myself to training on the Class V section of the Boiling Pot. I abandoned myself to learning to speak Nyanja and absorbing Zambian culture. I pushed down my discontent, hiding it under endless gin and tonics and spliffs of homegrown *dagga* until I contracted malaria and was sidelined for a month. I spent the whole of my bed rest reading *Love in the Time of Cholera* and playing the Indigo Girls, especially their version of Dire Straits' "Romeo and Juliet," over and over.

Once I recovered from malaria, Steve suggested I join him on a seven-day trip as a trainee on the Zambezi. He thought some uninterrupted time on the river might bring us closer, though he warned that he'd be the trip leader, busy with extra responsibilities. I agreed to go, hoping it would take my mind off Danny and help me find a way back to Steve. Trying to suppress memories of Danny while lying next to Steve was difficult, although not unfamiliar. I knew well how to suffer the pain of shedding lives past.

One morning halfway through the seven-day trip, I changed into river clothes, resolving to push my ruinous love life from my mind and focus on what was downstream: Chibango, the Class VI waterfall so treacherous, it couldn't be run without the threat of death. We would have to portage the rafts and gear around the rapid, experiencing its power from the safety of shore.

There was a lot of work ahead breaking camp and rigging boats. I crossed the white sandy beach toward the river kitchen and faked a smile as Steve handed me a cup of coffee, prepared exactly to my liking: plenty of cream and two spoons of sugar to hide the bitter taste of Nescafé. Even though I'd made the choice to give up Danny, Steve still couldn't look at me without glaring.

"How long are you going to punish me?" I asked.

"Sorry if I'm not eager to get my ass kicked again," he said. "It's just, what's to stop you from running off? Isn't that what everyone in your family does?"

The undercurrent of discontent between us was constant, assuaged only by the adrenaline that came with hurling ourselves down Class V whitewater. It was better than sex and the only place where trust between us remained.

After breakfast, our group of four rafts, three guides, four trainees, twelve American clients, and Joe, our videographer, loaded the boats and pushed off, then floated toward Chibango Falls. The site of a newly proposed dam, Chibango was our last road access until the take-out at the Matetsi River confluence about forty-five miles downstream.

As we floated, all thoughts of whitewater or the portage ahead were pushed aside because of the state of our American videographer. Joe, who was incredibly fair-skinned, with long flaxen hair, had been fine at camp that morning. He'd been darting around in his kayak videoing the rafts running through smaller whitewater, but suddenly he had begun shivering, despite the heat rising off the black-rocked river canyon. Usually chatty, with endless corny commentary for the camera, he had fallen into a kind of delirium, unable to speak or answer questions. We'd strapped his kayak onto one of the rafts and loaded him into the bow of the training boat that I was rowing. We were concerned he'd come down with malaria or bilharzia, a parasitic disease caused by freshwater snails, both potentially deadly. He vomited several times off the front of the raft, one of the symptoms of heat exhaustion.

As I pushed the oars through the crocodile-infested flats between rapids, Jono, recently promoted to head highsider, looked at me worriedly, not because of the crocs but because of how quickly Joe's condition had changed. No longer quavering, his tall, lanky body seemed to grow limper with each oar stroke.

"It is the *mzungu* food," Jono pronounced. The highsiders regularly regarded *mzungu* food disdainfully, preferring the culinary safety of their *nshima*.

"Maybe," I said, "but more of us would be sick, I think."

By lunchtime when we arrived at Chibango, Joe was utterly listless. His pupils were huge and glassed over. He moaned as we lifted him out of the boat, telling us to leave him alone.

While the group de-rigged the boats, Jono, Sunday, and I made a lean-to out of a tarp and some driftwood and placed Joe on a pad underneath it in the shade, checking in on him between schlepping the rafts and gear over the blistering rock shelf. The clients walked clear around him, speaking in hushed tones, foreheads drawn in concern. A sense of dread thrummed through the group.

"Guide meeting," Steve called out to the crew, and we gathered away from the clients. "Obviously, we have to get Joe out of here," Steve said. "Who is going with him, that's what we have to decide."

I was training on the trip, sharing a baggage boat with the highsiders, who could certainly handle the boat without me. Of the *mzungus*, I had the most experience with the local culture and language, and I was the most familiar with the gorge after Steve and Rich, another guide, both of whom were rowing passenger boats.

This was an opportunity to prove myself to Steve, to show him I wasn't going to run off, that I was trustworthy. If I could get Joe to a hospital and keep him from dying, things between Steve and me were sure to improve. I offered to go.

One of the highsiders, Sunday, would also stay behind, so there were two of us handling the evacuation. Our bags were pulled off the rafts, and we added supplies: painkillers, cool gel packs, acetaminophen, water, bread, and mangoes. I'd forgotten the powdered Gatorade at the house, a mistake I regretted since there was nowhere to get more, and it could have likely helped Joe. Sunday and I waved goodbye from shore as our river clan floated away.

We entered the lean-to shelter to find that Joe had turned blood red and his pulse was bounding. He was unresponsive, and although he had a fever of 104 Fahrenheit, he wasn't sweating.

"He's bad off," I said.

"Oh-uh-oh," Sunday said in agreement.

"Do you think there's a building or some sort of compound at the top of the road?"

Sunday shrugged.

"I think one of us should hike up. If there's a compound, they can get us transport to the hospital in Hwange." I'd gone on safari in Hwange

National Park to celebrate my twenty-first birthday the year before and knew it was a two-hour drive from where we were, on mostly decent tarmac. "You might have better luck arranging transport," I said to Sunday. "I'll stay with Joe."

We were on the Zimbabwe side of the river, where they spoke the clicking dialect of Ndebele, a language I didn't know but that Sunday spoke fluently. He turned toward me, but because of his lazy eye, I couldn't tell where he was looking. Unlike many of the other Zambians, Sunday was quiet, introverted. He had an understated presence that could be mistaken for apathy, but I'd come to understand that he was cautious, unused to brash *mzungus*, and measured and careful with his words, especially around me, the boss's "wife." Until now, ours had been a polite, somewhat distant, relationship. All of that was about to change.

Sunday pocketed a mango and eyed the crude road that led to what we hoped was a dam site compound at the top of the gorge. But we had no idea how far up the road it might be, since there were no maps of the gorge. They would presumably have a radio or telephone to contact the outside world, but we didn't know.

Sunday headed up the crumbling road, and I went to rouse Joe. He jolted awake, kicking me. "Fuck off, Mom! Why are you doing this to me? Leave me alone." There was no reasoning with him or calming him down. Eventually, he passed out from the pain, and I was able to lay a wet *chitenge* cloth over him to try to cool his core temperature. The heat radiating off the black canyon walls was crushing. Underneath the wet, colorful shroud, his body was as still as a corpse.

I was left alone with the roar of Chibango Falls and my fear. I sensed a presence, a mysterious foreboding. I scanned the water—it was too turbulent for hippos or crocs here, yet I felt as if I were being watched. After sitting with this feeling for a while, I sensed that the presence was the river god Nyaminyami, watching from within the falls. I spoke to him as I would the Snake, as a daughter asking for help. I begged him not to take my friend. I didn't want to call Joe's mother and girlfriend in the States to tell them he'd died in agony in the African bush.

Nyaminyami's ire rose on misty smoke as it spilled over Chibango Falls, his fury palpable. Since I'd arrived at the Zambezi last season, I'd been trying to deny that Nyaminyami was malevolent, but now, absent all distraction, there was no more pretending: Nyaminyami didn't give a shit about a suffering, sick *mzungu*.

I'd experienced communicating with other rivers, but whereas the Snake's voice had felt like a tickle on the inside of my forehead, Nyaminyami came into my skull like a freight train. Perhaps it was because the Zambezi, capable of running up to three hundred thousand cubic feet per second at its highest, was roughly ten times larger in volume than the Snake at its highest recorded level of thirty-eight thousand cfs.

She's gone. My wife is gone because of you. Nyaminyami was blaming me for what had happened decades ago, when outsiders like me had built the Kariba Dam, separating him from his wife, Kitapo. The dam—just upstream from Siavonga, where I'd paddled with Gary, Leonard, and Military—had displaced nearly all of Nyaminyami's people, and now a new dam was slated to be constructed here, at Chibango.

"I'm sorry," I said.

Make it right. A sacrifice.

Did he want a hostage? Someone to pay for the injustice he'd suffered? Did he want Joe?

"It won't bring her back." I stood up, showing Nyaminyami that I was prepared to defend Joe. More than five years had passed since I'd run to the closet when my father had come after me. I was now a grown woman, capable of fighting back.

If ever there was a river in need of anger-management therapy, it was the Zambezi. I moved to guard the lean-to entrance, shielding Joe from Nyaminyami with all the force I could muster, until I felt the river god retreat into the cave within Chibango.

With Nyaminyami quiet, I waited on the rock for what felt like hours for Sunday to return. I rummaged through Joe's waterproof camera case and ferreted out a stash of joints tucked alongside his malaria prevention medication, Deltaprim. Thank God for stoner video boaters.

Joe came to with a violent shudder as I was smoking a huge spliff.

"Where am I?" He was genuinely surprised and seemed somewhat lucid.

"We're at the dam site. You're sick. We're waiting for a vehicle to take you to the hospital. The others have gone downstream."

"Are you smoking all my joints? Those have to last the whole trip."

"I'd say the circumstances call for emergency usage." I passed him the spliff, and he took a shaky drag. "Have some water, okay?" I passed him a water bottle. His skin was still crimson.

"No! Don't make me drink it. I can't do it."

"How about a painkiller?" I suggested, trying to trick him.

"You have some?"

"Hell yes, I have some." I handed him a Tylenol with codeine and my water bottle. He managed to get a few swallows of water down, although it wouldn't do him much good. He needed IV fluids to recalibrate his system.

"When's the last time you had water?"

Joe thought hard. "Songwe camp."

"That was three days ago."

He reconsidered. "Yeah, it was at Songwe. I was too busy videoing to drink any water."

"Are you fucking kidding me, dude?" I stared at him, incredulous. "You have heat exhaustion. Probably heatstroke."

The regulatory functions of his body's cooling system had blown a gasket. This was the physical manifestation of the symptoms of heat exhaustion I'd read about in my first aid course, what the bullet points from my textbook looked like in real life.

Soon, Joe was unconscious again. I felt Nyaminyami watching.

"You're going to make it," I told Joe. Even though he was unconscious, I sensed that he could hear me. "You have to fight, Joe. You want to see your girlfriend again? Fight now. Like this." I picked up a rock fallen from the steep canyon walls and hurled it at Nyaminyami. "Stay away!"

I heard a crack against the waterfall shelf where the rock hit. Vengeance was the only language Nyaminyami spoke now. Years of disregard and disappointment had left only rage—we had that in common. I had generations of rage bred into my DNA. Rage was my motherfucking love language.

"You're not taking Joe. Go get your sacrifice somewhere else."

Chibango rapid surged then, coating me with a fine mist.

"You think you're tougher than me? Let's see it. There's nothing you can dish out that I haven't already survived."

I wanted Nyaminyami to understand that I would not be defeated. I'd learned the hard way that playing dead—as Mark had advised me long ago on the trail in New Mexico—didn't work with a predator. Predators only speak the language of dominance, and I'd grown tired of being mute.

"I'm still fucking here," I said, pounding my breastbone. For once, my past felt like an asset. I would not give up on Joe the way my parents had given up on me.

I turned to find Sunday, who had come down the road and was staring at me, his mouth agape. He looked scared at the sight of me: a *mzungu* witch on drugs doing battle with river gods.

"You are speaking to Nyaminyami?"

I nodded.

"Oh-uh-oh," he said. "Can you hear him?"

I jerked my chin and eyebrows up the way Zambians do. Yes.

"Can you hear other rivers?"

"Not as strongly as this one."

"That's because it's Nyaminyami." Sunday smiled. "There are witch doctors in my village who can hear him," he said. "You have been trained for this?"

I shook my head no. "In my culture, you're crazy if you talk to rivers. *Kafunta*." I spun my finger in a circle next to my head. "Where I'm from, some Native people still hear the voices of the land, the water, and animals."

"Oh-uh-oh," Sunday said. "To us, this hearing is a powerful gift. You do not hear with your ears but with your spirit. Perhaps your ancestors are calling you back."

"Nyaminyami doesn't seem to think so. He is angry with me and Joe, as if we are the ones keeping him from his wife by building the dam ourselves."

"His love for Kitapo is very strong. It is not right for them to be separated."

"I can't do anything about that," I said, then paused before asking, "What did you find at the compound?"

Sunday moved his upturned palm side to side: *Kalibe.* Translation: Empty. Not there.

"*Kalibe*? Sure?"

"No telephone," he said, wiping the sweat out of his eyes before sitting in the shade.

"Do they have a radio or transport?"

Sunday shrugged, meaning he didn't know. He pulled a crumpled cigarette out of his shorts pocket and motioned for my lighter.

"Are there people up there?" I leaned over to light his smoke.

He took a drag and nodded yes—there were people. Then he turned his head slightly away from Joe and me. When his cigarette was nearly finished, Sunday looked back at Joe, moving his eyebrows quickly up and down once, the way Zambians do when they are asking about the state of something.

"He's going to die if we don't get him out of here."

Sunday looked unimpressed. Death was a fact of life around here; there was nothing to be done to prevent it, no cutting-edge cures or insurance policies to pay for them. There was nothing but prayer. He took the last drag, then flicked his cigarette butt into the sand.

So that was it? Fuck that. Watching Joe check out was not on my to-do list. If there was one thing I was good at, it was mounting an escape for the sake of survival. I threw together some water and food, a headlamp, wads of Zimbabwe dollars and US cash, and zipped it all shut inside a pack.

Then I took my Nyaminyami necklace from around my neck and slid it over Joe's limp head.

Sunday looked at me, his face unguarded for the first time. "The trail, it goes more quickly," he said, pointing to a spur off the road.

"*Zikomo.*" Thank you. "Keep an eye on him," I said, meaning both Joe and Nyaminyami. As I cinched down my pack, preparing to leave, I asked, "Why doesn't Nyaminyami break the dam like he did before, instead of hanging around here feeling sorry for himself?"

"This, I do not know." Sunday laughed. "Maybe one day he will."

It was a bitch of a climb up the narrow game trail. There was barely room to pass between the crumbling earthen wall and the cliff. I kept going, thinking about Joe fighting for his life. I remembered the countless tight trails I'd shimmied back home in the crags of the Rockies while backpacking with Mark and my mom, flashed all the way back to my first hike at six with Mama and Sully—a ten-mile trek around Jackson Lake. When we returned to camp near twilight, Mama noticed blood on my shirt.

"Your backpack rubbed off your mole," Mama said, then looked at me, spooked. "You didn't say anything." Years later, I guided a backpacking trip in the Tetons with Mom, and while we were swimming in an alpine lake, she noticed my feet, blistered and bloody from wearing borrowed boots to save money. She gave me that same eerie look. "I had no idea. You never complain."

That wasn't true: I had complained plenty—about her leaving Sully for Mark, about Sal molesting me in my own bed—and had been told to get used to it. She'd trained me to carry the load despite the pain, to put one bloody foot in front of the other. Stopping on the side of the trail to complain about it wouldn't get me anywhere. I saw now that she had been training me for this moment.

As I traversed the trail out of the Zambezi gorge, I grew more determined each time I lost my balance and nearly fell headlong onto the rocks below. I had blood-soaked gashes on my shins and flaps of skin missing from my fingertips and knuckles, but this wretched trail would not prevent me from saving Joe. I had so much adrenaline coursing through me that I found it hilariously fitting when the trail dead-ended into a steep rock wall at the final lip of the canyon, just below where I guessed the dam site compound to be.

I couldn't see the compound—all that was visible was a sketchy, frayed rope hanging down over the lip, falling to where I was standing about thirty feet below. I pulled on the rope, testing it. It was attached to an unknown something up there. I reviewed my options: climb up the jury-rigged rope and arrive at the compound within minutes if I didn't fall to my death, or hike back down the shitty game trail and climb the road, losing precious hours in the process.

I pulled hard on the rope again, hanging all my weight to see if it would hold. I thought of Joe, unconscious below, unable to fend off Nyaminyami.

I leapt up to grab as high on the rope as I could and began pulling myself up, hand over hand.

Twenty

Telephone Chess

I pulled myself up the rope, as I had done as a kid in gym class during long Jackson winters. Despite the thick calluses I'd built from rowing, the rope's dry, dusty fibers burned my hands. I paused briefly, my palms on fire, and looked down long enough to see the canyon floor 350 feet below me. I had no harness or helmet, no long line, climbing chocks, or protection, nothing to prevent my death but faith in God and the Zimbabwean fishermen who had likely placed the rope. I kept climbing, praying the rope would hold, focusing all my energy on putting one bloody hand above the other. I reached the top and clambered over the rim, relieved to see a heavily fenced-in compound.

I took a moment to compose myself after nearly vomiting from anxiety on the climb, brushing the dirt off my clothes and rebraiding my disaster-struck hair, before striding over toward the armed guard standing near the gate of a barbed-wire enclosure. The lone cement-block building he was guarding looked like a prison in the middle of the savanna.

"Hello, my friend," I said to the guard. Looking at the ground, I lightly clasped my lowered hands together in a display of subservience and hunched my shoulders like an old woman over a cane.

234 of The River's Daughter

The guard's hand moved to the automatic rifle slung over his shoulder. I quickly realized I had no actual plan for getting inside the compound. I was totally winging it. As I was bent over looking at the ground, it occurred to me that Joe might not be the only sacrifice. I thought of something my father had said when I lived with him, when he criticized my mother's new anarchist lifestyle: you can't change the system by throwing rocks from outside. The only way to change it is to dismantle it from within. I needed to do whatever it took to get inside the compound, inside the guard's mind.

"From where did you come?" the guard finally asked, puzzled by the sudden appearance of a safari-wrecked Malibu Barbie climbing out of the gorge. He was taller than me, and unyielding, as if rooted in position. His large hands tightly gripped the rifle.

"From the river, my friend." I continued to look at the ground. Staring directly into the eyes of a superior was a sign of hostility in these parts.

"What is it you are wanting?"

"My friend is down by the river. He is very, very sick and needs to go to a hospital or he will die. With great respect, I am asking if we may use your telephone to arrange for transport to take him."

"Hmpf," he snorted. I snuck a peek past him and glimpsed an open door to the compound office. My heart quickened as I spied a fifties-style black rotary telephone on the desk. There was a fly-swarmed plate of *nshima* next to the phone. I heard papers rustling and a chair scuffling across the cement floor. Just out of my view, someone was inside, sitting at what I guessed was another desk.

"But you see," the guard began, then paused, sucking his teeth in a haughty display of authority, "the problem . . . is that we do not have a telephone."

I refrained from grabbing the chain-link fence and screaming, "What's that on the desk, you pompous ass? My friend is dying!" Instead, I chose to play his game of telephone chess.

I stayed silent. The guard looked me over.

"From where did you come?" he asked again.

"The river." This was going to take a while. I settled in.

"Yes, I know this," he said, annoyed. "How did you get to the river?"

"I have come from Mosi-oa-Tunya in a raft."

I kept my eyes downcast, but in my peripheral vision I saw him raise his eyebrows slightly.

"Through Nyaminyami's rapids?"

"Yes."

"And you are still alive? Were you feeling very scared?"

"I'm a good swimmer."

He laughed. Progress.

Speaking in clicking Ndebele, he addressed whoever was inside the office, a man, who answered back with "Oh-uh-oh"; the intonation sounded like "You don't say?" The man from inside appeared at the door then, dressed in a burgundy three-piece suit and shiny wing-tip shoes. He made his way across the clay yard, toward the fence.

"You are alone with your friend?" asked the suit.

"Our group left us behind because he is sick. There are two of us helping him." I kept my eyes on the ground.

"Oh-uh-oh," they said in unison.

"You are part of a whitewater rafting group?" Suit had taken over the questioning.

I nodded.

"I have always been very interested in this. Will you kindly tell me, is it very popular in your country? Have you experienced it on other rivers?"

For the love of God, we don't have time for bullshit chitchat. A man's life is at stake!

I smiled politely. "Yes, it is becoming very popular in the United States. It brings a lot of tourists and money to the village where I am from. Many people consider your river, the Zambezi, to be the best rafting anywhere in the world. Perhaps you would like to join my company on a trip someday?"

"Oh no," Suit laughed. "I cannot swim!"

"That doesn't matter. You wear a life preserver that floats you. I've taken many people on trips before who can't swim."

"And you are the one who captains the raft?" he asked disbelievingly. "There is no man helping you?"

"Only Nyaminyami himself." Still playing.

He smiled, then withdrew a little. "Well, you see, we have no telephone here. I am afraid we cannot help you."

"Do you have a radio, then, or transport of some kind to get my friend to a hospital?"

He jiggled his hand side to side, palm facing skyward: *Kalibe.*

"Can you tell me, my friend, how far is it to the main road from here?" Maybe I could hitch a ride on the highway, find a phone.

"A day's time."

"We cannot wait that long."

Moments went by. I continued looking at the ground and considered breaking out the cash.

"Which company is it that you work for?" Suit was still treating me like a human brochure.

"A company on the Zambian side of the river."

"Oh!" Suit's face broke open. "Zambia! My home country!" He chuckled.

"*Muli bwanji,*" I said.

Checkmate.

He stopped cold. "*Bwino, bwanji.* Oh! You speak my language!" Both Suit and the guard began laughing, as if I'd said the funniest thing they'd ever heard. This was a common response whenever I spoke Nyanja. People nearly fell on the ground, unable to control themselves. The first few times it happened, I asked if I had said something wrong. Perhaps my accent was bad? "No," they'd say, "we have never seen a *mzungu* speak Nyanja before."

Suit was laughing so hard he had tears. He opened the gate while wiping his eyes and led me into the office. "Here is the telephone," he said.

I called the office, and Dominic, the driver, answered. I told him what was going on. He said he'd drive across the border and find the 4x4 road to the river *manje manje*, meaning as soon as he could. Zeke and the high-siders had instructed me that in Nyanja, there is no word for "now," as the concept of time is quite different for Zambians: the same word, *mailo*, means yesterday and tomorrow, and the closest word for now, *manje*, means anytime in the next two weeks, or nowadays. Americans have countless words that mean "now": "right away," "ASAP," "immediately," "this minute," "directly," "instantly" . . . the list goes on and on. The fact that there is no such concept as "right now" drives *mzungus* crazy. The Zambians who worked with us understood this, and created *manje manje*, or *manje manje manje manje*, depending on the urgency, so that their impatient American coworkers would have something to grasp on to. I did my best to impress upon Dominic that this was a seriously *manje manje manje manje* situation before hanging up.

"*Zikomo*." I thanked the men for the use of their nonexistent telephone and was met by more chuckling. I left them slapping each other on the back in hysterics as I headed off by way of the 4x4 road. Once on the death rope was more than enough.

Twenty-One

Rescue Mission

I reached the river as the deep red sun slipped from view. It had been just over six hours since we had been dropped off at Chibango. Sunday was napping on a rock next to Joe's motionless body. He stirred as I checked to see if Joe had a pulse. It was so faint, at first I didn't detect it, but I moved my fingers around until I felt it trickling slowly, like a dripping faucet. Joe's dilated pupils were so huge they overtook any blue that used to be there. I squeezed a few drops of water from a moistened *chitenge* onto his sandpaper tongue, made a chair out of dry bags, and sat down to wait for Dominic to come save us.

"How did you get use of the telephone?" Sunday wanted to know.

"I spoke Nyanja." Of course, Sunday had done this also. "Who knows, maybe it was my angel face." I shrugged.

"Angel face." He laughed. "That is not why."

We sat uncomfortably with the truth: they let me in because I was *mzungu*. A little bit because I spoke Nyanja, but mostly because I was White.

Nyaminyami began to settle, and a coolness bathed the scorched gorge into a tranquil dream state. The Southern Cross rose over the canyon wall and moved across the sky, followed closely by Aquarius. We sat still, with nothing but burning stars and joints to mark the passing of time. Although Nyaminyami was quiet, I felt him slithering about, watching and waiting at the river's edge. Every so often, I threw a low, teeth-baring growl in his direction, just to let him know I was still on to his game.

As I dozed off, the grind of a Toyota Hilux cut through the roar of water bashing onto rock. Over twelve hours had elapsed since we'd put Joe in the lean-to. Erratic beams of headlights flashed around the canyon as the truck approached us, until finally it idled nearby.

"*Bwanji.*" I nodded to Dom as he came toward us. I wanted to hug him, but I'd been warned that only prostitutes hugged men openly here.

"*Bwino, bwanji.*" Dom's white smile glowed in the darkness.

Just before leaving, I slipped off to the river one last time and knelt before Nyaminyami. He was, after all, a river god.

I put my hand in his water. "Thank you," I whispered. "Thank you for sparing Joe."

He was quiet, and for the first time, I sensed the enormous loneliness beneath his rage. He wanted a hostage because he couldn't bear being alone, all his power unrealized, generation after generation.

"You're not alone," I told him. "*Tiza onana*, mighty one." *See you.*

Nyaminyami had shown me that wielding anger didn't bring back loved ones, or bring back a past version of the lives or selves we longed for. It kept us imprisoned, unable to move forward. But casting aside the anger felt like giving up; it made me feel powerless. I couldn't yet see how healing could come from surrendering. It worried me, how unwilling I was to give up my anger, and also: If the river god Nyaminyami was still mired in his anger over the transgressions against him, after all this time, what were my chances of breaking free?

I walked away from the river, toward the others. Dom lit a cigarette and stretched his six-foot-seven frame, weary from the five-hour drive from Livingstone. Sunday and I hoisted a still-unconscious Joe by his arms and legs onto a makeshift bed in the back of the truck.

"Get ready for a cowboy ride." Dom laughed as he began driving up the dam site road, engine grinding in the lowest gear. The grade was so boulder-ridden we were thrown into the air with each bounce. Joe came to and cried out in pain as his body was rag-dolled around in the back. It wasn't much better inside the cab. Mercifully, we reached the canyon rim and Joe fell unconscious again as the dirt road became flat.

I wasn't sure Joe would survive the two-hour trip to the Hwange hospital. He'd had only brief stints of consciousness throughout the day and had been unable to drink water in the hundred-plus-degree heat.

Dom handed me a grease-stained paper sack. "I brought *nkuku*."

I passed the bag to Sunday, offering the chicken to him first. He slid down in the back seat, chin to chest, shaking his head—the boss's "wife" should eat first. I tore off a wing and the smaller leg, giving the rest to Sunday, who smiled and looked at me sideways with his strong eye. We drove through the stillness of elephant sleeping grounds, taking in their shadowy forms beneath baobab trees. Wild elephants sleep standing up and get only a couple of hours of rest each night—it's too difficult for them to rouse their bodies after lying down. I knew that night we would be lucky to sleep at all.

We reached the small hospital outside Hwange National Park around 1:00 a.m. I followed Dom and Sunday as they carried Joe through the entrance and down the hallways lined with patients reclining on gurneys, into the lime-green waiting room. A couple of patients had sheets pulled over their faces; other sick and injured patients waited on plastic chairs. After placing Joe on an empty gurney, Dom and Sunday returned to the vehicle to rest, while I sat next to Joe.

Because Joe and I were *mzungus*, we were not required to wait as long as everyone else. Usually, I insisted on waiting in queue, but this time I didn't hesitate to cut the line. We were quickly ushered into a curtained-off corner and promptly greeted by a very young Zimbabwean doctor.

"He is suffering from malaria," said the doctor after looking inside Joe's mouth and listening to his breathing with a stethoscope. "We will send you with chloroquine tablets to relieve him." The doctor clicked Ndebele directions to an attending boy, who ran off to fetch the medicine.

"But my friend is taking Deltaprim," I said. During my own recent bout with malaria, I'd read that mixing Deltaprim and chloroquine could be fatal.

"That should not matter."

"Is it possible to do a malaria blood test first?" I asked.

"There is no need. This man most definitely is suffering from malaria. He has all of the symptoms I see every day as a doctor in this hospital." The doctor looked directly into my eyes—I'd insulted him.

"What about heat exhaustion or heatstroke? He has the symptoms for those also. Perhaps he needs intravenous fluids." I was beginning to feel that we'd made a big mistake in bringing Joe here. I kept thinking about the dead bodies in the entryway.

"Heat exhaustion?" The doctor looked at me as if I were perhaps suffering from something myself.

"It's something *mzungus* get when we are too hot," I said. "We are not used to the sun here. When our bodies do not have enough water, we become dehydrated and then go into shock. He has been in shock all day, as you can see." Joe was still unconscious, lying on the sagging gurney. "Also, my friend has not taken water for three days."

The doctor dismissed my suggestion with a wave as the boy returned without the tablets. There was more discussion in Ndebele before the doctor pronounced, "Madam, we are just now out of tablets. I will, instead, give him an injection of chloroquine." He reached for an unsheathed syringe from a nearby cabinet.

Moments earlier, I'd thought about asking the doctor if he could administer intravenous saline solution, but seeing the unsheathed needle made me reconsider. The last thing we needed was to leave this hospital with a case of HIV.

"Never mind," I said, putting my body between the doctor and Joe. "We're gonna go."

The doctor stepped toward me, alarmed. "You cannot just take him. You must first allow us to treat him."

I spread out my long arms, blocking the length of the gurney.

The doctor's voice deepened. "Your friend will certainly die if he is not treated." His words shot out in staccato the way the highsiders' speech did when they were quarreling.

As a river guide, I was required to regularly recertify in first aid, where heat exhaustion and heatstroke were covered extensively. I felt certain that that was what Joe had, largely on the basis that he hadn't drunk water for three days while being cooked in the extreme African heat. We needed to cool down his core temperature and rehydrate him with electrolytes. Every part of my intuition told me that we needed to get Joe the hell out of the hospital, *manje manje manje manje.*

"We'll take our chances," I said.

"You are responsible," the doctor said. "You understand, madam, that his life is dependent on your decision?"

I didn't know Joe very well outside of being his coworker for half a season. I'd done what I could to get him to the hospital. Why not hand him over to the doctor and be done with it? But I knew what it was to feel abandoned. Joe might die, but it wouldn't be because I gave up on him.

Moving Joe was a problem, since he was laid out flat on the gurney. Although taller than I was, he was skinny—weighing not much more than I did—so I was able to hoist him onto my shoulder and drag him back to the waiting room. I propped him in a chair before running to the truck for help. The doctor followed me out, shouting at Dom and Sunday in Ndebele as they carried Joe through the car park.

Once we were back in the truck, Dom looked at me expectantly. We couldn't go back to Livingstone, since it was the middle of the night and the border between Zimbabwe and Zambia was closed until 6:00 a.m.

"We need air-conditioning to cool him down, then we can rehydrate him. How about a hotel in Vic Falls?" I said. "On the side of town closest to the border." Dominic and Sunday looked at me like I was suggesting we charter a plane to the UK. This was a plan for rich people, which, to Dom and Sunday, we were. Ridiculously rich.

Dom drove us another hour to the tourist town of Victoria Falls and pulled into the driveway of the a'Zambezi River Lodge. Breaking out my wads of cash, I paid for a room with two double beds to accommodate the four of us. We got Joe situated, and I went to work cooling him down with wet towels, the air-conditioning blasting on high. I didn't dare try to give him water yet, since he was still unconscious and couldn't swallow. Dom and Sunday watched awkwardly from the doorway before opting to sleep in the truck. I left the room unlocked in case they changed their minds, and then I fell into a short, fitful sleep.

I awoke a couple of hours later, still in my river clothes. I was confused by the heavy red curtains and velvet wallpaper, and then I remembered Joe. Without saline fluids or any way to rehydrate him, there was a good chance he hadn't survived the night. I couldn't hear him breathing. I was scared to look over at his bed, to see his dead body.

Slowly, I turned over. His bed was empty. "Joe?" I called out in the cool, stale room.

There was shuffling in the bathroom. I knocked lightly on the door, pressed my ear to the wood. No answer.

I sat down on Joe's rumpled bed. Could he have crawled to the bathroom to vomit? Maybe he'd shit himself, then collapsed from fever? As I went to try the door again, it swung open and out walked Joe, freshly showered, his long white-blond hair dripping wet.

"I'm so fucking thirsty," he announced, gulping from a hotel cup.

I felt his forehead. His skin felt normal, no fever. His eyes looked like he'd been crying—a bit swollen and dull—but overall, he was himself. Relief flooded through me.

"Take it easy with the tap water. It'll give you the shits," I said. "We need to replace your electrolytes now. I've got Gatorade back at the house. We'll cross the border and get you fixed up."

Joe fell back down on the bed. "I feel weak."

"Duh. You, like, almost *died*." I packed up his waterproof camera case and collected the few things we'd thrown around the room. Despite minimal sleep, I felt energized. Joe was alive!

"Can you walk to the truck?"

"I think so."

We emerged from the cave-like room into the morning sun and were met by Dom and Sunday's stunned faces. They looked at Joe as if he were Lazarus, risen from the dead. Indeed, it was miraculous: the swift, heavenly power of air-conditioning.

Twenty-Two

None of Your Concern

O nce across the border, Dom dropped Joe and me off at the manager's house. It felt strange saying goodbye to Dom and Sunday after the intensity of the last day and night together, but I'd see them soon, maybe even tomorrow. Dom would drive us to the canyon rim, where we'd climb back into the same gorge we'd just worked so hard to leave.

Even though Joe was much improved, he was still shaky and weak, and I worried about a relapse if he didn't rehydrate with electrolytes. Plying him with Gatorade was all I could think about as we came through the front door. I expected to see Doreen, who in addition to being our house-keeper was my best friend in Zambia.

When I'd first met Doreen the previous season, she was a highsider, one of only two female highsiders in the twelve-year history of the company. She was barely five feet tall and weighed less than a hundred pounds, but she carried heavy coolers and rafts, matching the men load for load. They objected to her working in competition with them, making it harder for them to provide for their families. Doreen didn't have a family of her own, they argued, so she didn't need the money the way they did.

It was decided that Doreen must quit highsiding and become the man-ager's "house girl," so she came to work for us, doing the washing, ironing, and floor polishing. She joined our Zambian groundskeeper, Gabriel, and guard, Mr. Amos, bringing our total number of house staff to three.

"I don't want to play 'madam of the house,'" I'd told Steve. "It makes me uncomfortable." Back home, I'd cleaned plenty of motel rooms for money in between guiding seasons.

"What do you want me to do? Fire them?" asked Steve. "Then they won't have jobs."

Obviously, that wouldn't do, so I went from being a maid to having one.

Doreen and I had a few things in common besides scrubbing toilets for cash. We were both twenty-one years old and had grown up next to rivers: me in a small town next to the Snake, and Doreen in a Tonga village outside Choma, near the Lower Zambezi. Before meeting us, she'd never been around *wazungu*—White people—in her life. Before coming to Africa, I had rarely been around Black people in my life. We spent afternoons swapping dance moves while playing UB40's "Red Red Wine" over and over. We eventually broke the cassette tape, so Doreen brought in her tapes from home of Zairian *kwassa kwassa* and Lucky Dube, a South African reggae megastar.

Normally, Doreen arrived for work every morning promptly at eight. For some reason, she wasn't there to welcome Joe and me home from the gorge, but a *mzungu* guide from California, Sean, whom I'd first met three years earlier during my summer visit to the Kern, had let himself in and was stretched out on the brown velvet couch. Our bedroom fans—which he'd dragged into the living room—were trained on him as he watched a pirated version of the movie *Damned River*.

"What're you guys doing back?" Sean quickly sat up.

"We had to evacuate Joe. He got heat exhaustion, probably heatstroke."

"How'd you manage that, genius?"

"It was my first seven-day, man. I was super stoked on videoing everything," Joe said. "I forgot to drink water."

Sean shook his head. He'd been in Zambia for nearly five months but had thrown out his back the first month rowing the Boiling Pot and hadn't been on the water since. He spent most days hanging around our house watching movies, unless the power was out, and then he played my guitar or ambled to town for soft-serve ice cream at Eat Rite.

I got Joe situated in bed before digging out the stash of powdered Gatorade from my closet. I took it out to the kitchen and mixed up some.

"You've been holding out," Sean said. "I'll take some of that."

"It's for Joe," I said, trying not to glare. "He's sick."

"It's his own fault," he said.

"Hey," I said, changing the subject, "have you seen Doreen?"

"No, and I haven't seen Gabriel either. In fact, Gabriel hasn't been here the whole time you guys were on the water. If I was the manager, I'd fire him." Sean had been guiding for over a decade; he'd led the crew on the prestigious Class V Forks of the Kern. He was quick to give advice on how to run things in Zambia. He'd also offered to help me get hired at his company after the Zambezi season. Since Steve and I couldn't exactly go back to Idaho to work with Danny, California seemed like a good plan.

"Gabriel went to see his family in the village," I said. "His brother's sick." I left out that I had given Gabriel the bus fare to go—one less thing for Sean to pass judgment on.

He snickered. "He just doesn't want to work. Really, these people are just lazy." He stretched out on the couch again, his long legs dangling over the wooden armrest.

I brought the Gatorade to Joe, and after he drained the cup, he slipped into a deep, steady sleep. It seemed he was out of danger now, but I still monitored him, vigilantly scanning for signs that his condition might be backsliding.

I wanted Sean to disappear, but he showed no sign of leaving. I searched the house for an already rolled joint to take the edge off. I had nothing stashed, not even a roach. I went back into the living room toting a garbage bag full of uncleaned, Smugglers Camp *dagga*. At my rolling station, I sifted clumps of seed-and-stem-choked weed through a screen I'd pulled off one of the house windows to separate the smokable leaves. After the twenty-four hours I'd had fighting for Joe's life while not dying myself, I deserved to relax.

"Are you really going to start getting high?" Sean asked. "It's not even noon."

I clamped my lips together and continued sifting.

"Steve's right, you smoke too much," Sean said.

I was about to tell him to mind his own business—California job be damned—when Doreen sprinted in the door, breathless.

"Bleedget." Her face was furrowed in fear, her energy unusually frantic. Something was wrong. Really wrong.

"Come," she said. "Bring . . . your things." She motioned to my room. She meant my first aid kit, or "magic," as the Zambians had started calling it after I'd cured Gilbert's cold with Benadryl last season.

"What's going on?" Sean wanted to know.

Doreen looked at the polished floor. She didn't speak to any of the *mzungu* men, not even Steve. It wasn't proper. Whenever I told Steve about all the fun Doreen and I had, he didn't believe me because Doreen never looked at or spoke to him. She usually hid in the laundry room when he was around.

I ran outside with Doreen toward the gate, thinking how weeks had gone by with nothing to do but learn sad love songs on the guitar and think of Danny, and now, suddenly, I had a career as a paramedic.

Our guard, Mr. Amos, emerged from the bushes pocketing his sling-shot, which he preferred to a pistol. Mr. Amos worked from dusk to mid-morning, and mysteriously swathed his head with a T-shirt while on duty. His accuracy with a slingshot was unnerving, as were his stealthy mannerisms.

"Hello, Mrs. Steve." He was hunched over, looking at the ground. I'd told him repeatedly to call me Bridget, but he insisted on Mrs. Steve.

"*Bwanji*, Mr. Amos," I said as he held open the gate for Doreen and me.

I followed Doreen from the manager's house in the direction of Nakatindi Village, where I assumed we were going until we cut down a small footpath I'd never noticed before, leading to the company guide house a half mile away.

"It's Regina," she told me as we sprinted from the trampled grass onto the red clay road in front of the house. "Her husband . . ." Doreen shook her head, unable to say the words.

I was perplexed, since Regina, who worked in the office with Steve, didn't live in the guide house. She was married to the muscled, smooth-talking Thomas, one of the senior Zambian guides. Regina and Thomas had a daughter, Kuyanda, which means "love" in Tonga, and they lived together outside of town near Nakatindi Village. It was Regina who'd wanted to stay near the village, not Thomas. He was the most westernized of all the company staff and was one of the most popular guides with the Western clients because of it. Like most of the Zambian guides, Thomas had a tribal name, Sianga, and a *mzungu* name. The other Zambians I knew kept their tribal names hidden from us *wazungu*, but not Thomas, who used both openly.

Thomas had recently picked up with a rich, leathery German woman— a client from a one-day whitewater trip. She'd moved into a hotel flat in Livingstone and outfitted Thomas with a new, high-dollar wardrobe, including a black bomber jacket that he wore despite the heat.

Doreen and I passed through the guide house gate. Angela, the guide house maid, was in the dusty yard, her toddler son behind her legs, sucking his fingers. Angela's infant daughter jutted out from her hip.

"You have come," Angela said, relieved.

Angela, a widow, lived with her children in the cement lean-to behind the guide house. The gray walls of her one-room shack were adorned with glossy pictures ripped out of my old Victoria's Secret catalogs and fashion magazines. Cutout White vixens in black and red lingerie peered out seductively at Regina, who was curled up knees to chest on a mattressless twin bed frame pushed against the wall. Her head rested on her knees as she sniffed delicately.

"Regina?"

When she looked up at me, I saw tears mixed with the blood spilling from her nose and cracked-open lips. There was a deep gouge above her right eyebrow. Although the skin around her eyes was bruised deep purple and her eyes were nearly swollen shut, her gaze clung to mine, then hardened into resignation.

She stayed motionless while I examined her. My father had rarely hit my face when he beat me, focusing his blows primarily at my core. I remembered seeing my mother's face bruised and cut when we lived with him. What had been done to Regina was the worst beating I'd ever seen, and I'd seen more than my share.

I touched Regina's arm gently, then went to work, wetting some gauze with peroxide. Doreen and Angela breathed steadily behind me. Angela's kids were outside playing in the dirt yard, distracted.

"I do not know what I could have been thinking about," said Regina, "speaking to him that way. About *her*." Jaw set, she exhaled heavily out of her nostrils as I dabbed her cuts with the gauze. "I saw them coming out of the Fairmount Hotel, and it was as if I went mad."

"Even Kuyanda, their child, saw them," added Angela, clucking her tongue.

"What did you say to them?" asked Doreen. Along with being incredibly shy, Doreen was terrified of marriage, which was why she was still single and childless at twenty-one, practically a spinster.

"I waited until he came home, and then I begged him to stop seeing that woman, to do it for our child's sake." Regina covered her mouth with her hand, holding back waves of grief before continuing. "Do you know what he told me? 'Stop interfering, it is none of your concern.' Then his eyes turned a deep black. It was as if he disappeared from himself. Something took over his body. There was nothing that could be done to stop him."

"How long has he been hitting you?" I asked.

"It has been getting worse these last weeks since he started seeing her. Before, I could manage, but now, you can see, it has become a burden. Everyone is seeing me this way, and I do not want my child to feel me being so weak."

Regina winced as I pressed her split eyebrow together and taped it shut with butterfly closures.

"Why don't you leave him?"

From the doorway, Angela let out a cynical laugh and looked down, toeing the floor. "We are not like you women. We cannot just leave when the man is behaving like this. It is against the law for us to divorce our husbands. He is the one who can divorce us for any reason he likes, but we ourselves have no way to leave."

"What do you mean, it's 'against the law'?"

"It is true," said Regina. "The only way I can leave Thomas is if he divorces me, and then I must return to my family, if they will allow it. It is a very shameful thing when you are divorced, and it is most likely that my family will not take me back."

"But you and Kuyanda can go back to the village and . . ." I started formulating a plan to rescue her.

"No, no. *I* go back to the village. Kuyanda goes with Thomas. Then his new wife or mistress, *she* raises Kuyanda." Regina's head reared back. "I would rather take a thousand beatings than see *her* raise my daughter."

"So what can you do?" I asked. I had applied triple antibiotic cream to all her wounds and sealed the deep cuts with butterflies and waterproof tape.

"I must learn to keep my feelings hidden." She had finished crying. "Do you understand what I am saying?"

"Yes." I slid my arm across her rounded shoulders. "I do." How many beatings had I endured to avoid returning to my mother's? How many times had I pretended my father hadn't hurt me because it was easier than the alternative?

Searching for the words in Nyanja, I whispered, *"Nifuna kufa chifukwa nimvela impepo meningi."* I feel like dying because I am too cold.

Regina nodded, and the three of us held on to her, trying to warm her cracked, frozen heart.

A couple of days later, on the night before Steve and the seven-day trip were scheduled to return, the highsiders decided to throw a company-wide party at the boathouse, adjacent to the main office, which was a block away from the guide house.

"Let's go," I said to Doreen.

"What if we see him?" She was scared of Thomas after witnessing up close what he'd done to his wife.

"What's he going to do at a party?" Like Doreen, I'd been avoiding the boathouse, but for a different reason—I was afraid my anger would be uncontrollable and I'd make things worse for Regina at home.

Doreen, Angela, and I decided to go to the party together for added safety, in case we ran into Thomas. We weren't sure if he knew that we had aided Regina and whether our interference would provoke him. Regina stayed home. She didn't want to play the happy couple with Thomas at the party, especially with her face torn up.

We arrived at the warehouse as the setting sun shifted the sky from blazing orange straight into blackness. No matter how many times I'd seen the sun go down in equatorial Africa, the severity between day and night still surprised me. The boathouse was lit from within, and exuberant *kwassa kwassa* music lifted from the boom box speaker, lending a festive feeling to the dusty yard. Strapped to the back of a passenger lorry was a blue plastic drum barrel filled with *chibuku*. All the *mzungus* who'd tried this grain alcohol had gotten a brutal case of the shits, so I steered clear despite wanting a taste. I opted instead for a Mosi Lager along with my sensible friends, Doreen and Angela. A quick glance around revealed that we were the only women at the party, which was not unusual: there were only four Zambian women who worked for the company, and I was the only *mzungu* woman that season, bringing the total number of women at the company to five in a staff of around fifty.

In Zambia, men dance with men and women with women, so the three of us staked out a corner of concrete under the open-air structure across from the others. Doreen and Angela laughed as I practiced my *kwassa* dance moves, shaking my hips while throwing my arms open as if presenting a platter, my awkwardness a frequent source of entertainment for them. Over their heads, I spied one of the American guides, Alan, the only other *mzungu* at the party. Alan was a teddy bear of a guy, with sweet Southern charm to spare. Friendly and polite, he was well-liked by everyone. He was also ridiculously strong, with a thick, muscular build. I waved. He smiled and tipped his beer in my direction.

Alan was dancing *kwassa* worse than me alongside a group of highsiders, who were circled around, taking turns jumping in the middle for solos. Angela said something in Nyanja. The only word I caught over the music was "Sianga," Thomas's tribal name. He was here.

It had been two days since I'd bandaged the wounds he'd left, and the image of Regina's arched eyebrow split open with her nose and lips buried in blood was seared in my mind. At first, all I could see across the dance floor was his black leather jacket and the back of his six-foot-two frame. He had his arms outstretched above his head and was waving them around triumphantly. Then he turned around, gripping something in one of his hands. It was a gun.

I made my way over to where Thomas was, pretending I was going to see Alan, in order to justify joining the men's group.

"Hey, Thomas," I said nonchalantly. "Can I see your piece?"

Thomas smiled, swaying drunkenly. "Sure." He proudly plopped the 9-millimeter pistol into my palm.

"Thanks." I gripped it firmly next to my thigh, pointing it at the floor, and slowly danced my way to the edge of the boathouse, careful not to bump into anyone. I spun around with the music and, as if it were part of a dance move, chucked the handgun as far as I could away from the building, into the mango trees. I then walked away from the party, along the darkened side of the boathouse. Thomas followed me, agitated.

"What are you doing?" he yelled.

"You can't bring a gun to a company party, Thomas."

"Give it back."

"Go find it."

Thomas stumbled closer to me. "You fucking bitch." We were away from everyone, out of view and earshot, our voices drowned out by the loud, happy thrum of *kwassa* music.

"What are you going to do? Hit me?" I leaned in, so he could feel my breath on his face, see me looking hard at him, straight in the eyes.

Nausea rose in my stomach. I smelled sweat beneath his jacket, sensed how badly Thomas wanted to seize me by my long hair and smash my face into the metal siding of the warehouse. His body quivered with the desire to crush me between his fists.

"Go ahead," I whispered. "Take a shot." We both knew that if Thomas touched me, a world of hurt would rain down on him. Ruinous hurt—he'd lose his job, go to jail, never work as a guide again.

His eyes opened wide, and he was on the balls of his feet, ready to slam me.

"Jesus, what's going on here?" Alan's Southern drawl cut through the blackness, startling both Thomas and me in our hyper-adrenaline state. I let out a yell as Thomas punched the metal siding next to my face.

"Hey, back off, man." Alan grabbed Thomas from behind, pulling him away from me. "What the hell?"

"She's a bitch," Thomas shouted.

"You can't talk about her like that," Alan said, still holding Thomas, then turned to me. "Are you okay? Did he hurt you?"

"Nah," I said, turning to leave. "He's too chickenshit to hurt me."

Alan let go of Thomas and walked next to me. "It's late. You can't walk home by yourself."

"The fuck I can't."

"What was that about with Thomas?"

"He had a gun at the party, so I took it."

"Are you sure it was a real gun?"

"I'm from Wyoming. I think I know what a real gun looks like."

"Where is it?"

"I threw it in the mango trees."

Alan looked me over carefully. "Are you drunk?"

"No, but Thomas was hammered."

"Jeez. I had no idea Thomas had a gun," Alan said. "Do you think he'd use it? Is he violent?"

"Have you seen Regina?"

"Thomas did that?"

"Fuckin' A," I said. "The last thing that wife beater needs is a gun."

"Christ."

"Thanks for walking me," I said, when we reached my house. I could hear the cicadas singing clearly through the night air.

"Forgive me for saying this, it's not really my place," Alan stammered, "but I think you should try to take it easy. You're pretty wound up." He meant in general.

"I know. I'm working on it," I said, touched by his concern. "Don't worry." I said good night, closing the front door gently to reassure him.

Joe was awake watching videos. "How was the party?"

"Shit show." I lit a joint, inhaled as much as I could take, and passed it to him.

When Steve returned from the river the next day, he came straight home from the warehouse before unpacking the trip. He'd heard from Dom at the take-out that Joe's evacuation had been successful, and that there'd been some trouble at the party.

"Are you okay?" Steve's tanned arms flexed as he wrapped me in a hug.

"Well," I joked, "I'm a little bitter about missing the end of the trip. You better schedule me on the next one."

Steve kissed me. His beard stubble felt rough against my face. "Let's go out just the two of us tonight," he suggested. "It'll be fun, like a date." It seemed I was officially off the hook for my digression with Danny. Whether this was due to my evacuating Joe successfully or my being threatened by Thomas, I wasn't sure. Either way, I'd take it—I was tired of doing penance and eager to feel close to Steve again.

Once the gear from the trip was unpacked, we got cleaned up, put on our nicest clothes, and loaded into his company Jeep. The pall that had hung over us for months lifted, and we cruised giddily down the main drag, the pungent smell of savanna and woodsmoke wafting through the cab.

Steve parked in front of the nicest place in town—a crumbling, mango-colored colonial building on the far edge of Livingstone.

"The Fairmount?" I asked.

"We're celebrating." Steve smiled as he locked the Jeep.

A waiter in a red suit and white gloves seated us immediately. The place was empty except for one table at the far end of the dining room. There, a lone woman was seated. It was Thomas's German mistress. She was clad in a low-cut blouse, her freckled décolletage bursting forth. Box-dyed blond hair hung around her face in scraggly clumps. She and Steve exchanged waves as I looked away, pretending not to see her.

"Be nice," Steve whispered.

Scowling, I gave her the tiniest nod. I told Steve how I'd tended Regina's wounds after returning with Joe, and about Thomas waving a gun around at the party.

"That's horrible," he said. "But it's not really our business, aside from the gun part. We shouldn't get too involved."

"Too late," I said. "It became my business the minute I got Regina's blood on my hands."

"We can't get too emotionally invested. We don't know the whole story."

I wanted to explain to Steve that every woman who has ever been hit by a man knows enough of the story to be compelled to intervene. But Steve, a strapping six-foot-tall former high school football player, would never know what it felt like to be overpowered and demeaned because of his sex, despite his well-intentioned attempt to imagine it.

We ordered, drinking sour, off-label wine while we waited. I excused myself to go to the ladies' room.

While I washed my hands, Thomas's mistress came into the powder room.

"I'm Hilga," she said, pointing to her bosom. "I think you work with my boyfriend, Thomas." She spoke tentatively, her thick German accent rolling around like phlegm in her throat.

"Yes," I said, forcing a smile. "I also work with his wife. Regina's a good friend of mine."

"Oh." She looked down at the chipped tile, her heavy-lidded eyes shaded by bangs.

"What are you doing here?" I asked her, gesturing to the walls of the hotel. The place reminded me of the dilapidated house in *Great Expectations*, with Hilga in the role of Miss Havisham.

"Having a holiday," she said. "A bit of fun."

"It's not all that fun for Regina," I said. "Thomas beat her to a pulp when she asked him to stop seeing you. It's not fun for their little girl watching her father beat the shit out of her mother. And frankly, it's not really fun for me to see my friend suffering the way she is."

"Oh," Hilga said softly, "I didn't realize."

"She can't leave him, you know. It's against the law. You and I are free to come and go, throw money around, wreck lives, then leave," I said. "But she's trapped. She doesn't even have rights to her own daughter." I held Hilga's gaze. "What did you think, you and Thomas were going to live happily ever after, raising Kuyanda together? What happens after you stop footing the bill? You think he's going to stick around?"

"I just thought," Hilga said, "I thought . . . I don't know what I thought. I guess I wasn't thinking about it at all. I was lonely."

"Honey, you deserve to be more than somebody's sugar mama."

Hilga cleared her throat. "Thank you." She pulled out a cigarette and lit it.

I left her in the powder room. Our food had arrived, and Steve and I picked at our rubbery, overpriced bream. We didn't see Hilga again.

A couple of days later, Doreen, Angela, and I were having tea in the garden of the manager's house.

"That woman Thomas was seeing," Doreen said. "She left."

"She moved from the Fairmount?" I asked.

"She is no longer in Livingstone," Angela said. "She has gone somewhere, perhaps back to Germany. Nobody knows. It is as if she vanished."

Twenty-Three

The Sound of the Tribe

The rainy season arrived weeks early, bearing more moisture than the savanna could hold. Ribbons of rainwater streamed across the red plateau, and a swollen Victoria Falls sent plumes of mist so high they seemed to touch the sagging clouds. I was told it wasn't like this in past seasons, when the days burned hot and cicadas overtook the afternoons until the pressure of building clouds gave way to a quick release; then the rain would beat down for an hour or two of earnest drumming before subsiding into clear, quiet twilight.

Now the days began and ended with relentless rain, and the Zambezi ran so high that Steve canceled all rafting trips. There would be no work until there was a break in the downpour. We waited, the sticky humidity clinging to us as raindrops clung to the mango and jacaranda bark outside.

Highsiders waited in line under the dripping eaves outside Steve's office to ask him for loans of kwacha and *nshima*. They counted on the daily wages they earned to support not only their wives and children but also their extended families in the village. The rain had become a heavy burden. Just how heavy, we had yet to realize.

Finally, patches of blue sky emerged, growing larger until the whole sky became unbroken cerulean. Still, the water level remained too high to run trips. I brought lunch to Steve at his office desk, since he didn't have a chance to break away from the line of petitioning highsiders. While I was there, an overland truck of university students on holiday turned up. They were determined to see the Class V Boiling Pot at its most treacherous water level and wanted to put a deposit down for a trip. Steve hesitated, not wanting to compromise safety for quick cash. As a manager, he was often ridiculed by the competing Zimbabwean companies for being over-conservative with the company's safety policies. By contrast, the two newly formed Zimbabwean companies, both managed by White Africans, ran no matter the conditions, flipping more often than they stayed upright.

"If you can't bloody accommodate us," said the driver who'd brought the vacationing students, "we'll go to the Zimbabwe side and sign on with a company there."

Jono, the head highsider, had been waiting in line outside Steve's office. He whistled to get Steve's attention, motioning for him to come outside, away from the driver.

"It's nearly runnable," Jono told him quietly. Throughout the rain, Jono had monitored the water level with the highsiders, who knew the river better than anyone. "It will be very high," Jono said, "but we can manage."

The next day dawned pale blue. Steve kissed my forehead, and I woke with a start. I'd dreamed of Nyaminyami slithering along the banks of the Boiling Pot. People ran from him as he thrashed at whatever was in his way. I hid behind a rock to escape, and as he passed me, I saw that it wasn't malice that drove him. He'd been wounded and was in unbearable pain.

"Be careful," I said to Steve as he departed to launch the trip. I snuggled into the warm spot left by his body and flopped his pillow over my head to muffle the roosters outside.

An hour after Steve left, the phone rang. I answered it, groggy and disoriented. It was Regina calling from the office. "Something happened at the put-in," she said. "Someone is badly hurt."

I sat up straight under the sheet. My heartbeat pounded at the top of my skull. "Is it Steve?"

"They wouldn't say. Dom is coming to collect you," Regina said.

I threw on clothes, then waited outside by the gate.

Dominic couldn't provide me with any answers when I got into the truck cab. Instead, he handed me a greasy bag of samosas. I felt too sick from anxiety to eat anything, but I accepted the gift, not wanting to be rude.

"You're always feeding me during disasters," I said, remembering the bag of chicken he'd brought during Joe's rescue.

"You need more meat on you. Like Zambian women."

I laughed weakly and picked at the food during the twenty-minute drive.

When we pulled up at the Boiling Pot trailhead, we found a crowd of highsiders standing idly, a couple of them smoking hand-rolled cigarettes. No one working a river trip stood around at the put-in—ever. It was always a race to get the gear ready before the clients arrived. *Shit, this is bad*, I thought. I jumped out of the truck, intent on running toward the river, but Dom caught my wrist.

"We must wait here," he said. "Keep the trail free." I stood on the muddy ground with Dom near the tailgate of the truck. I regretted not telling Steve about my dream or trying more earnestly to warn him. In the past, he'd laughed whenever I mentioned premonitions I'd had or the river talking to me. I'd developed a habit of hiding my intuition from him.

A line of highsiders came into view, climbing steadily up the trail without their usual singing harmonies. They shouldered a body wrapped in a blue tarp laced together with white webbing.

I clutched Dom's arm, feeling like I was falling backward into a tunnel. Everyone began shouting so quickly in Nyanja; I couldn't understand what they were saying. The highsiders set the body down on the flatbed as the crowd pressed closer. Dazed, I turned my face away from the group and saw Steve walking up the trail alone.

I'd never noticed before that moment how deep the purple bags under his eyes were, and he was squinting as if he had a migraine. I was so relieved to see him, I nearly collapsed. He looked up, and as his eyes fell on me, a hint of relief flickered over his ashen face. He motioned for me to meet him away from the crowd.

"It's Gilbert," he said in a flat voice that didn't sound like his. Gilbert was the highsider who'd saved me from being attacked by baboons my first trip down the Boiling Pot trail. He was the sweet, gap-toothed young man who'd told everyone I was a witch when I cured his cold with Benadryl. "A huge rock came loose and smashed him."

"You saw it?"

Steve rubbed his forehead, as if trying to wipe it clean. "Not the accident, but I saw him after, when I pulled his body from the river."

Steve had seen too many dead friends for one lifetime. During his accident in the Tetons, he'd watched his best friend succumb to hypothermia and fall to his death. He had left his other friend behind in the snow in order to survive. Worse than losing his two friends was shouldering the burden of not having been able to save them. Steve had been twenty-four at the time, two years older than I was now.

All that work trying to escape the demons that had followed him from a snow-covered mountaintop in Wyoming eight years earlier, and still, the thing he'd tried to bury was right here in the African clay, wrapped in a tarp in the back of the flatbed.

"How am I supposed to deal with this?" he asked.

I held his face between my hands. "We're together in this. You're not alone."

"What am I going to tell them?" Steve motioned to the crew of highsiders, who had their eyes on him, looking for direction. As they stood around the truck, some—like Jono—wiped tears, but most stood silently, the grief not yet surfacing through the shock.

"The trip's fucking canceled, for starters," I said. "We'll figure out the rest of it together."

"We don't know what to do with a dead body in Zambia," Steve said.

Does anybody know what to do with a dead body anywhere?

I nodded toward the highsiders. "They do."

The rock that killed Gilbert was the size of a Volkswagen bus. As the highsiders had bustled over the basalt shelf, joking and singing, part of the canyon wall had shed itself, loosened by the rains. Those who were at the put-in said there was a loud crack overhead, like thunder, and they'd looked up to see a giant rock plummeting toward the rafts. Everyone ran for the forest or downstream, whichever direction they could go. Everyone except for Gilbert, whose foot was caught in the raft he was rigging. Realizing there was no escape, Gilbert stopped struggling and looked up just before the rock landed squarely on him.

Gilbert had belonged to the Lozi tribe. Highsiders Andrew and Kennedy, who were also Lozi, helped us take his body to a white building with green trim, a building I'd always wondered about. It turned out to be the morgue. We left Gilbert there, promising the man behind the desk we'd return with Gilbert's kin. Andrew and Kennedy drove with Steve and me to the village to translate the bad news to Gilbert's family. I couldn't get the image of Gilbert looking up out of my mind. What had he been thinking in those final seconds?

We traveled several hours northwest of Livingstone, then turned off the main highway onto the dirt spur leading to Gilbert's village, Maunga, the place of the thorn (acacia) trees. The worn tires of our rig struggled against the layers of wet clay. We drove around a wide bend and saw a lanky woman in a pink *chitenge* with a sleeping infant tied to her back. She stood in front of her thatched home, pounding groundnuts for the evening meal with a long, heavy pestle.

Who was she to Gilbert? I wondered as we drove past.

The highsiders had insisted on riding in the bed of the truck rather than in the cab. They gave a quick *tap, tap, tap* on the window separating us, indicating that we'd arrived at Gilbert's house. I turned to Steve. His blue eyes were several shades lighter than usual, washed out by grief. I pushed on the cab door, swung my legs around, and stood in the yard of Gilbert's family home. Steve opened his door but couldn't get out.

In front of the house, a muscled, gray-haired man sang to himself as he raked the yard in front of his rondavel. A smile filled in the lines of his worn face. As he raked, the hem of his navy trousers dragged in the dirt.

Andrew and Kennedy approached him very slowly while crouched low in a posture of respect. Although they didn't speak, the man understood why they had come. His face twisted in pain, and he crumpled at the knees. In unison, Andrew and Kennedy caught him on either side, holding him up by the armpits, so that Gilbert's father never hit the ground.

The man let out a high-pitched yowl that sounded like a trapped mountain lion. His weightless legs kicked back and forth through the air. Kennedy and Andrew held Gilbert's father up, absorbing his thrashing with their bodies. Andrew spoke in a low, smooth voice, saying something in Lozi that sounded like a lullaby.

I stood awkwardly on the edge of the yard, wishing I'd stayed in the truck with Steve.

Gilbert's father quieted for a moment. As his eyes came into focus, he looked at me. I didn't know how to say "I'm sorry" in Lozi or Nyanja, so I tried to say it with my body. I walked toward him with my left hand to my elbow and right arm out as Gilbert had the first time we'd met two years earlier at Songwe camp. I hunched my body forward to show respect, bending at the waist until my head was lowered.

The man lunged at me. Spit streamed from his mouth as he hurled rage-filled words. I jumped sideways, out of range of his kicking feet. Andrew and Kennedy gripped him tighter. They clicked their tongues, trying to soothe him. Gilbert's father's eyes rolled back into his head, in the same wild-horse way my own father's did when his anger overtook him.

"What's he saying?" I asked.

The highsiders hesitated before Andrew said, "He believes that you are the one who killed his son. He thinks that you and the *bwana* have beaten him to death."

I looked at Andrew, stunned.

"Sometimes *mzungus* beat their staff when they are unhappy with the work. People die from the beatings," Andrew said.

I searched Gilbert's father's eyes. I wanted to make him understand that I was mourning his son too. But the man couldn't see beyond the intensity of his pain.

I backed away and shuffled over to Steve, who was still hunkered in the driver's seat, pale and clammy. I held his weathered hand. It was hard to tell if he'd heard Andrew's translation. He sat with his head back and eyes closed, as if trying to disappear.

Andrew and Kennedy convinced Gilbert's father to get into the back of the truck so we could take him to retrieve his son. We made the trip to the morgue in silence. Steve and I waited on orange plastic chairs in the reception area. The smell of antiseptic was so strong it stung my eyes. Lurking just underneath was the scent of death, wafting on waves of heat. Andrew and Kennedy took the father in to see Gilbert's corpse. When they came out, the old man was wailing, his body once again collapsed into their arms.

They asked us to take them to Gilbert's aunt's house on the other side of Livingstone, then hopped onto the truck bed. We drove along the dirt road past shanty-like homes, and it was dusk when we turned into the aunt's neighborhood. We were going so slowly I could hear the tires cracking over gravel pebbles beneath us. The moon rose full and yellow overhead.

In the distance, we could hear a low whooshing that sounded like a strong wind scouring through a canyon. As we got closer to the sound, it took on the discordant tone of howling wolves. We crept closer to the heart of it—it was like nothing I'd heard before, an eerie bellowing, the sound *li, li, li, li, li* shouted in every tone. Our truck was quickly surrounded by scores of people, so many that Steve put the truck in park and lifted his hands off the wheel. It wasn't until the tearstained faces of Angela and Doreen appeared outside my window that I understood: it was the sound of the tribe mourning.

The three Lozi men in the back slipped off the bed and were absorbed into the throbbing crowd. The vibration of the group had a pulsing hum to it, like bees clustered around a hive. Angela pressed her hand to my window, and I wept as our eyes connected. In a drumbeat, she was gone, moving with the wailing procession down the dirt path. Her handprint remained on the glass, glinting in the moonlight.

A week after Gilbert's death, we were invited to attend his burial. After seeing the smashed raft and frame, Gilbert's father understood that Steve and I had not killed his son. There was no apology for the accusation, nor did we expect one. We threw ourselves into helping with the funeral. Two flatbeds were hired to transport the mourners to the cemetery.

Stan came down from Lusaka for the event. As was customary, he and Steve would bring bags of *nshima* to give the family after the funeral, on behalf of the company. Unfortunately, there was a severe cornmeal short-age in Zambia, and the shops only had coarse yellow cornmeal that people typically fed their dogs. It would be insulting to give Gilbert's family such low-quality *nshima*. Stan and Steve planned to buy finely milled white cornmeal across the border in Zimbabwe and meet us an hour later at the Zambian cemetery in time for the ceremony.

When it was time for the mourners to load into the flatbed trucks, I fell in line, gingerly holding my drab-colored skirt as I stepped onto the rig. The lone *mzungu*, I stood pressed together with Gilbert's kinfolk, who were adorned in brightly colored *chitenge* dresses and head wraps. As we drove through town, everyone sang together, clapping intricate rhythms to keep the beat, their voices cheerful and celebratory. It was as if we were holding a parade in Gilbert's honor, carrying his spirit along the highway to his resting place.

The cemetery was dappled with patches of red and white plastic flowers, the only objects marking the tightly spaced graves. We exited the truck and gathered around Gilbert's wooden casket. Angela and Doreen stood on either side of me, each holding one of my hands. I was brought to tears by the harmonized singing as the casket was lowered into the ground and wished Steve was there with me. I scanned the road, wondering why it was taking so long for him and Stan to arrive with the *nshima*.

One by one, the family and the Lozi highsiders walked forward to scoop a handful of earth and throw it onto the casket. Gilbert's brother was unable to let go of the dirt and clutched it to his chest. He fell onto his knees, sobbing next to the grave of his baby brother. He was gently lifted up and carried back into the fold of the tribe.

Men from the group were called up to speak. Angela whispered the translations for me. Several people said it was the father's fault that Gilbert had died. One of the mother's brothers claimed that someone had put a curse on his family because Gilbert's father had too many women and illegitimate children. People nodded in agreement.

In the middle of the speeches, someone called for a *mzungu* man to speak. They wanted someone from the company to eulogize Gilbert. Some men started yelling angrily over the casket, saying things that Angela wouldn't translate. Angela and Doreen both clicked their tongues loudly. Some of the Zambian guides and highsiders began tsking also.

"What are they saying?" I asked.

"They are saying bad things about *mzungus*, things that are not true," Doreen said. "They say it is disgraceful that no one from company management is here to speak. There is no respect for Gilbert, his family, or the tribe."

Angry calls of "*Mzungu!*" rose from the group.

"Where is Mr. Steve?" an elderly man asked me pointedly in English.

"He's coming *manje manje*," I said. I spun my Nyaminyami necklace anxiously around my neck.

The shouts for *mzungu* grew in intensity.

"Should I say something?" I asked Doreen.

"Women are not allowed to speak. This will only show greater disrespect."

Everyone at the funeral was now staring at me, while the demands of "*Mzungu!*" persisted. I was relieved when Stan and Steve finally drove up in Stan's car. The crowd turned from me to watch the two men approach the open grave, and Stan, the big *bwana*, was ushered to the front of the group. That Stan didn't know Gilbert didn't matter. Stan understood his role—he spoke at length about the loss the company would feel without Gilbert, how essential he'd been to the operation. His speech was translated into Lozi.

After the ceremony and speeches, shovelfuls of earth were moved to fill in the grave. Gilbert's was the first funeral I'd ever been to, and I was not prepared for the feeling of finality that smothered me as they sealed him in the ground. Steve remained on the periphery of the group, standing behind the Zambian guides on the other side of the grave. I stood with Doreen and Angela, crying, until the mourners thinned and we unclenched our fingers from one another. Doreen and Angela climbed back into the crowded flatbed with the tribe, and I walked over to the air-conditioned white hatchback with Steve and Stan.

Gilbert's father was the last to leave. Incapable of moving on his own, he was guided, wailing, away from his son's grave by tribesmen. Seeing these bonds of kinship made me long for my own father, even though I'd been estranged from him for five years. Would I be mourned so deeply?

After Stan dropped us off, Steve and I sat on our couch with no idea what to do next. I rolled a joint and we smoked it. Steve put on a Rickie Lee Jones album, and I drew a bath, lighting candles all around the tub. We left our funeral clothes in a heap on the bathroom floor and climbed into the warm water together.

Steve tenderly ran his hands over my skin as he soaped my back. It had been so long since we'd shared intimacy like this.

He stopped rubbing my back and asked, "Why do you think he died?"

Not wanting to lose the connection between us, I picked up a washcloth and squeezed water over his feet, gently caressing the scars where his toes used to be. "Who knows why things happen?" I asked. "If it weren't for your climbing accident, you'd be guiding mountains instead of rivers. We wouldn't be here in Zambia, or running whitewater." I turned to look at him. "We probably wouldn't be together."

Steve stood up so quickly, it startled me. "Gilbert would still be alive if it wasn't for us running trips here." He stepped out of the tub and reached for a towel. "He risked his life for what? So *mzungus* on holiday could have an adventure? We paid his family for their loss with fucking *corn flour*." Steve broke down then, clutching the towel as water pooled around his feet. It was the first time I'd seen him cry since Gilbert died.

I got out of the tub and held him as he buried his face in my shoulder.

"His father was right," Steve whispered. "We killed him."

I wrapped a towel around us. "It was an accident. Just like on the Grand."

"It's not fair."

I kissed him and smoothed the hair back from his forehead. Together, we'd been running rivers for three and a half years, two of them in a foreign country. I'd gone as far away from my family as I could get, looking for a safe place where I belonged, and all I'd managed to do was put myself in more danger.

Witnessing Gilbert's father had conjured my own father with such force that I couldn't stop thinking about him. My justification for leaving home was that I'd been mistreated. But the fear that kept me running was that I'd been mistreated because I wasn't lovable.

What if I'd been wrong? What if my father loved me so much, it brought him to his knees?

"It's time to go home," I said.

"Where's that?" Steve asked.

I had to find out if my father loved me in the way that Gilbert's father had loved his child. Otherwise, no matter where I was, or whom I was with, I'd always be an outsider on the run.

"California," I said.

Twenty-Four

If You Are Ugly, Know
How to Dance

We returned to the Kern River, the place where I'd made the decision to become a guide four years earlier. I felt nostalgic as we drove into the valley alongside the river, stealing glimpses of the boulder-choked whitewater and orange poppies covering the hillsides. Perhaps being only three hours from Ventura—where I was born and my father still lived—made it feel more like a homecoming. Along with Steve, I had been hired to work for the same premier whitewater company in California where he'd worked previously. At long last, we were being paid to work the same river together. The assembled crew that season had as many women as men. There was a sense of balance, something unfamiliar to me.

The season was barely underway when we returned from a two-day trip to a message waiting for Steve: his replacement on the Zambezi had quit and they wanted him back. Steve called the company's main office for more details. Afterward, we walked toward the wetland behind the guide house to talk about the offer.

"They'll pay me double my salary. You could come with me," Steve said.

"I thought we'd decided to work on a river that's *my* skill level."

"They offered me the Bío-Bío in Chile if I do it," he said. "A dream river."

"Sure, if you're a Class V guide." I was enjoying guiding Class IV. I'd gone straight from Class III on the Snake to getting my ass kicked on the Zambezi. I'd picked up some skills in Idaho, but there were gaps in my training. Working the Kern was where I needed to be to hone my confidence.

"This is our chance to break into the international scene." He faced me, eyes shining as he imagined the world-class rapids of central Chile. Over his shoulder, I saw a snowy egret lift from the marsh, its large body lurching as it began to take flight.

"Go ahead," I said. "I'm staying here."

After Steve returned to Zambia, I continued to think of Gilbert's father, until one day I picked up the phone and called my own father. He had no idea I was in California, or that I was a river guide.

"Joe's Bar," he said. Some things never changed.

"Hi, Dad." It was the first time we'd spoken in six years.

"As I live and breathe. My favorite daughter."

"Your only daughter."

"Still my favorite."

"Do you have plans for Father's Day? I was wondering if you, Shiray, and Garrett want to come rafting with me on the Kern River for the weekend."

"I don't have any plans, but if I did, I'd cancel them to be with you."

His answer gave me pause. I'd expected him to be angry with me for going missing for over half a decade.

"I can bring you on the river for free as my guests," I said. "But you might get bumped if the trip fills up." I was worried he'd change his mind if he had to pay. Although my dad was wealthy, he often balked at spending money on experiences. He preferred acquiring things.

"I don't think Shiray will want to come, and I'll pay full price for Garrett and me. I don't want to miss the chance to see you."

On the morning of the trip, I was overcome with anxiety and sat immobilized on the living room floor of the guide house, crying.

"What the fuck, Crocker?" Grant, our trip leader, was ten years older than I was and one of the first guides to raft the rivers in California. He had trained legions of guides all over the world, including on the Zambezi.

I didn't move from the floor.

Grant called out to Ashley, his girlfriend, who floated in as if on a runway. Years before, she'd abandoned a New York modeling career to shack up with Grant in the desert and guide the Kern.

"She's lost it," Grant said, pointing at me.

Ashley sat down on the carpet, followed by Rachel, a super-toned blonde with pouty lips who smelled like coconut oil. They each took one of my hands and held them.

"My dad's coming," I said. "I haven't seen him since I ran away at seventeen."

"Why not?" asked Ashley.

"He beat the shit out of me."

"Do you want him to ride in someone else's boat?" Grant asked. "Or I could bump him from the trip?"

"I thought I could handle this."

Lee, a "weekend warrior" who drove up from Hollywood on Friday nights to guide, came in to find us all on the shag carpet. "Am I packing this trip myself? 'Cause, honey, I cannot lift those rafts on my own." He fluffed his crimson hair into a perfect coif and inspected his manicure.

"Bridget's dad's coming. They're estranged. He used to beat her," Ashley recapped.

Lee, a well-bred Southerner, lifted his carriage slightly, assuming a regal air. "Girl," he said, looking at me, "you are courageous and luscious and strong. Hold your head up like the queen you are." He lengthened his neck and jutted out his chin, as if balancing a tiara on his head. "Everyone can see that you're a river goddess. If your father doesn't see that, well, we will drown that motherfucker in the river."

Rachel and Ashley lifted me under the armpits until I stood to my full height. I felt bolstered by Lee's use of the word "we."

By the time we arrived at the put-in, I'd managed to pull it together. I hid my puffy eyes behind dark glasses and scanned the passengers coming off the bus for my father and brother. When they appeared, I was struck by how much older my father looked. His blond hair still shone in the sun, but his skin was weathered, and he looked smaller. Garrett, whom I remembered as a kindergartner, was on the verge of puberty, tall, with thick blond hair and the same heavy Crocker brow my father and I have.

I waved as Grant herded the two of them under a sycamore tree with the other twenty-three clients for a safety talk. Dad gave me a thumbs-up, while Garrett flashed a half wave, carefully maintaining his cool middle-school demeanor.

"Is that your brother?" Lee said to me as we stood onshore by the boats. "He's fine."

I swatted Lee's arm. "He's *twelve.*"

I felt sick with anxiety. What was I thinking, bringing my father into the river world? Hadn't I learned my lesson with Mom in Hells Canyon? What if Dad made a scene with Lee like he had with Jai back in high school? The possibilities of all that could go wrong filled my head, until I feared I might actually puke.

"Stay strong, queen," Lee said, moving in front of me to divert the spotlight. He fixed a brilliant smile on his face and lifted his palms, as if stepping onstage to receive applause. If anyone understood overcoming obstacles, it was Lee. He was the first openly gay man I'd ever seen on the river, and the only one I knew who worked as a guide. Despite the homophobic comments and looks he endured, he remained centered in his own empowerment. I drew strength from his example. Lee was changing river culture history, and it gave me hope that I might be able to transform the culture in my own family.

After Grant's safety talk, the group was split into five paddleboats, with five or six paddlers per raft. My father and Garrett walked toward me along with three young professional women from LA. My dad winked at me, then reached to shake my hand, introducing himself as if we'd never met.

My father loved practical jokes. His favorite holiday was April Fools' Day. He put ads in the local paper for garage sales at his friends' addresses—early birds welcome!—to spice up the weekend. He also carried stickers with him that looked like bullet holes and put them on colleagues' cars when they went to lunch. "Holy shit, Ron," he'd say when they left the restaurant, "someone shot up your car." From the gleam in his eye, I could tell that Dad had something up his sleeve, so I played along. Being in on the joke instantly cut through my anxiety. Garrett mumbled a quick hi. Unlike my father, he was shy, and I could feel him quietly studying me. I wondered what he remembered. Did he know why I'd left?

After introductions, we pushed off and practiced paddle commands, with the three women paddling the bow and Dad and Garrett closer to me in the stern. We got underway, and I switched into my role as a guide, pointing out pictographs made by the Tübatulabal tribe along the river. "The Tübatulabal believe there are many worlds, some that have passed and some that are to come," I said. "In one world, the people all creep; in another, they fly. In another, they all swim like fish, or crawl like snakes. The people transform from world to world." I wondered if my father and I were capable of becoming different creatures in a new world.

"Have you been guiding long?" asked Megan, one of the women from LA.

"A few years. I just got back from working in Zambia."

My father looked at me, dumbfounded. "Really?"

"That's so cool," Garrett said. "Did you get attacked by any crocodiles?"

"No, but I got nailed by a scorpion and plenty of mosquitos. I got malaria."

We drifted around a bend in silence. Sandstone walls surrounded us. I loved this time of day, when the high desert sun reflected off flecks of quartz and iron pyrite, turning the canyon into a glittering oasis.

"I don't know about you," my father said, turning to Megan, breaking the easy silence, "but I'm a little nervous going down with a woman guide."

All three of the women paddlers whipped their heads around to stare at him.

"Not that I have anything against women," he said.

I had long believed that my father did have something against women. My father had never laid a hand on me until I started having my period, and every one of the beatings I'd received was provoked by my body's transition into womanhood, coupled with my likeness to my mother. I hoped that Garrett had been spared the physical abuse I'd endured because of his sex. All morning I'd been scanning his body, looking for marks. There was nothing.

My father had intended his comment to be unsettling; stirring the pot was his brand of humor. The women all turned to me. They wanted to know how I planned to deal with a sexist guest. Did they need to step in to defend me? I gave them a sly smile, assuring them that this was not my first rodeo. Managing sexist assholes was a regular part of my job. That this one happened to also be my estranged, practical jokester father changed the game for me a little. I delayed a takedown, weighing the risk-benefit ratio longer than I usually did.

"We're coming up to our first little rapid," I said. "Forward."

The crew worked together, paddling to avoid a large rock on the left. My father made a big show of diving onto the floor of the raft, where he remained until the bottom of the rapid.

"Are we through it?" he asked, feigning panic.

"No thanks to you," I said. "You can't hit the floor every time there's a little riffle."

Garrett laughed, enjoying seeing someone give our father shit.

While the women shook their heads, my father caught my eye and winked at me. Unlike the countless passengers I'd had who were truly terrified of whitewater (and women in charge), my father was having a grand time pretending to be a pain in the ass.

Lee's boat came up next to us then. "I hope you realize you have a river goddess as your guide. We all call her the Guidess." Lee's eyes were trained on my father as he paddled away.

"He sure is colorful," Dad said.

The women exchanged looks. *Who is this guy?*

"You're pushing it," I said.

Early in the afternoon, we stopped at Lower Camp, and I led the swim that had transformed me into a river guide years before. Garrett, a burgeoning surfer, couldn't get enough. As we floated next to each other about to take the drop, he looked over, face wide open with glee. "This is the funnest thing ever."

I laughed. I'd said the exact same thing the first time I'd done it. Garrett and I swam through the Class II rapid over and over, lapping it like it was a waterslide. We kept at it long after everyone else had gone up to change and set up their tents. Only Dad remained, watching us from shore as he sat on a rock near the rafts.

"My two water kids," he said to us when we finally got out.

Garrett walked toward camp to get changed. I took off my PFD and stashed it in my boat. Even though I wore a modest one-piece swimsuit with shorts over it, I wrapped a Zambian *chitenge* cloth around me like a towel to hide my body, remembering a beating my dad had once given me for wearing a bikini to a pool party. I then checked all five boats' bowlines, shoring them up for the evening. As I worked, my father stood awkwardly near me.

"There's something I want to say."

I turned to face him.

"I fucked up," he said. "I mistreated you."

I pulled the *chitenge* tighter around my shoulders. "Yes," I said. "You did."

"It was so hard for me to accept that you were growing up," he said. "I missed so much of your childhood."

"That wasn't my fault."

"I'm not trying to make excuses here, I just want to be honest." He shuffled nervously from one foot to the other. "I had no idea what to do with a young woman."

"Obviously."

"I've been working on getting ahold of my anger since you left. Going to counseling twice a week, taking anger-management classes. All I want is to be a better dad." He looked me in the eye. "I'm so sorry. I want to be the dad you deserve."

I hadn't expected him to apologize, and I certainly hadn't expected him to take responsibility for what he'd done.

"Nobody wants their kid to suffer the way you did," he said, tearing up. "Your mother and I put you through so much. No parent wants to admit they failed. But I want to put this right." He wiped his tears with the back of his hand. "Losing you was the most painful thing I've ever experienced. Please give me another chance." He broke into sobs that emanated from his core.

I thought of Gilbert's father, how he'd do anything to have his boy back again. Here was my own father before me, propelled by his suffering to become a better man. But it was scary to consider letting down my guard. I was afraid I'd be hurt again, maybe worse this time. I looked at the river, noticing how the main current piled onto rocks and strainers before finding ways around them. The river was a master of reinvention, capable of adapting to overcome any obstacle. I bent down, put my hand in the water, and prayed for the courage to change course.

I turned back to my father. "Thank you for apologizing. I'm willing to try again."

His head lifted. "I've got another shot?"

"Don't fuck it up."

My entire body was zinging with hopeful surrender, which was exactly the way I felt before dropping over the horizon line into a Class V rapid.

The next morning, we loaded into the boats and made our way to the first Class IV rapid of the trip, White Maiden's Walkway. Unbelievably, the rest of our group hadn't yet caught on that my dad, Garrett, and I were related, so our charade continued, although I wasn't sure why we were still at it. When we reached White Maiden's, the passengers waited with the boats while the guides walked downstream to scout the rapid. The water was at a tricky level, and the razor-sharp rocks at the bottom stood out like a goalpost.

I felt the prickly buzzing of adrenaline entering my bloodstream, spreading through my arms and legs. I was learning to distinguish the difference between fear and excitement, since they often felt the same in my body. I reminded myself that adrenaline was a tool that helped me do extraordinary things. When faced with dangerous situations in the past, I had mostly responded by fleeing. I had learned from running rivers to use the tool of adrenaline to fight instead.

I stood next to Grant as we surveyed the rapid. The entrance was a mess of rocks to pick through before lining up to shoot through the goalpost rocks. Directly below sat a giant house-sized rock that funneled most of the current right, into a fierce recirculating eddy known as the Room of Doom. At this medium water level, boats flipped on the undercut wall there, pushing swimmers down to where they could easily become entrapped and potentially die.

"Got your line?" Grant asked me.

"Hey diddle diddle," I said. *Right down the middle.*

"Until the goalpost. Then you have to push hard to go left of the house rock. The Room of Doom is a no go at this level. It's a death chamber in there." Grant looked me square in the eye to make sure I understood.

I put on my best Valley girl accent. "So, like, is there a DJ in the Room of Doom?" I grinned at him and we both burst out laughing. Usually when Grant and I worked together, we spent most of the time giggling like teenage girls.

"Why are you guys laughing? White Maiden's makes me wanna puke," Rachel said.

"Seriously," agreed Ashley. "I can't look anymore."

We headed back toward the boats and passengers, hopping across boulders and dodging poison oak. As we neared the rafts, I paused to study the entrance at river level, something I'd learned from Steve. It was easy to get disoriented running the rapid when you'd only seen it from a high vantage point. Nailing the entrance was the most important move, and if you didn't recognize anything, you could quickly get lost and blow the line.

As I studied the current flowing into the rapid, a yellow swallowtail butterfly swished across my forearm, then flew over the rapid, dipping low over the left side of the funneling tongue at the entrance. If I angled the boat toward the left side of the current, where the butterfly was, it would set me up to sail between the goalpost rocks.

We untied the boats and paddled out of the eddy, Grant taking the lead.

"Let's dip our hands in the water and ask the Kern for safe passage," I said to my paddlers.

"Is that some kind of African voodoo?" asked my father.

"Can you hear that? The sound of the river?"

"Yeah. So?"

"The river can hear you too."

Everyone touched the water except for Dad.

"All forward," I called out.

I recognized the fold of current the yellow swallowtail had pointed out and eased the boat next to it. We dropped into the rapid and became engulfed in the roar of water all around us. I kept my focus on the current and used my paddle as a rudder to hold the line. We slipped effortlessly between the goalpost rocks, but as we dropped down between them, we hit bottom hard enough to knock everyone to the floor. As the soaked paddlers scrambled to recover from the hit, we were thrust hard to the right, toward the Room of Doom. I considered calling a turn to get to the left of the house rock, but it was too late. The current had decided for us: right.

"Back-paddle," I hollered. The group vigorously cranked on their paddles to keep us off the wall. I hoped that we could hug the house rock and
squeak past the undercut wall, but every single molecule of water was
pushing us into the Room of Doom. My mind made the shift from *This
can't happen* to *This is happening*.

"Highside, highside, highside!" I shouted. I grabbed Garrett and pulled
him high up on the left tube as our raft hit the rock wall sideways. The rest
of the crew followed us, moving their weight toward the rock to prevent
the upstream tube from getting pushed down by the current.

"Grab the perimeter line. Don't let go of the boat. Don't swim," I
yelled. Swimming here would mean getting dragged through the undercut caves, possibly never coming out.

We sat perched along the outside tube of the raft as it fluttered in the current. Every moment, the tube crept farther up, threatening to flip. I scanned
the left shore to see if the other boats were mounting a rescue or giving me
signals. They were too far away, with the house rock looming between us.
All they could do was watch. No one was coming to save us. It was up to me.

Every obstacle in the river has a shadow, a place of respite that's shielded
from the flow. Behind the house rock was a calm eddy in the exact shape
and size of the rock. If we could get there, we'd be safe. I wedged my feet
all the way under the boat's back thwart and leaned off the stern. I could
almost reach the eddy behind the rock. I extended my arms as far as they
could stretch, and with my elbows locked, I thrust paddle strokes toward
the eddy. I did it over and over until sweat dripped into my eyes and my
breath came out in splinters.

"We're movin'," Dad called to me after several minutes of clawing for
the eddy.

I dug deeper, my eyes fixed and jaw set. As I paddled, my mind shifted
into a gear that existed beyond pain, a place I knew well, as did my father,
mother, their parents, all the way down the line. Over the years, I had
spent a lot of time ruminating about what my family had not given me,
overlooking what I'd inherited as my birthright: the ability to transform
suffering, rise up, and survive.

I summoned a fury to match Nyaminyami's. There was a release, like a pop, and the boat came free of the rock wall. I continued grabbing with my paddle at the eye of the eddy—the place in the center that's closest to the rock—until I'd pulled the boat all the way out of the Room of Doom.

I looked over at my father, my breath still ragged.

"I guess we didn't mean to go there," he said.

"That was pretty ugly." I unclipped my water bottle and took a long swig. "As they say in Zambia, 'If you are ugly, know how to dance.'"

Megan pointed at my dad. "It's because you didn't listen to her," she said. "You didn't ask the river for safe passage."

My father opened his mouth to say something, then closed it again.

We ran Sundown Falls, Deadman's Curve, and Preparation H rapids, making it without incident to the Royal Flush, a Class VI portage.

"Can we run it?" Garrett asked me.

"Hell no."

"C'mon. You could pull it." After White Maiden's, my little brother seemed to think I could get us through anything.

"It's Class VI—meaning unrunnable. You should talk to my friend Grant. His buddy ran it in a kayak and got stuck underneath that undercut wall on the left, see it?" I pointed to the scoured sandstone overhang. "His kayak was fully submerged, and he couldn't move. The only thing that wasn't underwater was one of the guy's hands poking out from under the ledge. A guide took his throw bag and threw it across the river. It landed right in the guy's hand, and they were able to pull him out."

"Good thing he caught it," Garrett said.

I put my arm around his shoulder, which was nearly as tall as my own. "He got lucky."

We ate lunch below the portage. While I was cutting up a pineapple, Grant came over and gripped one of my biceps, then the other. "I can't figure out how you got out of the Room of Doom. You must have superpowers in these arms."

"Her arms are so long." Rachel pantomimed powerful paddling strokes. "*Voom, voom, voom.*"

"Bridget's superpower is that she's relentless," said Lee.

They all looked at me, smiling. I placed my hand over my chest, absorbing their love.

⁓

After lunch, we still had five Class IV rapids to go. In between Hari Kari and Horseshoe Falls, my father pointed to Grant and asked, "How come he's always in the lead?"

"He's the trip leader," I said.

"That makes sense. He's a man." Dad was back in the pot-stirring game.

The glares from Megan and her friends were merciless. They looked at me, begging me to do something.

I flashed a smile. "This next rapid has a huge hole in the center. Imagine a crashing wave in the ocean that's eight feet high," I said. "We're going to have to take a piece of it. I'll need some extra power in the back to help stabilize the raft." I looked at my father. "You're a big strong guy. Would you mind helping me?"

"Of course," Dad said, switching with Garrett.

"Paddles ready now," I said. "All forward."

We dropped through the entrance and swung around the bend in the river, building momentum. The hole came into view, and I lined the boat up to take the edge of it, adding enough angle to collapse the back left side where Dad and I sat. When we slammed into the hole, the raft folded. I crouched down and held on for the hit, but I neglected to tell my father to do the same. He was knocked into the river like an eight ball in a corner pocket.

He came up next to the boat, his eyes huge.

"Grab on to the perimeter line," I yelled to him while navigating the rapid's second drop.

"Pull me in," Dad shouted.

The crew all turned to see my father clinging to the side of the boat.

"Are you sure you want a woman to pull you into the raft? I might not be strong enough."

"Fucking pull me in."

"I could hurt myself. Maybe we should wait and get Grant to do it."

I reached down and grabbed him by the shoulder straps of his PFD, then hoisted him into the raft.

"You did that on purpose," Dad said.

"What do you mean?"

He shook his head. "Putting your own father in the drink."

"He's your *dad*?" Megan said, her mouth agape.

"Along with being a pain in my ass."

Garrett snickered. "Admit it, Dad," he said. "You had that coming."

Dad tried to stay mad, but he couldn't keep a straight face. Soon we were all crying with laughter.

We pulled into the large, cove-like eddy on the left below Horseshoe Falls, at the jump rock perched above the river. Lee was already tied up and slicing into a watermelon onshore. "What's so funny?" he asked.

"He's her *dad*." Megan could barely talk, she was laughing so hard. "We thought he was some random asshole this whole time."

"No, he's my asshole," I said.

I tied up our raft, and Lee served us all melon. As we slurped the juicy sweetness, we watched Grant jump off the rock across the eddy and land a cannonball behind the boats, soaking half the group.

"Come on," I said to Dad and my brother. "Let's jump."

"Are you going to push me off the ledge?" Dad asked.

"Maybe." I started climbing the trail to the rocky point. My brother followed.

"You've got to do it." Grant grinned at my father from the water. "It's part of the experience."

Dad got up and followed Garrett and me up the trail. We made our way through the dust and cheatgrass. When we reached the top, we had a full view of Horseshoe Falls.

"That's where you fell in." I pointed to the hole.

"Jesus Christ." Dad scanned the half-mile-long rapid from its entrance to the pool below, where our boats were. "You could get lost in there," he said. "But you knew *exactly* what you were doing, you little shit."

"Consider it my Father's Day gift."

Garrett walked to the edge of the rock and looked down. He lifted his hand in a salute, then jumped into the pool below, spinning his body like a corkscrew.

I turned to Dad. "You going?"

He hesitated. This was beyond his comfort zone.

"Let's go together," I said.

He shot me a determined look. "What the hell? We've come this far."

We jumped at the same time, landing next to each other in the jade-green pool below. Under the water, I opened my eyes to see him rise up, reaching for the gleaming green cattails and cottonwoods swaying just above the mirrored surface.

Epilogue

Run like a River

In the spring of 2020, during the height of the COVID pandemic, my dad, my mom, and I all had cancer at the same time. It was the first time since my parents' divorce forty-six years earlier that I'd thought of the three of us as a family unit.

Three years after the Kern River trip with my dad and Garrett, when I was twenty-five, I married Steve in Montana. His father officiated the ceremony as a spring storm delivered sideways sleet. My father walked me down the aisle, squeezing my arm as I fought off a panic attack, while my mom spent most of the day doing bong loads in her hotel room. Two years later, I became the first Crocker on my dad's side of the family to get a college degree.

At thirty, I suffered a series of severe panic attacks that landed me in the hospital, unable to breathe. After I scored "extreme" on an anxiety test, a doctor asked if I self-medicated. It turned out that responding to anxiety or any other feeling by drinking or using qualified as a yes. The doctor suggested I seek help through a therapist and a twelve-step program. Shortly after getting into recovery, I divorced Steve, settled in California, and pursued a writing career. At thirty-seven, I married a lifeguard I met on a boat to San Miguel Island, off the coast of Santa Barbara. I was on a writing assignment for a magazine, and Johnny was traveling alone to explore the northernmost of the Channel Islands. As I boarded the boat, I looked up the stairs onto the upper deck and straight into his gentle blue eyes. *Wow*, I thought. *That's the kindest, most loving man in the world.* He had a barrel chest and a deep belly laugh, and his reverence for water was breathtaking. We were married next to the ocean and moved to a state beach in Malibu, where Johnny worked and where we've raised our two daughters.

Just before his cancer diagnosis, Dad and I met for lunch, as we often did. I drove up the coast from Malibu to meet him at a sushi shop we loved in Ventura.

"I'm feeling a little bored," he said over a baked scallop roll. "I need a challenge."

Typically, when Dad craved a challenge, he bought a new car, launched a real estate project, or took off on his motorcycle. He'd call me from San Francisco, Louisiana, or Utah, having left on a whim for a weekend ride.

"Why don't you retire?" I asked. He was seventy-five, and his fourth wife—a truly lovely woman—was keen to enjoy their golden years traveling.

"Let's not get carried away."

I knew Dad would use business as an excuse not to travel for as long as possible. Working was how he stayed out of trouble. Idle hands were dangerous for my father.

A month after our lunch, Dad's wife called to tell me he was in the hospital with sepsis. He'd eaten some bad lobster outside Zion National Park, she told me. I was at his bedside in under an hour and, after a series of tests, we quickly learned that he also had pancreatic cancer.

My father and I had worked through a lot of hard things since our river trip on the Kern twenty-five years earlier. We'd gone to counseling together, and sometimes he made therapists cry with his ferocity, afterward proclaiming them to be "dumber than a box of rocks." My father was a live wire of hurt, and as with Nyaminyami, his anger was a cover-up.

"How bad is it?" Dad asked when we were alone.

"After surgery, you've got a one-in-four chance of making it past five years," I told him.

"Son of a bitch."

"You're the one who asked for a challenge." I reached for his hand, but he pulled it away, not wanting sympathy. "Nobody fights like you," I said. "You're going to be the one who makes it."

After being estranged from my mother for the better part of my thirties and forties, I began calling her with regularity at the beginning of the COVID pandemic. Over the years, I'd tried to talk about the events that had harmed me during my upbringing, but she wasn't willing to discuss or even acknowledge them. She responded by sending eleven-page manifestos via certified mail detailing what she described as my lifetime problem with lying. In her letters, she urged me to seek help.

"Good idea," I said. "Let's go together."

"I don't need therapy," she said. "Managing your mental health is your responsibility. I didn't cause your problems."

Without her willingness to work on the breakdown between us, I struggled with our relationship. I loved my mom, but I couldn't endure being told I was lying whenever I talked about the past. I also didn't want my children to experience the family disease, so detaching felt like the best way to protect them too.

For decades, my mom and Mark have lived on their own in the Montana wilderness, isolated from modern society. They have caches of supplies stashed on their land and relish the demise of humankind, as it will give other species a chance to recover.

"How are you guys doing with the lockdown?" I asked when I called to check on them.

"We've been ready for the apocalypse since before Y2K," my mom said. "We're rooting for the pandemic. Nature bats last."

Mom told me that she'd been battling skin cancer for over ten years. She could no longer go outside without long clothes and a wide-brimmed hat. Then, just after my dad's surgery, she found out she had breast cancer.

"I told the doctor just take them. Cut them both off. I'm so done with the male gaze," she said. "But the doctor said I only needed a lumpectomy plus chemo and radiation."

I began to cry.

"This is why I didn't want to tell you," she said. "People always make it about themselves when you tell them you're sick."

"I think it's okay to feel sad."

"Well, don't do it around me," she said. "I need only positive vibes right now."

Both my parents began chemo at the same time and, oddly, remained on parallel schedules. I alternated days checking in with them, as talking to both on the same day rendered me immobile. I'd sob on my patio, thumbing through travel magazines while looking at the ocean until it was time to take my kids to swim practice at the outdoor pool.

And then I had a skin cancer diagnosis—melanoma. I went in for my surgery consultation.

"Where did you get all the sun exposure?" asked the surgeon.

"I worked as a river guide year-round for seventeen years. Mostly in the tropics," I said. "And I've lived on the beach in Malibu for fifteen years."

The doctor shook his head in disbelief, as if this was the most idiotic thing he'd ever heard. "We should be able to get clear margins on this one, but you have a 50 percent chance of developing another melanoma, even if you never get another drop of sun on your skin."

It felt like too many hard things at once: the constant work of caring for my young children during the pandemic, my dad and mom each fighting for their lives, my outdoor lifestyle upended. I couldn't run away from my problems to alleviate my anxiety and anger as I had in the past.

But I could run.

I had always processed emotions through my body, and I began running on the high school track at night during my kids' outdoor swim team and water polo practices. As I accumulated laps, Orion loomed over the ridge-line of the Santa Monica Mountains, just as he had over the Batoka Gorge in Zambia all those years ago. Under a dome of stars, I recalled my friends in Zambia who'd endured worse hardships every day. My body grew stronger, and I channeled that strength toward my mom and dad. I became more comfortable carrying the fear that I might lose one or both of them.

As the running continued, my understanding of what my parents and I had accomplished in this lifetime took on more clarity. My father had eradicated poverty for our family in a single generation, without the ability to read or write beyond an elementary-school level. My mother, who was beaten relentlessly by her own mother, never once abused me physically. Through implementing what she'd learned in parenting classes and books, she'd shifted the course of our family's legacy of abuse. They both had run the hell out of their legs of the race, setting me up to finish strong.

For my part, I've sought the help of therapists, twelve-step programs, parenting classes, and countless mentors in the interest of breaking the cycle of poverty and abuse. I'm most proud that my own children have never known either. They've only ever had a sober mom, one set of parents, and the same home. That's not to say there hasn't been adversity. We've had to evacuate multiple times for wildfires, mudslides, flooding, and tsunami threats. After the Woolsey Fire decimated Malibu, requiring our community to rely solely on survival skills, I called my mom and Mark to thank them for teaching me how to effectively navigate disaster.

Over the years, I'd gone through several periods of estrangement—or detachment—from both my parents. A dispute would erupt, and I would throw up my hands, claiming it was too hard to deal with a crazy mother or a raging father. I'd be better off without them, I reasoned. I'd even gone so far as to tell myself it would be easier if they died.

When the three of us got cancer and I began to think of us as a family again, I realized how wrong I'd been. I'd been devastated by the prospect of losing them. As I continued running laps, I grew to see the three of us as the warriors we were. Breaking the family cycle was grueling work, requiring time-outs, readjustments, and shifts in perception. Like when my dad had finally been properly assessed for learning disabilities in his sixties. At the time, I'd worked at a school for kids with learning deficits and arranged for Dad to get a full workup. We knew he struggled to read and write, but we didn't know why.

My boss sat down with me before Dad came in for his results. She wanted to prepare me. "Does your dad struggle with anger?" she asked.

"A lot."

"I honestly don't know how your father is capable of functioning in society. He has huge auditory and visual learning gaps, dyslexia, and extreme ADHD. People with his diagnosis are usually in prison or homeless."

"My father hates homeless people. He yells at them."

"I can't figure out how he passed the real estate licensing test," she said.

"He took it seven times."

She smiled. "Sheer determination."

Dad came in and we went over the results. Some of the tests revealed that his functioning skills weren't even at a kindergarten level. If only he'd been diagnosed sooner, gotten the help he needed as a kid, would our family have been spared his rage and abuse?

Afterward, I suggested we go out for ice cream to lift our spirits. On our way into the shop, we passed a homeless man sitting at an outdoor table. My dad treated him to a triple scoop of ice cream and gave him fifty bucks.

Along with new information came compassion and gratitude.

After years of struggling to understand my mom's personality change, I stumbled on a book about personality disorders. The book described her symptoms in exact detail, citing untreated trauma from childhood neglect and abuse as the cause.

As a grown woman with twenty years of recovery, I came to see my parents clearly within the context of their stories. And then, the story changed.

"There's something you don't know," Dad said one day while we were having lunch at a restaurant near his home. He was little more than a skeleton,
doing his best to polish off a cup of gelato and a beer. It was a shitty lunch
for a stage 4 cancer patient, but what the hell.

"When I fought for joint custody of you, I made sure there was a clause
in there that your mom couldn't take you out of state without my permission. She always wanted to move to the mountains, and I wasn't going to
stand for her and some other guy taking you away. So, you couldn't move
to Jackson unless I signed off on it."

"It's okay, Dad."

"I'm not finished." He took a sip of beer. "Before you moved to Jackson,
whenever I'd go to get you, there'd be chaos. Fights. Cops. Screaming."

"I remember."

"I'd look at you crying and torn up, and the realization hit me hard that
we'd been doing that to you every weekend *for years*. You were so little, and
that heavy burden of hatred, like a war, was all coming down squarely on
you." His eyes teared up. "I signed the papers for you to move to Jackson
because I knew you'd have stability. Your mother and I would never have
to see each other. Even though it killed me to let you go, I did it."

"I always thought you didn't want me, that's why you didn't fight
harder for me," I said.

"I know you did, honey," he said.

"Why did you wait so long to tell me?"

"I thought about it. I didn't want you to blame your mother for taking
you away. Things are hard enough between you two as it is. I *was* fighting for you—to have a better life, one with stability, which is what you
needed."

I remembered Regina and Thomas, how Regina had said she'd rather
take a thousand beatings than see Thomas and his mistress take her daughter. My father had done what Regina wasn't willing to even consider: he'd

handed over his child and let his enemies raise her. As a parent, I couldn't imagine bearing that kind of sacrifice.

⁓

Two weeks before he died, I sat with my dad on the enclosed porch at his lake house in Maine, in the town where he was raised, and watched the loons dive for mollusks buried in the murky clay.

"I'm worried about the family," he said. He peered at me from under the hat he wore to cover his bald head.

"We've got a strong family, Dad." Through the window, we could see Garrett and his wife in the water, arms outstretched to catch their two children as they jumped off the dock. Nearby, our stepmom, who was in every way my dad's soul mate, was blowing up inflatable lake toys.

"You know who's the strongest?" Dad pointed his gaunt finger at me.

"Only because I got my ass kicked the most."

"That's true." He raised his hand as if to testify.

I walked over to him and sat on the arm of his recliner. "I used to be super resentful," I said, "but now, I'm grateful for the strength it gave me." As I hugged him, I could feel his ribs poking through his shirt, and the warmth of his heart underneath.

"My favorite daughter," Dad said, kissing my cheek. "I'd do it again with you in a heartbeat."

"Me too."

⁓

Recently, Johnny woke me with the news that he'd secured a private permit to run the San Juan River in Utah. "It will give us something to look forward to," he said. "We'll bring sunshades, umbrellas, hats, rashguards—make sure you stay protected from the sun."

When Johnny and I first started dating, I took him on the Kern and dumped him in Horseshoe Falls. A solid waterman, he self-rescued and said it was the best date he'd ever been on. Ours is a love born of water, and we've rafted as a family since our youngest daughter had a Binky lashed onto her miniature PFD. Our children have run hundreds of river miles on trips in the US and Costa Rica.

From my desk overlooking the Pacific Ocean, I think of the Snake River, where I almost drowned as a girl, where I first guided, and where I began to find my power as a woman. Rivers have shaped not just my callused hands but the course of my life. I remember the Zambezi, Nyaminyami, and the Kern, where I dumped the two men I've loved most in Horseshoe. I imagine the San Juan River in Utah, the muddied smell of ancient sediment blowing upstream on an afternoon headwind. In my mind's eye, cottonwood leaves rustle as bald eagles swoop in to build their nests. I've run the San Juan twice with my daughters—it's where I taught them how to swim out of the current and into an eddy in order to survive, just as I did when I was their age.

Some people think that Johnny and I are crazy to take our young children on multiday whitewater expeditions through remote wilderness areas. Isn't it dangerous?

We're all dying. I want my daughters to learn that part of living is being willing to embrace adventure, whether it's a river trip or improving connections with loved ones, even when it's hard. I want them to learn from rivers—as I did—to be relentless in finding their own line and, when they flip, not just to survive but to recover strong.

I asked my mom, Mark, and my brother David and his wife to join us on the eighty-four-mile wilderness run, but they said they couldn't make it. I plan to keep inviting them.

The day my father died, I flew from California to Maine to be with him.

"Thank God you're here," he said as I scooched onto the edge of his bed.

I smiled. "Where else would I be?"

He patted my hand, then dozed off. A few minutes later he awoke with a start. "Why are you here?"

"I'm here for the Big Adventure, Dad."

"Don't talk about that." He sank down deeper under his quilt. "I'm not ready."

"Well, it's happening." I kept my tone steady, determined not to break down. I was there to encourage him and walk beside him, not to make it about me.

Dad grabbed my shoulder, pulling me closer. "Promise me," he said.

"I'll take care of the family," I interrupted.

"Thank you. I know you will. I'm not worried about that," he said. "I need you to promise me that you'll publish your book." I'd been working on a memoir for twenty-two years.

"You don't look very good in it, Dad."

"I don't give a shit how I look." His blue eyes held mine. "What's important is that you publish it."

I looked at him hesitantly. I was afraid that publishing my story would alienate me from my family again.

"There's no shame," Dad said. "You worked hard. You have a beautiful life and family. Enjoy it. Don't let shame stop you."

I worried that affixing the story to the page would keep us stuck within one narrative, frozen in old versions of ourselves, when the truth is, just like rivers, we are becoming the next incarnation of ourselves with every breath.

My dad's final words were, "Love you."

He said them twice to make sure we—my stepmom, my brother, and I—got it. As he took his last breath, the loons gathered along the lakeshore feet away, erupting in rounds of *whoo-oo-oo-oo-oo*. I glanced toward them as they swam through the darkened water, the reflection of a full, radiant moon shimmering in their wake.

Acknowledgments

A dear friend and mentor of mine, Judy Fairchild, once observed that my wealth is in my relationships. I've been incredibly fortunate when it comes to friends and colleagues and have been uplifted more times than I can count by some of the world's kindest people, whom I'd like to acknowledge here.

Thank you to Todd Shuster and Aevitas Creative Management for believing in the strength of my work, and to my remarkable agent, Lauren MacLeod, for her lightheartedness and prowess at selling my manuscript to my dream publisher. I don't know what stars aligned to bring Cindy Spiegel onboard as my editor, but she and the entire team at Spiegel & Grau—including Julie Grau, Liza Wachter, Nicole Dewey, Andrew Tan-Delli Cicchi, Jess Bonet, and Nora Tomas, as well as their associates Jeff Farr, Mona Hauck, Anne Horowitz, and Meighan Cavanaugh—are a delight to work with. I am also particularly grateful to my lawyer Melissa Nasson for her legal expertise and compassionate heart.

My deepest gratitude to Greg von Doersten and Tony Demin for allowing their images to appear alongside the story. I've been blessed to work with world-class photographers, and these two have been incredibly supportive and generous to me throughout my career. Big love.

For going above and beyond in pursuit of seeing this dream realized, I am deeply indebted to my friends Roko Belic and Gael Firth, Jeffrey Gettleman, Rick Ridgeway, Murray and Margot Carpenter, Randall Wallace, Moira Gilbert and Dan Sarrow, Christina Haag, Elle Johnson, Tom Urban, Tracy Ross, Shellan and Rob Isackson, and my wonderful brother, sister-in-law, and stepmom.

Enormous thanks to my writing groups: Judy Fairchild, Rita Batchley, Karin Just, Lisa Gizara, and Amanda Beno of the Carpet Sniffers; and my Travel Writer Bros, Jim Benning and Jeremy Kressmann, for being talented developmental editors and lovely, caring men. Members of the Malibu Writers Circle—particularly Robert Kerbeck and Asher Sund— have my heartfelt gratitude for fierce loyalty to the story and never once going easy on me: Jane Garnett, Tom Moore, Susan Tschudi, Liz Ziemska, Michal Lemberger, Sandra O'Briant, John Struloeff, and Liane Starr. A special shout-out to my Brave Women Writers group for carrying me through the scariest part of publishing my story: Angela Barton, Sasha Cagen, Kirsten Ott Palladino, Shawna Ayoub, Amy Jo Burns, Melissa Banigan, Sedona Lynn, Darlene Kriesel, and Kim Jorgensen Gane. Deep gratitude goes to my first writing and editing partner, Bo Fuller. The day I walked into a Barnes & Noble and saw her book on display, I fell to my knees in complete awe that people like me could publish books. In that moment on the bookstore floor, I made the commitment to write this book. Thank you, Bo, for your tremendous courage and inspiration.

To the teachers and professors who had a significant impact on my critical thinking and writing skills: Patty Chlebeck, Roni Adams, Linda Karell, Andra Witkin, and Steve Chapple. Extra special thanks to Alanna Brown for giving me a D and telling me she was going to grade me based on the work she knew I could do. Thank you to Tim Cahill for pulling me aside at the Livingston Writers Workshop and telling me that I had the makings of a real writer. Thanks to Don George for convincing me to invest in my professional development by attending Book Passage Travel Writers & Photographers Workshop.

Unrelenting gratitude goes to my long-standing Patagonia crew: Michele Bianchi, Megan Marble, Kasey Kersnowski, John Dutton, Kim Myers, Carin Knutson, Nora Gallagher, Vincent Stanley, Yvon and Malinda Chouinard, Joanne Dornan, Val Franco, Cheryl Endo, Lisa Williams, Helena Barbour, Jim Little, Alison Ferguson, Mary Osborne, Bill Klyn, Lynn Siodmak, Sunday Rylander, Chris Gaggia, Hillary Fleming, Chipper Bro, Stuart Ruckman, Kelly Cordes, Karla Olson, Brittany Griffith, Morlee Griswold, Karen Bednorz, Jane Sievert, Diane French, Barbara O'Grady, and many, many more. To find long-time employment writing about the natural world and outdoor sports while working alongside so many brilliant thinkers has been an incredible boon.

To the nurturing sisterhood that's walked beside me throughout this journey of healing and spiritual transformation: Jill Olivares, Jenny Karns, Keleigh Gomez, Jennifer Rice, Mary Mac Gonzalez, Denise Peak, Audrey Newman, Dusty Lovejoy, Betsy McIntyre Cornell, Christine Kapetan, Jeanette Calliva, Dawn Dana, Susanna Brisk, Julie Merkell, Laurel Rice, Liz Galvan, Mimi Camarillo, Kelli Loughman, Cushla Leonard, Kris Krengel, Evy Wild, Kim Ledoux, Kevin Hanna, Randee Bieler, Denise Salazar, Megan Bergkvist, Ann Ryan, Aylin Cook, Robyn Dalbey, Leslie Haaland Dominick, Verla Dynneson, Julie Mermelstein, China Isler, Carolina Morgado, Leslie Pierce, Doreen Hamangaba, Jan Hayse, Andrea Lee, Heather Harris, Dinah Hayse, Estela de Wulf, Barbie Herron Conkling, Cathy Bauers, Elizabeth Riddick, Desi Bradley, Linda Zielski, Brittany Walker, Diane Malecha, Lizzy Baldwin, Aubree Holmes, Heather Gardner, Juliana Leite Dos Reis, Daria Matza, Nisahna Engel, Erin Joy Henry, Kelly Graham, Hannah Lamonea, Lydia Graham-Stiegler, Judith Stine, Peggy Garrity, Laura Brown, Heather Cappiello, Jean Rosecrans, Lisa Chinnery, Myra Ingersoll, and countless others. I love you wholeheartedly.

To my many friends and colleagues who championed, guided, and celebrated each success alongside me: Bill Robinson and Sheryl Luera, David and Rixt Clifford, Matt Daly, Amy Kathleen Ryan, Nancy Idler and the Regan family, Hank List, the Brady family, Kelly and Ian Kincaid,

Roslyn Satchel, Elsje and John Kibler, Jude and Brenton Brown, Joe Sichta, Julie and Doug Jones, Brit and Sandy Horn, Rainbow Pharaon, Greg Bonann, Sarah Doyle, Carmen and Ryan Shain, Ryan and Darlene Addison, Amanda "Binky" Urban, Jayme Moye, Michael Shapiro, Julia Scheeres, Larry Habegger, Lavinia Spalding, Torre DeRoche, James Michael Dorsey, Tony Cohan, Anne Van, Sarah Katin, Kimberley Lovato, Abbie Kozolchyk, Betsy Gaines Quammen, Liberty Clinton, Dave Forsyth, the Holzapfel family, Tara Ellison, Ako Eyong, Alison Singh Gee, Mary Jo McConahay, Jessica Mecklenburg, Joe Albanese, Tara Walch, Marcus Hibdon, Brett Norris, Naomi Deibel, Kay Gabbard, Tim Coates, Daisy Colborn Mastroianni, Kevin Bommer, Kassondra Cloos, Martin Zitzelberger, Gary Ananian, Claire Fullerton, Debbie Prince, Marianne Rogoff, Barbara Burke, Julie Ellerton, Ilene Cherrie, Dave Talsky, Barry Kearson, Tom Clements, Michael Benge, John Rasmus, Krista Langlois, Andrea Guevara, Ronlyn Domingue, J. Faye D'Avanza, David "Dewey" Weber, Catherine Malcolm Brickman, Don Love, Bryan Burk, Jennifer Johnston Jones, Kathy Eldon, Tom Jackson, Lisa Hagan, Justin and Gloria Dreyfuss, Karen and Brian Kelly, Colin and Jackie Anglin-Simon, Tony Hotchkiss and Audrey Shubin, Jessica and Tony Mark, Erik Shaw, Erik Landry, Jason and Laurel Dinkler, Donald AuCoin, Iliana Carballo, Isais Badilla, Antony Gomez, Trisha and Eric Johnson, Cornelia van den Houdt, Ignacio Just, and so many more.

One of the greatest blessings of my life was being adopted into the river family, with whom I felt an immediate kinship, particularly Jeremy Anderson, Bill McGinnis, Morgan James, Jamie "Jinky" Johnston, Frederick Reimers, Ken Streater, Alison French Steen, Arturo Oropeza, the Cervilla family, Nicole Silk, Leonardo Vazquez, Tac Leung, Arvind Bhardwaj, Mark and Marta Hammond, Marc Goddard, Laurence Alvarez-Roos, Mara Drazina, Michael Fairchild and Kim McCampbell, Gene Evans and Steven Messer, Susie Dodge, Erik Meldrum, Damara Stone, Amy Flynn, Melissa Ward, Brian Mauer, Luther Stevens, Barry Kruse, Susan Maida, Phil and Mary DeReimer, Nino Dai, Arun Ray, Tilak Borah, Luz Holguin, Rod Raunig, Kevin Thompson, Liam and Breck O'Neill, Dmitri and Melissa Pruyn, Ari Kotler, Greg McFadden, Amanda Szecsei, Wendy Higa and Pietro Ortiz, Aileen Burgoyne, Gary "Firestarter" Thornbrugh, Emily Norton Kessler, Kelly Wiglesworth, Heather Tork, Toni and Terry McQueen, Corey and Jessica Milligan, Jonathan Benak, Drew Meyer, Nikki Cooley, Charlie Ross, Brian Stevenson, Heidi White Franks, Beth Thomas and Joe Dengler, Dominic Mubika, Sunday Ngwenya, Beth Rypins, Kelley Kalafatich, Sue Norman, Rachel and Andy Rost, Mark Kocina, Dave Seibt, Dan Grant, Will and Karin Hoida, Abby and Neal Guthrie, Molly Nellman, Danielle Rees, Coeylen Barry, Jim Miller, Maria Blevins, Risa Shimoda, Dave Cernicek, Kirstin Heins, and the legions of boaters I've worked with who've had my back and literally saved my life.

I am profoundly grateful for the special gift of being raised in Jackson Hole, and to my hometown community and the bond we share. I'm grateful to my mother, who, as the world's most prolific reader, instilled in me a deep love of literature and learning. Thanks goes to my first stepmother for recognizing and believing in my talent as a writer, to my stepdad for anchoring me in love, and my other stepdad for teaching me how to be at home in nature. Thank you to my one-of-a-kind father, who had a remarkable gift for storytelling and championed this book with everything he had, even from the hereafter.

Above all, I am thankful to my husband, Johnny, for his steadfast devotion to my development as an artist and the sacrifices he's made in providing me the space and time to pursue my craft. His constant enthusiasm and encouragement are unparalleled. I treasure our beautiful children and the life we've created—my deepest desire realized.

Finally, for every river that's brought me here, every flip and broken oar that taught me how to make my boat right again, for my Creator who never abandoned me, but filled me with hope and strength to carry a difficult load, survive it, and come to inhabit joy, I am humbled and grateful.

About the Author

A leading whitewater explorer, Bridget Crocker has guided expeditions down many of the world's greatest river canyons in Zambia, Ethiopia, the Philippines, Peru, Chile, Costa Rica, India, and the western United States. She is a graduate of Montana State University, Bozeman. Her work has been featured in *Outside*, *Westways*, *Men's Journal*, and *National Geographic Adventure* magazines among others, and she is a contributor at Patagonia, Lonely Planet Guidebooks, and The Best Women's Travel Writing. She lives with her family in Malibu, California. Visit her at www.bridgetcrocker.com or follow @bridgetcrocker for information about book events, river trips, and writing courses.